Productivity 13

Process + principles the same for 17
  — but see 31

×14
×15

Occam's Razor , p. 33

Purpose of book , p. 34

TG model based on orthography 36

Opek, op?S , 36

Memory complex; access simple, 39
Lex: knowing what? , Grammar: knowing how to
exaggerate~ted (waited) overlapping morphs? 29
42 ??

prediction of change: 49

basic contrast of theories: 49
occam solves the problem of arbitrariness 49

→ Dewey: p. 51
Details of memory are irrelevant 52
  Phoneme = basic alternant 50 (B's idea)
    ignores contrast 53

  Phonemic system learned – age 3 54
Grammar must accommodate change – 57
  what are schemas? 63–64
No alphabetic units 65
Lg. specific vs. un_____ of phonetics 66–67
procedural knowledge (phonology?? 70, 40
Anterior !? 72

(N) is round 74
Principle of evidence — not simplicity
Nonalphabetic notion of speech - 75
Dynamic view of lg - vocab
At cell/neuron level, effects are all-or-none
     not gradual
Compensatory lengthening 74
Syl-final Cs a subset of syl-init. 88
Why p/#s_ is not aspirated 89
Frequency + memory effect, 91-92
Clarity - 1st conjugation - 99
Local generalization 10#6, 121, 124
Words in storage 109
Frequency effects 111, 172
Memory vs. Lexicon 113, 172
Plural unmarked 115

No example 128
Prefix derivatives not regular? 135
Nice frequency example 154
I dunno Know in lexicon 160 etc, 161
speedy speech not + Proton? 165
Against morpheme 166
Humboldt's Universal 169
Schema 175?! What is it? 176
Memory of phrases 186
Sound change is regular! 190

PHONOLOGY AND LANGUAGE USE

A research perspective that takes language use into account opens up new views of old issues and provides an understanding of issues that linguists have rarely addressed. Referencing new developments in cognitive and functional linguistics, phonetics, and connectionist modeling, this book investigates various ways in which a speaker/hearer's experience with language affects the representation of phonology. Rather than assuming phonological representations in terms of phonemes, Joan Bybee adopts an exemplar model, in which specific tokens of use are stored and categorized phonetically with reference to variables in the context. This model allows an account of phonetically gradual sound change that produces lexical variation, and provides an explanatory account of the fact that many reductive sound changes affect high-frequency items first. The well-known effects of type and token frequency on morphologically conditioned phonological alterations are shown also to apply to larger sequences, such as fixed phrases and constructions, solving some of the problems formulated previously as dealing with the phonology–syntax interface.

Joan Bybee is the author of several books and articles on phonology, morphology, language universals, and linguistic change. Most recently, she served as a coeditor for both *Essays on Language and Function Type* (1997) and *Modality in Grammar and Discourse* (1995). Dr. Bybee is Regents' Professor of Linguistics and Chair of the Department of Linguistics at the University of New Mexico.

CAMBRIDGE STUDIES IN LINGUISTICS

General editors: S. R. ANDERSON, J. BRESNAN, B. COMRIE,
W. DRESSLER, C. EWEN, R. HUDDLESTON, R. LASS,
D. LIGHTFOOT, J. LYONS, P. H. MATTHEWS, R. POSNER,
S. ROMAINE, N. V. SMITH, N. VINCENT

Phonology and Language Use

CAMBRIDGE STUDIES IN LINGUISTICS

In this series

Supplementary volumes

Earlier issues not listed are also available

Phonology and Language Use

JOAN BYBEE

University of New Mexico

CAMBRIDGE
UNIVERSITY PRESS

PUBLISHED BY THE PRESS SYNDICATE OF THE UNIVERSITY OF CAMBRIDGE
The Pitt Building, Trumpington Street, Cambridge, United Kingdom

CAMBRIDGE UNIVERSITY PRESS
The Edinburgh Building, Cambridge CB2 2RU, UK
40 West 20th Street, New York, NY 10011-4211, USA
10 Stamford Road, Oakleigh, VIC 3166, Australia
Ruiz de Alarcón 13, 28014 Madrid, Spain
Dock House, The Waterfront, Cape Town 8001, South Africa

http://www.cambridge.org

© Joan Bybee 2001

First published 2001

Printed in the United States of America

Typeface Times Roman 10.25/13 pt.   *System* QuarkXPress [BTS]

A catalog record for this book is available from the British Library.

Library of Congress Cataloging in Publication Data

Bybee, Joan L.
     Phonology and language use / Joan Bybee.
         p.   cm. – (Cambridge studies in linguistics ; 94)
     Includes bibliographical references and index.
     ISBN 0-521-58374-8
     1. Grammar, Comparative and general – Phonology.   2. Linguistic change.
     3. Grammar, Comparative and general – Morphology.   4. Universals (Linguistics)
     I. Title.   II. Series.
     P217.3 .B93   2001
     414 – dc21

                                                                00-045525

ISBN   0 521 58374 8   hardback

To my parents

Contents

Figures

Tables

Acknowledgments

The idea for this book and the perception that it was needed arose in the context of the community of researchers who investigate the way language use gives rise to grammar. Indeed, it was these workers in usage-based functionalism, most notably my long-time friend Sandy Thompson, who first supported and encouraged a book that would show how principles that had been successfully applied to the explanation of morphosyntactic patterns could also be applied to phonology. This book was originally intended for these linguists and their students. However, the encouragement and support of phonologists was also forthcoming once the idea of the book was broached. I am grateful to Janet Pierrehumbert in her role as editor for Cambridge University Press for supporting this project and for giving me extensive comments and suggestions on the first draft of the manuscript. I am also much indebted to Martin Haspelmath, José Ignacio Hualde, and Carmen Pensado for their careful reading of the first draft and their detailed comments and questions. I am particularly grateful to José Ignacio Hualde for comments that caused me to rethink certain issues. In addition, suggestions from Jürgen Klausenburger and Robert Kirchner also led to revisions of the manuscript. Discussions with each of these individuals helped me develop a deeper understanding of the phenomena treated here, as well as an improved presentation of my ideas.

For assistance in researching and editing, computing, and formatting, I am grateful to Dawn Nordquist and Catie Berkenfield. Also, Dawn Nordquist coded and helped me analyze the data discussed in Section 6.3.3, with the assistance of Rena Torres-Cacoullos. Aaron Smith also assisted at various stages of the project. Thanks are also due to my colleague Caroline Smith for consultation on various issues in the phonetics literature. To the many students who have posed interesting questions and problems over many semesters and to those whose research answered some of these questions, I am extremely grateful for the stimulation.

The University of New Mexico has provided research support in the Regents' Professorship I was awarded in 1996, and the College of Arts and Sciences has provided teaching relief in the form of a Research Semester in the spring of 1999. My parents, Robert and Elizabeth Bybee, have provided donations, matched by the Exxon Foundation, that made possible research assistance. Without these sources of support, this work would certainly have taken much longer to emerge.

And, finally, many thanks to Ira Jaffe, for the generosity and good humor with which he contributes to the peaceful home and working environment that we share.

1

Language Use as Part of Linguistic Theory

1.1 Substance and Usage in Phonology

This book introduces into the traditional study of phonology the notion that language use plays a role in shaping the form and content of sound systems. In particular, the frequency with which individual words or sequences of words are used and the frequency with which certain patterns recur in a language affects the nature of mental representation and in some cases the actual phonetic shape of words. It is the goal of the present work to explore to the extent possible at the present moment the nature of the relation between the use of linguistic forms on the one hand, and their storage and processing on the other.

To someone approaching linguistics from other disciplines, it might seem odd that language use has not been taken into account in formulating theories of language. However, since language is such a complex phenomenon, it has been necessary to narrow the field of study to make it manageable. Thus we commonly separate phonology from syntax, synchrony from diachrony, child language from adult language, and so on, constantly bearing in mind that interactions exist that will eventually have to be taken into account. We then go on to formulate theories for these domains – a theory of syntax, a theory of phonology, a theory of language acquisition – knowing all the while that the ultimate goal is to encompass all these subfields in one theory of language.

Early in the twentieth century, a proposal was made to distinguish the shared knowledge that a community of speakers has from the actual uses to which that knowledge is put (de Saussure 1916). Many researchers then focused their attention on the structure of that shared knowledge (called 'langue' by Saussure and 'competence' by Chomsky

1

1965) and paid little attention to language use in real time. The focus on competence, or the structure of language, turned out to be extremely productive. Structuralism provided linguists with a workshop of analytic tools for breaking down the continuous speech stream into units, and these units into features; structuralism postulated hierarchical relations among the units and assigned structures to different levels of grammar, organizing language and the people who study it into subfields – phonology, morphology, syntax, and semantics.

The present work proposes to demonstrate that the focus on structure needs to be supplemented with a perspective that includes more than just structure, a view that includes two other important aspects of the language phenomenon – the material content or substance of language, and language use. The SUBSTANCE of language refers to the two polar ends – phonetics and semantics – that language molds and structures, the two ends between which language forms the bridge. Language USE includes not just the processing of language, but all the social and interactional uses to which language is put. For present purposes, in the context of phonology, the frequency with which certain words, phrases, or patterns are used will be shown to have an impact on phonological structure. I will return to a discussion of these two aspects of language and the role they play in past and future theories after describing some recent developments in linguistics and related fields that suggest a need for an enlarged perspective on language.

In the domain of morphosyntax, a substantial development beyond structuralism has already taken place. The content of grammatical categories has been studied as a substantive rather than a structural matter, for example, in crosslinguistic studies of subject, topic, noun, verb, tense, aspect (Comrie 1976, 1985, Dahl 1985), mood, and so on. Also use is being studied as a prime shaper of syntactic structure (Givón 1979, Haiman 1994, Hopper and Thompson 1984, and others) and morphological structure (Bybee 1985, Bybee et al. 1994, DuBois 1985). So far, no comparable development has occurred in phonology, but there are several indicators that it is time to open up the field to new questions and new sources of data and explanation.

Despite having looked carefully at matters of structure, having defined and redefined units such as phoneme and morpheme (or formative), having shifted and reshifted levels such as phonemic and morphophonemic, we find that problems and questions still remain. Units and levels do not submit to definitions that work for every case. We still do not have strict definitions of even the most basic units, such as segment, syllable, morpheme, and word. Instead we find variation and gradience commonplace in empirical studies, and we find phonological phenomena intimately bound up with lexicon and morphology, syntax, discourse, and social context.

Developments from outside linguistics also point to a new view of language. Studies of natural categorization by psychologist Eleanor Rosch and her colleagues have had an impact on the way that linguists view categories, including word meaning (Lakoff 1987), grammatical classes such as gender (Zubin and Köpcke 1981), verb classes (Bybee and Moder 1983), grammatical functions such as subject and topic, and phonetic categories (K. Johnson 1997, Miller 1994, and other 'exemplar' approaches to phonetic categories). In particular, these studies show that the way human beings categorize both nonlinguistic and linguistic entities is not by discrete assignments to categories based on the presence or absence of features, but rather by comparison of features shared with a central member. All category members need not have all of the features characterizing the category, but a member is more central or more marginal depending on the number and nature of shared features. Moreover, Nosofsky (1988) has shown that the perceived center of a category can shift toward the more frequently experienced members.

A second development important to linguistic modeling is the development of computer models that can reproduce apparent 'rule-governed' behavior as well as probabilistic behavior using parallel distributed processing (Daugherty and Seidenberg 1994, Rumelhart and McClelland 1986, and others). In such models, labeled connectionist models, structures are not given in advance (i.e., innate), but take their form from the nature of the input, just as neurological matter is structured by the input it receives. Connectionist models, then, are quite compatible with usage-based theories of language. Langacker (1987) and now Ohala and Ohala (1995) argue that storage of linguistic percepts should be like the storage of other mental percepts.

Yet a third recent development applicable to a large array of sciences is the study of complex systems and their emergent properties. The basic idea behind emergence as it will be applicable here is that certain simple properties of a substantive nature, when applied repeatedly, create structure. Lindblom et al. (1984) are, to my knowledge, the first to apply the notion of emergent structure in linguistics. They illustrate emergence in the following way:

Termites construct nests that are structured in terms of pillars and arches and that create a sort of 'air-conditioned' environment. The form of these nests appears to arise as a result of a simple local behavioral pattern which is followed by each individual insect: the pillars and arches are formed by deposits of gluti- nous sand flavored with pheromone. Pheromone is a chemical substance that is used in communication within certain insect species. Animals respond to such stimuli after (tasting or) smelling them. Each termite appears to follow a path of increasing pheromone density and deposit when the density starts to decrease. Suppose the termites begin to build on a fairly flat surface. In the beginning the deposits are randomly distributed. A fairly uniform distribution of pheromone is produced. Somewhat later local peaks have begun to appear serving as stimuli for further deposits that gradually grow into pillars and walls by iteration of the same basic stimulus-response process. At points where several such peaks come close, stimulus conditions are particularly likely to generate responses. Deposits made near such maxima of stimulation tend to form arches. As termites continue their local behavior in this manner, the elaborate structure of the nest gradually emerges. (Lindblom et al. 1984: 185–186)

Lindblom et al. point out that the importance of this notion for lin- guistics is that structure can be explained without attributing a 'mental blueprint' to the creatures creating the structure – that substance and form are intimately related (see also Hopper 1987, Keller 1994). Note further that in this example and others of emergence in complex systems, substance and form are related via the PROCESS by which the structure is created.

If we apply emergence to language, the substance and use interact to create structure. The substance in question includes both phonetics and semantics. Phonetic substance has always been included in the field of phonology. Only a few phonologists have ever proposed that phonology is independent of phonetics (see Postal 1968). On the con- trary, most phonologists see phonetics as motivating phonology (for a recent statement, see Hayes 1999). They have perhaps not always been serious enough about pursuing the phonetic facts, however. One promi- nent feature of generative phonology has been its disdain for the 'low- level' phonetic properties of speech, properties that presumably border on performance.

Semantics, on the other hand, has been considered irrelevant to phonology. This would not seem to be such a serious allegation to level at phonologists, except that phonological descriptions and theoretical works are full of references to notions such as morpheme and word boundaries – both of which delimit meaningful units – as well as to specific grammatical categories or specific morphemes. Generative phonologists and Optimality Theory phonologists have proceeded as though the content of these categories did not matter. I have shown in Bybee (1985) that the phonological fusion of morphemes reflects their degree of semantic fusion, and in the chapters of this book, I will explore further the relation between grammatical and lexical units and phonological structure. Generative theories have largely neglected such topics: even though morphological decomposition has played an important role in the development of generative theories from *The Sound Pattern of English* to Lexical Phonology and Optimality Theory, the semantic derivations that should parallel the phonological ones have never been attempted.

While substance has found its way into phonology from both the phonetic and semantic end, USE has been systematically excluded from structuralist theories altogether. As mentioned earlier, distinctions such as langue versus parole (de Saussure) and competence versus performance (Chomsky) were specifically designed to set up a mental object that is separate from the uses to which it is put and to designate the mental object as the proper domain for linguistics. Of course, there is some value in distinguishing mental representations from the social activities upon which they are based, but totally excluding factors of use from consideration ignores the potential relation between representation and use. It is certainly possible that the way language is used affects the way it is represented cognitively, and thus the way it is structured.

In fact, a good deal of progress in morphology and syntax has been made in explaining specific phenomena by making just this assumption. It has been shown that syntactic structures are the result of the conventionalization of frequently used discourse patterns (e.g., DuBois 1985, Givón 1979), and that grammatical morphemes develop from lexical morphemes in particular constructions through increases in the frequency of use and through extension in use to more and more contexts (Bybee et al. 1994, Haiman 1994). Greenberg (1966) has demonstrated that markedness effects are directly related to frequency of use, with unmarked members of categories being the most frequent, and Tiersma (1982) has shown that this hypothesis also explains cases of local markedness in morphology. Psycholinguists have long known that high-frequency words are accessed faster than low-frequency ones, and I have argued that high-frequency irregular morphological formations tend to maintain their irregularities precisely because of their high frequency (Bybee 1985, Hooper 1976b). In all of these findings we have a dynamic aspect – language structure is becoming or remaining because of the way language is used. Thus the emphasis on the static, synchronic language as the object of study has given way to the view of language as slowly, gradually, but inexorably mutating under the dynamic forces of language use.

Very little attention has been given to phonology in this usage-based approach to language, yet these same ideas CAN be applied to phonological phenomena with very interesting results. It is the purpose of this book to explore the phenomena that have traditionally been studied as phonology, reevaluating structural notions in terms of use and substance. The successes of structuralism in its various guises are not being discarded. Rather structural notions will first be empirically evaluated to ascertain their viability, then the basis of such notions will be considered, and the role that substance and especially, use, plays in the phenomena will be discussed. The phenomena discussed here point to a deep involvement of phonology with lexicon and grammar, and a role for both token and type frequency in shaping phonological structure. A dynamic view of language is taken here, one that integrates both synchronic and diachronic sources of explanation.[1]

1.2   Some Basic Principles of a Usage-Based Model

The ideas that I will apply to phonology are for the most part already present in the literature and are now shared by a number of linguists, phoneticians, and psychologists. A brief statement of these ideas follows.

1. Experience affects representation. The use of forms and patterns both in production and perception affects their representation in memory. High-frequency words and phrases have stronger representations in the sense that they are more easily accessed and less likely to undergo analogical change. Low-frequency words are more difficult to access and may even become so weak as to be forgotten. The lexical strength of words may change as they are used more or less in different contexts. Patterns (represented as schemas, see below) that apply to more items are also stronger

---

[1] The phonological theory developed here is quite different from Natural Generative Phonology (NGP) (Hooper 1976a). For while NGP had very concrete lexical representations, much involvement of morphology and the lexicon with phonology, and the same view of the relation of synchrony to diachrony, it was a structuralist theory and provided no means of representing the impact of language use on language structure.

and more accessible, and thus more productive than those applying to fewer items. This is in contrast to modular approaches in
which representations and rules or constraints are all static and
fixed, and in which all rules or representations in the same component have the same status (for instance, all being equally accessible no matter how many forms they apply to).

2. Mental representations of linguistic objects have the same
properties as mental representations of other objects. Of course,
this is the simplest assumption we can make – that the brain
operates in the same way in different domains. One consequence
of this assumption is that mental representations do not have
predictable properties abstracted away from them, but rather
are firmly based on categorizations of actual tokens. As
Langacker (1987) and Ohala and Ohala (1995) have pointed
out, if predictable properties are taken away from objects,
they become unrecognizable. (See Chapter 2 for further
discussion.)

3. Categorization is based on identity or similarity. Categorization
organizes the storage of phonological percepts. What form this
categorization takes is an interesting question and one that can
be approached through phonetic and psychological experimentation as well as through analogies with findings in other perceptual domains. From structural linguistic analysis we can already
identify many different types of relations among linguistic objects
– for example, the relation between two phonetic tokens of the
same word, that between tokens of the same morpheme in different words, and that between two similar phones in different
words in the same or different contexts.

4. Generalizations over forms are not separate from the stored
representation of forms but emerge directly from them. In
Langacker's terms, there is no 'rule/list separation' (see Chapter
2). Generalizations over forms are expressed as relations
among forms based on phonetic and/or semantic similarities. New
forms can be produced by reference to existing forms, but most
multimorphemic words are stored whole in the lexicon.

5. Lexical organization provides generalizations and segmentation
at various degrees of abstraction and generality. Units such as
morpheme, segment, or syllable are emergent in the sense that
they arise from the relations of identity and similarity that
organize representations. Since storage in this model is highly

redundant, schemas may describe the same pattern at different degrees of generality (Langacker 2000).

6. Grammatical knowledge is procedural knowledge. Anderson (1993) and Boyland (1996) distinguish declarative or propositional knowledge (e.g., 'Washington, DC is the capital of the United States') from procedural knowledge (how to drive a car, tie your shoelaces, and so on). While linguistic knowledge is in part declarative (in the sense that we can cite the meanings of words, for instance), much linguistic knowledge is procedural (Boyland 1996). A native speaker can form an acceptable sentence quite automatically, yet be unable to explain how this was done or to list what the properties of an acceptable sentence are. Thinking of grammatical constructions as procedural units has profound consequences for our view of phonology. Phonology then becomes a part of the procedure for producing and decoding constructions, rather than a purely abstract, psychological system.

1.3   The Creative Role of Repetition

Usage-based functionalism emphasizes language as a conventionalized, cultural object. In order to understand the nature of language, we need to understand what it means for behavior to be conventionalized. Haiman (1994, 1998) discusses grammar as ritualized behavior and points to various properties of both ritual and grammar that are the result of repetition. It is useful here to distinguish between a ritual and a convention: though both represent repeated behavior, a ritual can be individual and idiosyncratic, but a convention is agreed upon socially and evokes a consistent response in other members of a society (Tomasello et al. 1993). What both concepts have in common is that their structure is shaped by repetition. The following is a summary of some aspects of language that are shaped by repetition.

Through repetition we get lexical strength – strong, easily accessible representations, such as a greeting when you see someone you know or responses such as 'thank you' and 'you're welcome'; that is, any kind of learned automatic response. It is repetition that ritualizes these responses and makes them readily available. These are just extreme examples of a general phenomenon that pervades linguistic representation – repetition leads to strength of representation (Bybee 1985).

Repetition also leads to reduction of form. This is true of nonlinguistic gestures such as making the sign of the cross. It is true in nonhuman rituals: among chimpanzees (according to Plooij 1978, cited in Haiman 1994) the original gesture of lying down is reduced to just leaning slightly backwards. And it is true of language in many obvious cases. Greetings become reduced, (*how are you* becomes *hi*), grammaticizing phrases with increasing frequency reduce and compress (*going to* becomes *gonna*), and, in less obvious cases, there is a general frequency effect in reductive sound changes (see Section 1.4).

Repetition also leads to the reduction of meaning. This reduction or bleaching of meaning can be related to what Haiman calls habituation, or the loss of impact due to repetition. Habituation is also a general phenomenon, not restricted to language or to humans. It is 'a decline in the tendency to respond to stimuli that have become familiar due to repeated or persistent exposure' (Haiman 1994:7). We recognize habituation in the trivialization by repetition of great music (Beethoven's Fifth Symphony) or great art (Van Gogh's sunflowers). We also find it in language in cases where the emphatic becomes the normal. For instance, in the French negative construction *ne . . . pas*, *pas*, literally 'step', was once an emphatic added to the original negative *ne*, but is now obligatory and nonemphatic.

Finally, and perhaps most importantly, repetition leads to emancipation. In emancipation, instrumental actions are disassociated from their original motivation and are free to take on a communicative function instead. The military salute derives from the more instrumental gesture used in the Middle Ages when knights in armor greeted one another. They raised the visor of their helmet to show their faces as an indication of a peaceful greeting. The armor is gone, the visor is gone, but a reduced form of the gesture remains, though without its instrumental function. It no longer raises the visor, but it has been imbued instead with the function of communicating respect for the military hierarchy.

Applications of the principle of emancipation through repetition in language involve all sorts of cases of conventionalization, and most commonly, cases in which one communicative function is replaced by another. For instance, the inquiry into someone's current state of being, *how are you*, is not just reduced phonologically to *hi*, but also is emancipated from its original communicative value and now serves simply as a greeting. (A more conservative function of *hi* is found in some dialects of Black English where speakers commonly respond to *hi* with *fine*). Emancipation is also richly illustrated in the process of grammaticization during which words lose their categoriality. For instance, verbs become auxiliaries and sometimes affixes, and also become disassociated from their lexical meaning and take on pragmatic or grammatical functions, as when *be going to* loses its motion sense and becomes a future marker.

Haiman (1994) demonstrates that the development of ritual is a common process in the animal kingdom, and by no means restricted to humans, or even primates, as dog and cat owners can attest. He further argues (Haiman 1998) that ritualization is the basis for the development of grammar. The process of grammaticization depends upon repetition and is characterized by the reduction of both meaning and form, by strong entrenchment of patterns, and by emancipation in the sense that forms in their grammaticizing constructions often shift from propositional meaning to discourse-oriented functions (Traugott 1989). Our understanding of the ritualization process can be applied to syntax, as Haiman has shown, but also to phonology, as we investigate the role of repetition in the structuring of phonological patterns and lexical representations.

1.4 Frequency Effects

Much is already known about frequency effects in language, and much remains to be learned. In this section, I will lay out the basic notions and terminology that will be taken up again in later chapters.

There are two ways of counting frequency of occurrence that are applicable to language: token frequency and type frequency. TOKEN FREQUENCY is the frequency of occurrence of a unit, usually a word, in running text – how often a particular word comes up. Thus *broke* (the past tense of *break*) occurs 66 times per million words in Francis and Kučera (1982), while the past tense verb *damaged* occurs 5 times in the same corpus. In other words, the token frequency of *broke* is much higher than that of *damaged*.

TYPE FREQUENCY refers to the dictionary frequency of a particular pattern (e.g., a stress pattern, an affix, or a consonant cluster). For instance, English Past Tense is expressed in several different ways, but the expression with the highest type frequency is the suffix *-ed*, as in *damaged*, which occurs on thousands of verbs. The pattern found in *broke* has a much lower type frequency, occurring with only a handful of verbs (depending upon how you count them: *spoke, wrote, rode,*

*[handwritten: * or: frequent thing occur in context with a lot of redundancy?]*

etc.). The penultimate stress pattern of Spanish has a very high type frequency, occurring with about 95% of nouns and adjectives that end in vowels (*abuéla, camíno, pronómbre*), while antepenultimate stress has a much lower type frequency (*claúsula, fonológica*). One can also count the token frequency of such patterns – that is, how often the pattern occurs in running text.

1.4.1 Token Frequency

Token frequency has two distinct effects that are important for phonology and morphology. In one frequency effect, phonetic change often progresses more quickly in items with high token frequency. This effect is particularly noticeable in grammaticizing elements or phrases that undergo drastic reduction as they increase in frequency. Thus *be going to*, which is becoming a future marker in English, is reduced to ['gʌɾə] or even further reduced in phrases such as *I'm gonna* to ['aiməɾə]. Similarly, the conventionalized contractions of English are reduced due to their high frequency: *I'm, I'll, I've, can't, don't, won't*, and so on (Krug 1998). But the effect occurs on a more subtle level as well: regular sound change in many cases progresses more quickly in items of high token frequency. There is a tendency in American English for syllabicity to be lost in sequences of unstressed schwa + resonant, as in *every, camera, memory*, and *family*. This reduction is more advanced in words of higher frequency (such as those just named) than in words of lower frequency, such as *mammary, artillery, homily* (Hooper 1976b). The loss of final [t] or [d] after a consonant is also more common in words of higher frequency, such as *went, just*, and *and*. In fact, a general effect of token frequency on the rate of deletion has been found for 2000 tokens of final [t] or [d] (Bybee 2000b).[2]

[handwritten: Is this regular?]

If sound changes are the result of phonetic processes that apply in real time as words are used, then those words that are used more often have more opportunity to be affected by phonetic processes. If representations are changed gradually, with each token of use having a potential effect on representation, then words of high frequency will change at a faster rate than will words of low frequency.[3] The streamlining of

---

[2] Further discussion of these examples and further references for other similar examples can be found in Chapter 3.

[3] This suggestion is found in Moonwomon (1992). Factors other than simple frequency are important, too. These are discussed in Chapter 3.

*[handwritten: at a given frequency/v truth. If some tendency exists, it will affect frequent items more, at their rate of their frequency. *]*

high-frequency words and phrases has the effect of automatizing production. Any motor activity that is repeated often becomes more efficient. The first effect of frequency, then, is to automate production
(Boyland 1996). (For further discussion, see Chapter 3.)

The second effect of frequency seems to contradict the first, since it
makes items more resistant to change, but it concerns change of a different kind. High frequency encourages phonetic change, but it renders
items more conservative in the face of grammatical change or analogical change based on the analysis of other forms (Phillips 2001). For
example, high-frequency forms with alternations resist analogical leveling: while English *weep / wept, creep / crept,* and *leap / leapt* have a
tendency to regularize to *weeped, creeped,* and *leaped,* respectively, the
high-frequency verbs with the same pattern, *keep / kept, sleep / slept*
show no such tendency (Bybee 1985, Hooper 1976b). As a result, morphological irregularity is always centered on the high-frequency items
of a language. This conservatism of much-used expressions can also be
found on the syntactic level (Bybee and Thompson 2000). It has often
been observed that pronouns show more conservative behavior than
full noun phrases. English pronouns, for example, maintain distinct
forms for nominative and oblique case, while nouns have lost these case
distinctions. The position of pronouns sometimes reflects an earlier
word order. Similarly, verbal auxiliaries, which are very frequent, often
retain conservative syntactic characteristics. The English auxiliaries, for
instance, retain the ability to invert with the subject, and they precede
rather than follow the negative, both properties once shared by all
verbs (Bybee to appear).

This conserving effect of frequency places some items outside the
domain of the regular combinatorial patterns of the language. Their
frequency gives them a high level of lexical strength. That is, they are
so engrained as individual patterns that they are less likely to change
even if general changes are occurring in the language. To account for
this entrenchment effect, I have proposed (Bybee 1985) that representations are strengthened whenever they are accessed. This strengthening makes them subsequently easier to access and also more
resistant to some forms of change.

1.4.2 Type Frequency and Productivity

Another major effect of frequency and thus of usage is the effect of
type frequency in determining productivity. Productivity is the extent

to which a pattern is likely to apply to new forms (e.g., borrowed items or novel formations). It appears that the productivity of a pattern, expressed in a schema, is largely, though not entirely, determined by its type frequency: the more items encompassed by a schema, the stronger it is, and the more available it is for application to new items. Thus, the English Past Tense -*ed* applies to thousands of verbs and is much more productive than any of the irregular patterns, which are highly restricted in the number of verbs to which they apply (Bybee 1985, 1995; MacWhinney 1978; see also Chapter 5).

Since type frequency is based on the number of items matching a particular pattern, it is also relevant for determining the relative strength of phonotactic patterns, stress patterns, and other phonological patterns applying at the word level. Recent studies have shown that subjects' judgments of the relative acceptability of nonce items with occurring and nonoccurring phonotactic patterns are based on the distribution of these patterns in the lexicon. Patterns with high type frequency are judged to be more acceptable than patterns with low type frequency (Pierrehumbert 1994b, Vitevitch et al. 1997, and others; see Chapter 4.7). In addition, for classes defined by morphological, phonotactic, or stress patterns, type frequency interacts with the degree of similarity of the members of the class such that a smaller number of highly similar items (a 'gang') can also evince limited productivity (Aske 1990, Bybee and Moder 1983, Frisch et al. 2001; see also Chapter 5).

The importance of productivity of both phonological and morphological schemas to our understanding of cognitive representations of language cannot be overstated. Productivity provides us with evidence about the generalizations that speakers make, and it is important to stress that speakers' generalizations are not always the same as those devised by linguists on the basis of distributional evidence. Distributional evidence often recreates past stages of a language and does not reveal the restructuring and reanalysis that the patterns might have undergone. Productivity can be used as a diagnostic to determine which patterns are fossilized, and which represent viable schemas accessible to speakers.

1.4.3   Frequency Effects in Other Theories

The proposal that frequency of use affects representation suggests a very different view of lexical storage and its interaction with other aspects of the grammar or phonology than that assumed in most current theories. Structuralist and generative theories assume that the lexicon is a static list, and that neither the rules nor the lexical forms of a language are changed at all by instances of use. Similarly, as Pierrehumbert (1999) points out, all versions of Optimality Theory (Hayes 1999, Prince and Smolensky 1993, 1997) posit a strict separation of lexicon and grammar that makes it impossible to describe any of the interactions of phonology with the lexicon that are attested in the literature, many of which have just been mentioned: for instance, the fact that many phonological changes affect high-frequency items first, and the fact that the strength of phonotactic constraints is directly related to the number of items they apply to in the existing lexicon. Hammond (1999) identifies an effect of frequency in cases of the application of the Rhythm Rule and proposes that an Optimality Theory account of the facts can include item-specific constraints inserted into the constraint hierarchy. But such a proposal neither fits well with other properties of Optimality Theory nor does it provide an account for why words and phrases of different frequencies of use behave differently.

1.5   Phonology as Procedure, Structure as Emergent

If we conceptualize phonology as part of the procedure for producing and understanding language, the phonological properties of language should result from the fact that it is a highly practiced behavior associated with the vocal tract of human beings. To move away from the more abstract views of phonology, it is perhaps useful to compare speaking to other fairly complex but repetitive neuromotor activities, such as playing the piano. When a person learns to play the piano, he or she learns not just to strike notes, but to strike notes in sequence. Each piece of music has its own sequence of notes that must be learned. Practice is essential; the motor patterns that lead to the fluent striking of longer and longer sequences of notes must be automated for a piece to begin to sound like music. With practice, the transitions between the notes become more fluent, and the speed of execution automatically increases. In order to maintain the correct rhythm and tempo, the player must at times hold back and not play every note as fast as possible.

    An important result of learning to play several pieces is that new pieces are then easier to master. Why is this? I hypothesize that the player can access bits of old stored pieces and incorporate them into new pieces. The part of a new piece that uses parts of a major scale is much easier to master if the player has practiced scales than is a part with a new melody that does not hearken back to common sequences. This means that snatches of motor sequences can be reused in new contexts. The more motor sequences stored, the greater ease with which the player can master a new piece.

Storage and access to motor sequences implies categorization in storage. Even after the A Major scale is mastered as an automated unit, subsequences of the scale can still be accessed for use elsewhere. Connections are made between intervals that recur in different pieces.

Some analogies with the acquisition and use of phonology are obvious here. Children learn phonological sequences as parts of words, never independently of words. Articulatory routines that are already mastered are called forth for the production of new words, leading to a tendency of children to expand their vocabulary by acquiring words that are phonologically similar to those they already know (Ferguson and Farwell 1975, Lindblom 1992). This tendency leads to the structuring of the phonological sequences across words and the limiting of the potentially immense phonetic inventory. Put another way, the repetition of gestures and sequences across words allows relations of identity and similarity to develop in stretches of speech, giving rise to segment, syllable, and foot-sized units.

With practice, speakers become more fluent in stringing words together, and this fluency and automation is characterized by the smoothing of transitions and overlapping of movements constrained by the need to retain information value. Some repeated sequences become highly automated and reduced in form. At the same time, speakers must be able to access and recruit sequences into new combinations to express their thoughts and intentions. With practice, the ability to produce new combinations is also enhanced, probably by the storage of multiword constructional schemata (Bybee 1998, Pawley and Syder 1983). The use of novel combinations, however, does not constitute as large a percentage of spontaneous speech as one might suppose. Erman and Warren (1999) estimate that about 55% of the spoken and written texts they analyzed consisted of prefabricated multiword sequences.

Grammatical and phonological structure emerge from the facts of co-occurrence in language use. Words that commonly occur together – for instance, nouns and their determiners, or verbs and their objects –

begin to behave as constituents. The more commonly they co-occur, the tighter their constituency becomes (Bybee and Scheibman 1999; see also Chapter 6). Phonological structure is affected by use in that articulatory accommodations occur as the result of real language use. This is the sense in which grammar can be said to be emergent.

Emergence in language is much more complex than the emergence described earlier of the structure of the termite nest. The main difference is that human beings are much more intelligent than termites. First, the experiences of human beings in using language are registered in the brain, are categorized there, and gain some of their structure from categorizing capabilities of the mind. Second, the use of language by humans is goal-oriented or purposeful. The purpose is to communicate thoughts, perspectives, needs, desires, and so on. Note that the purpose of communicative acts is to communicate, not to create grammar. Yet the result of innumerable communicative acts is to change language and to create and recreate grammar (Bybee et al. 1994, Keller 1994).

Thus, functional constraints are manifested in specific languages through individual acts of language use. If there is a constraint comparable to the NO CODA constraint of Optimality Theory, it is a result of the phonetic tendency to reduce and coarticulate coda consonants more than onset consonants. This tendency manifests itself in every instance of language use in languages that have coda consonants, reducing these consonants by very small degrees. Eventually, coda consonants are lost in such languages, leaving a language with a reduced number of coda consonants or none at all. Since no comparable tendency operates on onset consonants, the result is that some languages lack codas, but that no languages lack onsets. Thus, the intersection of phonetic grounding and language-specific and typological properties takes place in the individual speaker in multiple instances of language use.

1.6   Organization of the Book

The goal of this book is to propose a unified account of some of the major empirical phenomena that have been examined in phonological theory in recent decades as well as less familiar phonological phenomena that provide evidence for the importance of usage in understanding phonological structure. In Chapter 2, I present the model of representation proposed for morphology in Bybee (1985) and show

how it can be used to accommodate phonological representation and to model various usage effects. Chapter 3 argues for the need for phonetic detail in lexical representations and shows how variation and sound change can be modeled in an exemplar representation. Chapter 4 discusses patterns of phonetic implementation in terms of articulatory gestures and argues for certain strong constraints on sound change. Here also, the acceptability of phonological patterns in the lexicon, or phonotactic patterns, are discussed in terms of their distribution in the existing lexicon. Chapter 5 presents what is known to date about the interactions of morphology with phonology; it includes a discussion of morphologization, of the differences between patterns based on morphology from those based on phonology, and of the role of type and token frequency and similarity in the formation of productive classes. Chapter 6 treats sequences larger than a word and demonstrates through the study of sound change in progress that words are the basic units of memory storage, but that longer sequences of high frequency as well as constructions can also be stored in memory and processed as chunks. Chapter 7 studies lexicalized sandhi alternations, using French liaison as the example, and demonstrates that the loss of liaison in certain contexts corresponds to morphological regularization in that high-frequency contexts maintain liaison longer. The implication of this finding is that phrases and constructions with liaison are stored in memory much as morphologically complex words are. Finally, Chapter 8 delves into the theoretical status of universals or crosslinguistic tendencies, arguing that there is an essential diachronic component to any attempt to explain linguistic structure or to account for universals of language.

1.7   Language as a Part of Human Behavior

A basic assumption of this book is that the cognitive and psychological processes and principles that govern language are not specific to language, but are in general the same as those that govern other aspects of human cognitive and social behavior. Our enormous memory capacity, fine motor control, the ability to categorize experience, and the ability to make inferences may be fine-tuned for language, but are all clearly used in other domains as well. This means that the principles underlying language could be studied using the methods and theories of psychologists or even biologists. It also means, however, that the discoveries of linguists could unveil principles useful in the more general understanding of human psychology. This book is a linguist's book: it applies the established methods and data of linguists to the understanding of language as an emergent system resulting from the general cognitive capacities of humans interacting with language substance over many instances of language use.

2

A Usage-Based Model for Phonology and Morphology

2.1 Introduction

The goal of phonology as conceived by generative theory is to describe the following phenomena: (i) the relations among similar but physically distinct sounds that are nonetheless taken to be 'the same' in some sense (allophonic relations), (ii) the relations among variants of morphemes as they occur in different contexts, (iii) phonological units of various sizes – features, segments, syllables, feet, and so on, and (iv) language-specific and universal properties of these relations and units.

Assuming that the proposed methods for accomplishing these goals in generative phonology are familiar to readers, I will briefly show in this chapter that an alternate model, which does not make the same assumptions as generative phonology, can accomplish these same goals as well as accommodate other facts about phonological structure that are left unexplained in generative theory. The evidence in favor of this model is not all presented here, but rather is developed in later chapters, since this chapter is intended to provide a frame of reference for proposals discussed later in the book.

The model sketched here is based on my proposals in Bybee (1985) concerning relationships among morphologically related forms – proposals that were derived from the study of the crosslinguistic properties of morphological systems and the characteristic ways in which morphological forms change over time. It is augmented by the theoretical statements contained in Langacker (1987, 2000) and other works. The model also incorporates findings on phonetic categorization reported by Miller (1994) and K. Johnson (1997) and on lexical relations reported by Pisoni et al. (1985). The model contains gradient categories and relations and is heavily affected by the nature of the input;

it thus contains properties that can be subjected to formal modeling and simulation using connectionist architecture.

2.2   The Rule/List Fallacy

Perhaps the most fundamental difference between the model to be explored here and structuralist or generativist models is the rejection of the notion that material contained in rules does not also appear in the lexicon and vice versa. Structuralist frameworks placed great emphasis on the systematicity of language, and it was thought appropriate to reduce the enormous complexity of language by extracting regularities that could be captured in general statements (i.e., rules), thereby only representing truly idiosyncratic material in a list (i.e., the lexicon). In this view, the major goal of linguistic analysis is to determine which features of a unit are idiosyncratic, and which are predictable by rule, with the additional desideratum of having as many features predictable by rule as possible.

However, there is no particular reason to believe that human language users organize or process linguistic material in this way. It is clear, for instance, that a child cannot learn that *-ed* marks the regular past tense of English without first learning a number of verbs containing this suffix, such as *played*, *spilled*, *talked*, and so on. When the generalization is formed, these words are not necessarily flushed from memory (Langacker 1987:42). Nor do new words formed in this particular way fail to be recorded in memory. New instances of regular past tenses can also have an impact on the representation of language. Our reaction to linguistic percepts is like our reaction to other perceptual experiences: our brains record even the predictable pieces of the experience. Granted, our reaction to the predictable features of experience differs from our reaction to the unpredictable: the predictable properties are mapped onto the memory representation of previous similar or identical experiences, whereas new, unpredictable properties must create new memories. However, this is very different from saying that predictable properties are not stored in memory at all, but are present only in rules.

Langacker (1987:392) describes phonological representations in Cognitive Grammar as follows, 'phonetic details are no less properties of an individual morpheme by virtue of conforming to general patterns.' A parallel statement concerning a nonlinguistic percept would be that the presence of two ears is still an important property of a dog, even though all dogs have two ears. Langacker (1987:392) goes on to say, 'If all the regularity is factored out of a linguistic structure, the residue is seldom if ever recognizable as a coherent entity plausibly attributed to cognitive autonomy.' That is to say, if our memories for dogs excluded all the predictable features (two ears, a muzzle, fur, a tail, wet nose, etc.), what is left would not be a recognizable or coherent entity. Similarly, if all predictable features are removed from a word, it would not be recognizable as an English word, or as a linguistic object at all (see also Ohala and Ohala 1995).

The point is not to deny the presence of regularities, but rather to say that predictable features need not be excluded from representation in individual items. The presence of a feature on a list does not exclude it from being predictable by rule. Rather the notion of rule takes a very different form. Linguistic regularities are not expressed as cognitive entities or operations that are independent of the forms to which they apply, but rather as schemas or organizational patterns that emerge from the way that forms are associated with one another in a vast complex network of phonological, semantic, and sequential relations.

2.3 Organized Storage

Linguistic items are not stored in a long, unstructured list. Rather, the regularities and similarities observable in linguistic items are used to structure storage. Experiments on lexical access have shown that subjects can identify a word presented with masking noise more successfully if the preceding word they heard (without masking) is phonetically similar. Moreover, the greater the degree of similarity, the more it aids in recognition of the masked word (Pisoni et al. 1985). The interpretation of this result is that the activation of a word also activates phonetically similar words. One way of accounting for this pattern of spreading activation is to propose that the similarities among words cause them to be organized lexically as spatially proximate. Pisoni et al. say:

Phonetic Refinement Theory assumes that words in the lexicon are organized as sequences of phonetic segments in a multi-dimensional acoustic–phonetic space. In this space, words that are more similar in their acoustic–phonetic structure are closer to each other in the lexicon. Furthermore, it is possible to envision the lexicon as structured so that those *portions* of words that are similar in location and structure are closer together in this space. For example, words that rhyme with each other are topologically deformed to bring together those parts of the words that are phonetically similar and separate those portions of words that are phonetically distinct. (1985:87, emphasis in original)

Bybee (1985) presents a similar proposal using a two-dimensional visual representation that is easier to render on paper than topological deformation; in this proposal, identity relations are represented by connecting lines. Activation of one item spreads to other items connected by such lines. In Bybee (1985), I proposed that these lexical connections can be phonological or semantic, since the type of priming relations just described also occur among semantically related words. When words are related by parallel semantic and phonological connections, the resulting relations are morphological, as with a series of words expressing past tense that all end in [d].

In effect, generalizations about linguistic units are discovered by speakers as they categorize items for storage. Such generalizations can be described in schemas, which are non-process statements about stored items. The schemas represented in Figures 2.1, 2.2, and 2.3 correspond to the following generalizations, though it is not necessarily the case that these have a cognitive representation independent of the forms that participate in them.

(1)   [ɛ̃nd] is a possible syllable rhyme: [$__ɛ̃nd$]
(2)   [b] is a possible syllable onset (in effect, [b] is a phoneme): [$b__]
(3)   [[VERB] d] means Past Tense: [[VERB] d]Past Tense

Thus, it is possible to represent the generalization of patterns without removing predictable information from the representation of particular items.

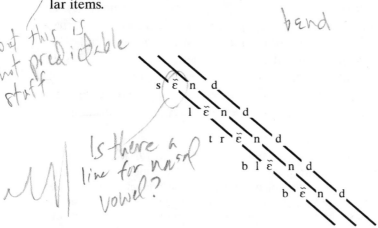

Figure 2.1. Lexical connections for [ɛ̃nd] in *send, lend, trend, blend, bend.*

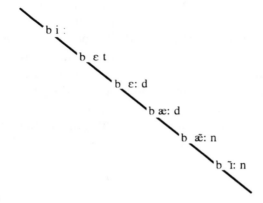

Figure 2.2. Lexical connections for the [b] in *bee, bet, bed, bad, ban, bin.*

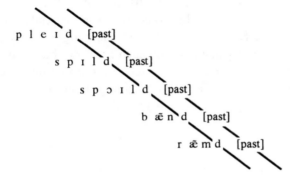

Figure 2.3. Phonological and semantic connections yield Past in *played, spilled, spoiled, banned, rammed.*

The type of representation described here can be thought of as an associative network. In such a network, storage can be redundant in the sense that words are stored even if they are predictable from the combination of morphemes. In some cases, words are stored multiple times, depending on contexts of use. Similar or identical properties of meaning and form are associated with one another across items, and these associations give rise to generalizations such as those in 1–3.

2.4   Morphological Structure Is Emergent

Since phonologically and semantically similar words and phrases are categorized and stored in relation to one another, morphological relations give rise to internal structure. Using connecting lines, we can see in Figure 2.4 that stems and affixes emerge naturally once appropriate associations have been made (Bybee 1985). The stems and affixes that are apparent in this diagram are never extracted from the words in which they occur. There is no separate morphological component nor a list of morphemes anywhere in the grammar. Nevertheless, new formations are possible on the basis of the type of organization illustrated here. The schema in (4) that describes this pattern can be applied to new verbs.

(4)   [[VERB] ɪŋ] Progressive Participle

Strictly speaking, a morpheme is a unit with semantic content, but various morphlike elements, which either fail the meaningfulness criterion or do not recur in other words, also litter the scene. As shown in Bybee (1988a), it is possible to capture such partial relations using connecting lines. For example, certain meaningless formatives with uniform behavior can be identified such as those that recur in *receive*, *reception* and *deceive*, *deception*. Is *-ceive* a morpheme? The answer is no, because it has no identifiable meaning. However, some speakers might still be aware that *-ceive* recurs in verbs and furthermore alter-

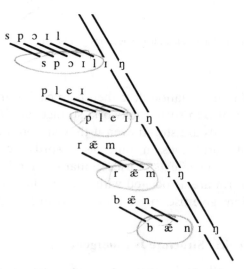

Figure 2.4. The emergence of the *-ing* suffix in *play*, *playing*; *ban*, *banning*; *ram*, *ramming*; *spoil*, *spoiling*.

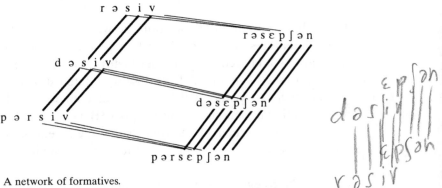

Figure 2.5. A network of formatives.

nates with *-cep-* before *-tion* in nouns. These submorphemic relations can be represented as in Figure 2.5.

Another type of defective morph occurs in cases in which one part of a word is identifiable as a morpheme, but the remainder of the word is meaningless and does not recur. Such morphs (often called cranberry morphs) occur as the first part of the days of the week. The *-day* part of these words is transparently meaningful and identifiable as the word *day*, but *Mon-, Tues-, Wednes-, Thurs-,* and so on do not occur elsewhere and cannot be assigned any meaning except that of designating a day of the week. We need not ignore the fact that these words contain a meaningful element, *day*. Connecting lines can show this relationship without necessitating the assignment of morpheme status to the residue (Bybee 1988a).

Experiments reported in Gonnerman (1999) indicate that priming relations among morphologically related words are simply a consequence of the phonological and semantic similarity between words. While it is well known that *teach* primes *teacher*, Gonnerman shows that this is due to the parallel phonological and semantic similarity of the words by showing that priming relations are also evident between words with phonological and semantic similarity, but no morphological relationship, such as *jubilant, jubilee* or *trivial, trifle*. Thus the morphological structure of words is not a given, but rather is derived from relations of similarity.

Thus, the notion of morph or morpheme can be treated as gradient, depending upon whether or not the element has meaning assigned to it and whether it recurs. However, gradience is not limited to the defining of linguistic units, such as morpheme; gradience also characterizes two types of categorization used in the model proposed here.

First, the strength of association between items with identical or similar features may vary according to the number and nature of the features, and according to other factors, such as token frequency of the item (see Chapter 5). Thus, loosely related derivational pairs such as *despair, desperate* will have weaker connections than transparent inflectional pairs such as *shoe, shoes* (Bybee 1985, Derwing and Baker 1977). Gonnerman (1999) reports that the extent of the priming reflects the degree of semantic and phonological similarity between words.

Second, the categorization expressed in the schemas has a prototype structure, with some members qualifying as more central and others as more marginal members of the same category (Bybee and Moder 1983, Köpcke 1988, Prasada and Pinker 1993). Examples of this type of gradience will also be discussed in Chapter 5.

2.5   Rules and Schemas Compared

A debate ongoing in the literature for about a decade concerns the treatment of the English regular and irregular Past Tense in network or connectionist models, which lack explicit rules, versus models that posit explicit symbolic rules (Pinker 1991, Rumelhart and McClelland 1986, and others). This debate has helped to clarify the nature of symbolic rules and how they differ from the emergent generalizations referred to here as schemas. The basic point of disagreement in this debate is as follows. Connectionist and network models (Bybee 1985, 1995, Daugherty and Seidenberg 1994, Rumelhart and McClelland 1986, and others) claim that all grammatical generalizations are solidly based on particular forms and, as a result, can only be emergent patterns, not explicit rules. On the other hand, the dual-mechanism model (Marcus et al. 1995, Pinker 1991) claims that regular and irregular forms are treated differently. While irregular forms are listed in the lexicon and may be subject to treatment by schemas, regular forms are generated by a symbolic rule. As evidence, proponents of this theory point to the productivity of the English regular Past Tense versus the relative lack of productivity of the irregular formations. Proponents of the associative networks model point to the difference in type frequency to explain the higher productivity of the regular versus irregular Past Tense in English (Bybee 1995).

Rules represent pervasive schemas.

   One effect of this debate has been to clarify the notion of a symbolic rule, especially in contrast to emergent generalizations or
schemas. Four points of difference are evident in this debate. First,
schemas are organizational patterns in the lexicon and thus have no
existence independent of the lexical units from which they emerge. In
contrast, rules are postulated to exist independently of the forms to
which they apply. In fact, symbolic rules are thought to belong in a component or module that is separate from the lexicon.

   Second, schemas are highly affected by the number of participant
items: a schema ranging over many different verbs, for example, is more
productive than one ranging over only a few. Also, in this view, productivity is gradient; besides productive and unproductive patterns,
there may be intermediate degrees of productivity. Rules, on the other
hand, are not affected by the number of types to which they apply.
Since rules are independent of the forms that they affect, there cannot
be any relationship between the rule and the number of items it applies
to. Productivity of rules is determined by 'default' status. Once learners observe that a certain rule is used in default situations (e.g., for new
formations such as verbs derived from nouns), they determine that this
rule is the default or productive rule (Marcus et al. 1992).

   Third, schemas are highly affected by the particulars of existing
types. Bybee and Moder (1983) observed experimentally that the
closer an English nonce verb was to *strung*, the prototype, or best exemplar, of a small irregular verb class, the more likely it was that the subjects would form its Past Tense by changing the vowel to /ʌ/. Similarly,
Köpcke (1988) found that German subjects tended to pluralize nonce
nouns that ended in full vowels with -*s*, since that is the form used in
existing German nouns with full vowels (e.g., *Autos*, *Pizzas*). A symbolic rule, on the other hand, applies to a whole category, such as verb
or noun, without regard to the particular shape of individual members
(Marcus et al. 1995).   An emergent rule — P P

   Fourth, schemas may be gradient categories, based as they are on
particular types. Individual types may be closer to or farther from the
best exemplars of the category. Thus, speakers would exhibit probabilistic behavior in assigning nonce forms to one schema or another.
In contrast, rules are discrete in their behavior: a form either is or is
not subject to a rule because a form either belongs or does not belong
to the relevant category.

   As for the evidence for selecting schemas over rules, the preceding properties of schemas are just what we observe both in

experimentation and real language behavior. For example, even a pattern that affects many forms, such as the diphthongization in stressed syllables in Spanish verbs, is not easily extended to nonce verbs, but rather seems to be closely tied to the particular verbs with the pattern (Bybee and Pardo 1981, Kernan and Blount 1966). Experiments with nonce forms also confirm the relationship between the number of forms participating in a schema and the productivity of that schema (Bybee and Moder 1983, Bybee and Slobin 1982, Lobben 1991, Wang and Derwing 1994), as do productivity in child language (Guillaume 1927/1973) and intuitive judgments of productivity (Baayen and Lieber 1991). The effect of the particular shape of forms and the gradient nature of schemas are also confirmed in nonce probe experiments (Bybee and Moder 1983, Köpcke 1988, Prasada and Pinker 1993). Finally, there is evidence of effects of token frequency in regularly inflected forms, such as regular English Past Tense, which cannot be accounted for if regular forms are derived by rule rather than being stored in memory (Alegre and Gordon 1999a, Bybee 2000a, Hare et al. 2001). See Chapter 5 for more details about schemas over morphologically related forms.

2.6   Frequency Effects

The frequency effects mentioned briefly in Chapter 1 find a natural expression in this model. Since tokens of use map onto existing representations, high-frequency items grow strong and therefore are easier to access. The other side of the coin is that little-used items will tend to fade in representational strength and grow more difficult to access. The conserving effect of high token frequency, which protects high-frequency items from regularization on the basis of productive schemas, is represented as lexical strength. Since regularization only occurs when existing forms are difficult to access, high-frequency forms are not prone to regularization. The other effects of high token frequency will be discussed in later chapters.

Schemas, which are organizational patterns across lexical items, gain strength from the number of different items participating – that is, by their type frequency. Stronger schemas are more productive; that is, they are more likely to be used to produce new words. It is, of course, an empirical question how many items are required to constitute a schema. Empirical testing of productivity of patterns with different numbers of participants suggests that the minimum may be around six, but factors such as phonological similarity and token frequency of individual items also affect the formation of a schema. These issues are discussed in Chapter 5.

2.7 Units of Storage

The phonological shape of all words and frequent phrases that a person uses are stored in memory along with information about their meaning and contexts of use, both linguistic and nonlinguistic.[1] The storage is not a simple list, but entails a network of connections to related items that makes storage more efficient. Two issues concerning the nature of the stored elements often arise. First, are all the words of a language stored? This becomes an issue for languages with complex morphology, where a single verb might have thousands of possible forms. Second, what is the size of the units stored? How do we determine what is a word in a language, and what types of phrases are appropriate for storage? Sketches of answers to these questions will be given here.

Hankamer (1992) argues against the position that all possible words of a language are stored in the lexicon on the basis of agglutinative languages such as Turkish, where, by his calculations, a single verb root has, at least in principle, the possibility of having over a million forms. Sadock (1980) makes a similar argument for languages in which incorporation of a noun root in a verb form is common. These authors treat the issue of lexical listing as a clearcut dichotomy: the form is either in the lexicon or not. Moreover, they assume that each word adds complexity to the lexicon. However, if the lexicon is viewed as a complex network structure of the type described earlier, a word is not necessarily an independent unit, but is instead deeply embedded in the organizational structure. In this case, a regularly inflected word, say, *exaggerated*, whose stem is already present in some other word, *exaggerate*, adds no complexity to the lexicon and takes up very little 'space,' since all of its parts overlap with existing items. In fact, in a case such as this, it probably does not make sense to ask if *exaggerated* is 'in' the lexicon or not. It is there as a unit

---

[1] In Chapter 6 it will become clear that constructions are stored in the same way as words, and that their phonological material is subject to the same organizing principles as words are.

if it has been used, but the two portions of it overlap with other items and it has low token frequency, so it has little autonomy. The complex verb forms of Turkish or the incorporated nouns of Mohawk can be treated the same way – as highly embedded in a complex system.

However, all morphologically complex forms are not equal. Certain combinations of morphemes, for pragmatic and semantic reasons, may be used much more than other combinations. The complex forms of high-frequency combinations may stand out in various ways in lexical representation: they might resist regularizing change, they might undergo special reduction, or they might move away from semantically related forms (as *went* moved away from *wend*). Thus even the topology of regular, agglutinative morphology, like that found in Turkish, will not be uniform and flat, but instead will show a varied texture (see Gürel 1999).

The second issue concerns the size of the storage units. I have been using the term 'word' here, which raises two issues: the issue of words versus morphemes as units of representation and the question of the definition of 'word.' Many phonological and morphological theories use the word as the base unit. I will define 'word' as a unit of usage that is both phonologically and pragmatically appropriate in isolation. As such, words are plausible cognitive entities; they are units of production and perception that can undergo categorization. It is this cognitive autonomy that motivates my choice of words as storage units, though other arguments will be given in Chapter 6. While morphemes are derivable from words, they show considerably less autonomy.

How much of a stretch of speech constitutes a word? This is an empirical question that I hope to answer in this book, using phonological data and data from usage. Note first that the notion of word is also gradient and heavily based on use. We might define a word as a frequently recurring stretch of speech. Such a definition would include sequences that are orthographically several words. For instance, *want to*, *have to*, *going to*, and *would have* would be considered words under this definition, even though the elements involved occur elsewhere as words. In fact, the same phrase can be one word in some uses and multiple words in others. Consider the phrase *I don't know*. In some discourse-oriented uses, it is a single unit ([airəɾo]), while in its more compositional, transparent meaning it consists of three units (Bybee and Scheibman 1999, Scheibman

2000a). Similarly, all words of the same category may not be segmented the same way. For instance, some nouns might occur with a definite article (*the sun, the moon*), some with an indefinite (*a nap, another*), and so on. I will argue in Chapter 6 that the unit of storage is a processing unit or neuromotor routine and heavily influenced by actual usage.

2.8 Phonological Units

The articulatory and acoustic stream that constitutes speech is continuous and does not yield to exhaustive segmentation. Yet recurrent parts of the continuum can be associated to yield units of different sizes – namely, features, segments, syllables, and rhythmic units. A gestural score representation (Browman and Goldstein 1992) specifies the magnitude and temporal duration of gestures produced by the active articulators and their temporal coordination with one another. Lindblom (1992) argues that if anatomically and temporally identical control functions are stored only once, then given a set of CV syllables, identical syllable onsets and identical steady states (vowels) will be associated in a network such that units corresponding to segments will emerge. He further points out, however, that given the nature of speech, it is possible that chunks of different sizes will also emerge. There is no necessity that the speech stream be exhaustively segmented into alphabet-sized units; some units may be simple, like a pure vowel, others complex, like a diphthong or affricate. See Chapter 4 for further discussion.

Syllables have often been thought of as the basic organizing unit of articulation. According to Browman and Goldstein (1995:20), 'syllable structure is a characteristic pattern of coordination among gestures.' Once the nature and timing of particular gestural coordinations are described, in effect, syllabic structure has also been described. Generalization to a notion of syllable, however, occurs through schema-formation. Similarities among stretches of speech in terms of the temporal coordination of gestures will lead to an abstract notion of possible syllables for a language.

2.9 From Local to General Schemas

The architecture provided by the type of lexical organization envisioned here allows for many different analyses of the linguistic data. In fact, as Langacker (1987:28) argues, there is no reason to suppose that there is only one correct analysis and, hence, cognitive representation of any set of data. Rather, grammars may encompass different types of generalizations. The types of analyses that are preferred by speakers may be discovered by various empirical means, and the properties of the model can be appropriately revised. Relevant data include evidence from language change, the treatment of new words or loan words, and psycholinguistic experimentation. Some facts about schemas are already established, while others require more research.

Schemas may be formed at many different levels of generality. The representation of a particular word, such as *send*, would be a very specific or local schema. A schema for the rhyme *-end$* is at a more general level of representation. Then there could be a more general schema for *-Vnd$*, and a still more general – *vowel-nasal-voiced stop$*, or even more general *-vowel-sonorant-stop$*, and so on. The presence of any of these levels of generality for a schema does not preclude the existence of others.

Furthermore, the sequential domain of schemas is potentially open and only constrained by the input: schemas are formed over frequently occurring stretches of speech. Given the string *atmosphere*, what makes us think it is more likely that a schema will be formed over the sequence *-at-* than the sequence *-tm-*? Given the verb phrase *hit the ball*, what makes us group *the ball* rather than *hit the*? In both cases it is the fact that items that occur together frequently are grouped together into storage and processing units (Boyland 1996). That is, the input, or experience of the language user, determines much of what we have come to regard as linguistic structure. Saffran et al. (1996) have recently reported that eight-month-old infants learned to recognize three-syllable 'words' embedded in random sequences of syllables, with no other cue than that these three-syllable sequences occurred frequently in the input. It is important to note that this ability to segment arises before infants are aware that sequences of spoken language are referential.

The notion that frequency of co-occurrence in the input determines constituency has not been applied extensively at different levels of grammar (but see Bybee and Scheibman 1999). Once it is clear what patterns occur in linguistic usage, we will be able to separate the necessary properties of the human language faculty from the properties that are derivable from the input.

Evidence for prototype categorization has been reported for various hierarchical levels of linguistic structure.[2] Miller (1994) presents evidence that categorization of phonetic tokens has a prototype structure, with particular tokens being stored and categorized as more or less central members of categories. Judgments about phonotactic patterns have been shown to be based not on abstract rules, but on the frequency of distributional patterns of actually occurring words of the language (Coleman and Pierrehumbert 1997, Pierrehumbert 1994b, Vitevitch et al. 1997, see also Chapter 4). Morphological classes of words that behave in the same way, such as the verbs in English that follow the pattern of *string, strung* are organized into prototype categories and describable by schemas (Bybee and Moder 1983, see also Chapter 5). Syntactic constructional schemas also have prototype structure, are more productive if they apply to more items, and are based on patterns of usage (Goldberg 1995). Finally, of course, the earliest findings of this type were that semantic categories are not discrete, but rather have a prototype structure in which some members of the category are judged to be better exemplars than others (Rosch 1973, Lakoff 1987).

The same principles apply at all levels. Linguistic objects – phonetic sequences, words, phrases – are categorized in the same way as nonlinguistic objects – birds, chairs, noses. The structure of the categories is such that nondiscrete members may be more central or more marginal, frequency in experience influences the importance of particular features, and features may be more or less important to defining the category, but no feature is redundant and thus dispensable.

2.10 Conclusion

Many of the traditional questions of phonology, then, can be answered in terms of categorization. Allophones are phonetically similar and thus are categorized as belonging to the same or related cognitive units, provided no contexts of contrast are present. Relations among allomorphs are also relations of similarity involving not just phonetic but

---

[2] The term 'prototype' categorization is used here to refer to categorization that relies not on the presence or absence of discrete features, but on the organization of tokens of experience into groups based on similarity to a central member. Whether the categorization is based on similarity to an actually occurring exemplar or to an abstract prototype is not of concern at present.

The point is Occam's Razor

semantic properties as well. The units of phonology – syllables and segments – emerge from the interaction of the properties of gestural coordination and the frequency with which these gestures are combined sequentially. Crosslinguistic similarities can be attributed to the universal properties of the vocal tract and neural storage and to the fact that all cultures use language in very similar ways.

In addition to accounting for these traditional issues of phonology in a way that is consistent with what is known about psycholinguistic processing and cognition in general, this usage-based model goes beyond structuralist models to show how language use gives rise to structure. The model can explain how internal morphological structure arises through lexical organization. It can predict reductive phonetic changes in high-frequency forms and the susceptibility of low-frequency forms to morphosyntactic change based on productive patterns. It can also predict degrees of productivity based on type frequency and changes in constituency due to the frequent repetition of combinations of elements.

All of these proposals require further investigation, further articulation, and testing with empirical evidence from multiple sources. It is the purpose of this book to take a step in that direction.

3

The Nature of Lexical Representation

3.1 Introduction

In this chapter, I argue for a model of phonology which does not canonize the distinction between predictable and contrastive features in phonology with phonemic underlying representations. It is proposed instead that individual tokens of experience are stored and organized into categories without redundancies removed, as suggested in Chapter 2. In the following, I present evidence for this position by examining the following types of cases: (i) cases of phonetic variation that are specific to particular words (Section 3.4.1), (ii) cases of distributionally predictable features that are lexically contrastive (Section 3.4.2), and (iii) cases showing the involvement of variable sound change with morphology (Section 3.6).

In this chapter I also demonstrate the use of schemas for phonological generalizations and present a model for the effect of sound change on the lexicon that allows for both phonetic and lexical gradualness as well as for the tendency for high-frequency words to change faster than low-frequency words.

3.2 The Phonemic Principle

A principle basic to our understanding of phonology and, in fact, of all aspects of linguistic structure, is the phonemic principle – that objectively different sounds form relations with one another and that some of them can be considered at some cognitive level to be very similar, or even the same. This basic insight can be expressed in different ways by different models.

The structuralist models we are all familiar with, probably based on the success of alphabetic orthographies, postulate that mental representations of sound structure are written out in phonemes; only phonemes exist in mental representations and variants of phonemes emerge only in surface forms. This mode of representation accounts for the contrastive value of the abstract unit and also for the fact that the variants of the phoneme are predictable from features of the surrounding context. The complementary distribution of the variants is accorded great importance. Such models are not without problems, however. Once we move away from the phonetic level, decisions about representation become more and more arbitrary. For instance, is the phonemic representation for the English voiceless bilabial stop one of the phonetic variants – that is, either the aspirated [pʰ] or unaspirated stop [p] – or is it something different entirely, a segment unspecified for aspiration?

Generative phonology expanded on the idea of phonemic representation by further postulating that there should be only one mental representation for each morpheme, using the distribution not just of phones but also of phonemes as evidence for single mental representations and the predictability of variants. This expansion exacerbates the problem of arbitrariness and also makes claims about the predictability of variants that are not always substantiated. That is, it is a long leap from the claim that the variants of the phoneme /p/ are rule-governed and predictable to the claim that the variants of the stem *opac-* (e.g., [opeɪk], [opæs]) are rule-governed and predictable.

Although the phonemic principle should probably not be pushed as far as generativists have tried to push it, there is undoubtedly something valid in the basic insight that certain objectively distinct sounds are related to one another. But this insight can be modeled in other ways; writing out underlying representations in abstract phonemes is not our only choice. Furthermore, there is evidence that even at the phonemic level, the basic principle is not as categorically applicable as previously thought. First, and not surprisingly, there are cases where evidence for phonemic representation is decidedly mixed and points to no unique decision. Second, there are cases where lexical and morphological factors interact with phonetic ones in ways not predicted by the phonemic principle. In this chapter, I will discuss the evidence that contradicts the phonemic principle and argue that the usage-based model outlined in Chapter 2 can capture what is valid about the principle while also representing, in a nonarbitrary manner, the full range of facts.

3.3 A Cognitively Realistic Model of Phonological Representation

As mentioned in Chapter 2, instead of viewing linguistic representations as different from other types of cognitive functions, a growing number of researchers are working under the plausible assumption that linguistic representations have the same properties as other types of stored mental percepts. For instance, as mentioned in Chapter 2, Langacker (1987, 2000) has proposed that cognitive representations of linguistic forms and the generalizations over them are maximally redundant, arguing that phonological segments with redundancies removed cannot plausibly constitute cognitively autonomous units. The phonological sequence [pa], which has real physical instantiations both acoustically and motorically, cannot be recognized in the boiled-down representation [LABIAL] and [BACK].

Ohala and Ohala (1995) have also argued that redundancy in representations is essential to categorization, citing the fact that the perceptual cues for the identification of many consonants lie in the transitions of their onsets and offsets, which are predictable from a postulated 'steady-state' portion of the consonant and surrounding segments. They compare linguistic percepts to visual ones:

Intuitively, the mental representation of things we perceive and recognize seems to include predictable details: in our conception of the shape of the letter *G*, do we omit the entirely predictable left side? Our intuitions tell us "no"; the reader can follow his or her own intuitions, but whatever they are, these intuitions should apply to speech perception as well as letter shapes. (Ohala and Ohala 1995:58)

Similarly, Miller (1994), summarizing the results of several experiments on perceptual categorization of phonetic segments, concludes that phonetic categories are both context-dependent and multiply specified. That is, the abstracted prototype of a phonetic category is sensitive to context. In fact, a given linguistic category (say, /p/) will not have just one prototype, but may have several – one for each frequent context. In addition, hearers make use of multiple acoustic cues in assigning stimuli to phonetic categories. As Miller (1994:272) puts it, 'the processes that map the acoustic signal onto categorical representations of speech do not necessarily produce a loss of detailed information about particular speech tokens (cf. Pisoni 1990).' Instead, the process of categorization produces complex categories that

= claim

?,

are centered around several prototypes or good exemplars weighted for frequency, and that are represented in considerable detail.[1]

These arguments for redundant storage from phonetics and cognition were preceded by more than a decade by arguments made by Theo Vennemann from more traditional linguistic data. He argued that lexical representations must be pronounceable, which entails that the unit of storage must be the word (rather than the morpheme), and that the level of detail must correspond to the 'systematic phonetic representation' (Vennemann 1972a, 1974).[2] One of the arguments that Vennemann made was that the explanation for certain distributions of sounds could depend upon features that were predictable and hence not available at the level at which the explanation should be formulated. One example he cites is the case of Icelandic, where the reduced vowel phonemes /ɪöɑ/ occur only in unstressed syllables, while stressed syllables may contain these as well as six other vowels and six diphthongs. Since stress is predictable, and thus not entered in lexical entries, the regular distribution of these vowels must be stated in terms of affixes or of noninitial syllables, even though it is clear that the real causal factor is the stress. If whole words, with stress indicated, are listed in the lexicon, then the appropriate statement of distribution can be formulated and applied (Vennemann 1974:357).

check this

Recently, other phonologists have come to support this view. In the context of Optimality Theory, Burzio (1996) argues that if the grammar is not a set of rewrite rules, then much of the motivation for underlying representations is lost. In addition, he argues that certain patterns, such as English stress, are only partly predictable from segmental patterns, making the storage of stress marking necessary. Kirchner (1997) argues for a gradient view of contrastiveness derivable from the ordering of constraints in Optimality Theory, rather than a strict division between predictable and contrastive features. Steriade (2000) argues against the distinction between phonetic and phonological features by showing that certain features that are usually considered phonetic (predictable), such as English flapping, have lexically specific behavior (see also Hooper 1981). Burzio (1996) and Steriade (2000) point out,

wrongly considered

---

[1] Johnson (1997) argues that an exemplar model of perception, in which a perceptual category is defined as a set of all experienced instances of the category, can also be used to account for the ability to decode speech produced by different voices, without the need for speaker normalization.

[2] As we will see in Section 3.4, the level of phonetic detail necessary in the lexicon is even more specific than the systematic phonetic representation (see also Hooper 1981).

as did Hooper (1976a) (see also Chapter 4), that the effects described by the phonological cycle can also simply and naturally be described by having lexical forms identical to surface forms. Booij (2000), Cole and Hualde (1998), and Janda (1999) argue from language change that lexical representations are changed permanently by sound change, such that old underlying representations do not resurface when rules become unproductive (see also Hooper 1976a). Cole and Hualde further argue that sound changes do not ever refer to underlying forms that differ from surface forms.

The view of phonemic categorization being developed in the studies mentioned so far is quite different from the one that led to the establishment of the phoneme as the unit of mental representation. The main arguments for the abstracted phoneme as a significant unit were linked to its contrastive function: phonemic contrasts were identified as those phonetic contrasts that distinguished words (Jakobson and Halle 1956). Predictable features were considered unimportant for identifying words and, thus, phonemic systems could be boiled down to a simple set of oppositions. Since this view of perception is not accurate, one of the main arguments for phonemic representation, and the theories based on it, must be dismissed (Ohala and Ohala 1995).

One way of seeing the difference between structuralist theories and the more recent theories of categorization in phonetics is formulated by Johnson and Mullennix (1997) as follows. We previously viewed memory representation as simple and access as very complex; we now view memory representation as very complex and access as relatively simple. A parallel description applies to phonology. In generative phonology, underlying representations are very simple and rule systems are considered to be quite complex. In the theory developed here, stored representations are complex and interact in complex and interesting ways, but access to these representations is relatively direct and not mediated by derivational rules, since the patterns found in these stored forms are represented in schemas, which are emergent generalizations over complex representations. (For similar statements, see Booij 2000 and Burzio 1996.)

Adding to the complexities of stored representations is the fact that linguistic representations are not just categorizations of perceptual events; in fact, it is simplistic to view language as just a decontextualized mental activity. We cannot really apply a mind-body separation to language, as language use consists of physical events taking place in a social context (Fox 1995). The events or percepts that have to be

categorized for storage contain simultaneous information on motor
activity, perceptual activity, meaning and social context. In fact, one
could argue that linguistic knowledge does not so much resemble
propositional knowledge as it does procedural knowledge, such as that
used in highly practiced skills (Anderson 1993, Boyland 1996, Bybee
1998). One of the main criteria for distinguishing these two types of
knowledge is that propositional knowledge can be reported, while procedural knowledge cannot. Language users can report on the meanings
of particular lexical items and explain the meanings of sentences, but
they cannot easily report on the meanings or use of grammatical morphemes or constructions, nor can they report on phonological patterns
without first learning analytic techniques. It thus appears that lexical
meaning may be propositional (though I think that in many cases, the
choice of lexical items may also be procedural, as suggested in Pawley
and Syder 1983), but that the rest of language, surely all of grammar
and phonology, is procedural knowledge.

3.4   Linguistic Evidence for Detailed and Redundant Storage

Even if one accepts the basic insight of the phonemic principle – that
objectively different sounds form relations of similarity with one
another – that does not mean that we must also accept the postulates
that mental representations are phonemic, that all speech sounds in a
language are uniquely assignable to one of the phonemes of a language,
that unpredictable features appear in stored representations, and that
lexical items cannot have subphonemic detail or variation. In fact,
trying to apply these postulates to a model of language creates problems and leaves some data unaccounted for. In the following sections,
I will discuss these problems and demonstrate how the valid aspects of
the phoneme can be derived from a usage-based representation.

3.4.1   Lexical Variation

There seems to be widespread agreement that phonetic change is
gradual and produces variation. There also seems to be agreement that
sound change interacts with the lexicon and morphology, changing
lexical items and creating alternations. Some argue that sound change
may become involved with the lexicon and morphology quite early in
its development (Bybee 2000a, Guy 1991a, 1991b, Harris 1989, Hooper
1976b). As an example of lexical involvement, many, if not all, sound

Table 3.1. *American English Schwa Deletion: Poststress Vowels Preceding Unstressed Sonorant-Initial Consonants Tend to Delete (Hooper 1976b)*

No Schwa		Syllabic [r]		Schwa + [r]	
every	(492)	memory	(91)	mammary	(0)
		salary	(51)	celery	(4)
		summary	(21)	summery	(0)
evening	(149)			evening	(0)
(noun)				(verb + ING)	

Frequencies per million from Francis and Kučera (1982) are given in parentheses.

changes diffuse gradually through the lexicon, affecting some words before others (but see Labov 1981, 1994). If a change is both phonetically gradual and lexically gradual – that is, if words change gradually, and if each word changes at its own rate, then each word will encompass its own range of variation. A number of cases of change in progress that show both lexical and phonetic variation have now been discussed in the literature (Booij 2000, Bybee 2000a, Hooper 1976b, Johnson 1983, Phillips 1984, 2001).[3]

As an example, consider a case of what has been described as schwa deletion in American English by Zwicky (1972) – the tendency to delete a poststress schwa followed by a nonword-final /r/, /l/, or /n/. The deletion is most common before /r/, next most common before /l/, and then /n/. For example, words such as *memory, family* and *opener* undergo this deletion variably. In Hooper (1976b), I reported on a study of words of this shape that suggests that high-frequency words undergo the deletion to a greater extent than do low-frequency words. A few examples are given in Table 3.1.

The important point for present purposes is the fact that there are at least three distinct ranges of variation exemplified in these words:

---

[3] Labov (1981, 1994) and Kiparsky (1995) make certain generalizations about the sound changes that have a pattern of lexical diffusion. However, these authors do not take into account all the cases of lexical diffusion cited here. As Phillips (1984) argues, Labov's (1981) account of which changes are 'lexical diffusion changes' does not fit the facts. Kiparsky's claim that lexical diffusion is the same as analogy is belied by the fact that analogy affects infrequent words first, while the changes discussed here and by Kiparsky affect high-frequency items first.

Not a stage of
variation

 (i) *every* is consistently a two-syllable word; that is, it has nonsyl-
       lablic [r]
 (ii) *memory* is variably pronounced as two syllables or with a
       syllabic [r]
 (iii) *mammary* has three full syllables and does not undergo
       reduction.

It is arbitrary and overly simplifying to divide all words of this type
into three discrete categories, but it serves to illustrate the current
point. The distributional evidence usually cited in the literature points
to a lack of contrast between syllabic and nonsyllabic [r]. But in fact,
there is no reason to even posit a contrast between [r] and [ər] given
the evidence usually noted. Nonsyllabic [r] occurs pre- and postvocal-
ically, as in *rat*, *trap*, and *tar*, and syllabic [r] occurs elsewhere – that is,
between a consonant and a word boundary, as in *writer*. All instances
of [ər] can be taken to be syllabic [r].

The data, then, present a problem for phonemic representations,
since some words show subphonemic variation. Since this variation is
lexically specific, the representations for particular words must contain
subphonemic detail. The evidence suggests that each word is represented with a range of variation that corresponds to the actual tokens
of use experienced by the language user. The center of this range
contains the most frequently occurring variants, which constitute
the prototype for the category. The center for the range of variation
may gradually shift as words are used, leading in this case to the loss
of syllabicity for the poststress syllable, as has occurred in *every* and
evening.

Other cases where gradual shift in particular lexical items occur in
connection with sound change are the vowel shifts in San Francisco
English studied by Moonwomon (1992), vowel reduction in Dutch (van
Bergen 1995), *t/d* deletion in American English (Bybee 2000a) and *d*
deletion in New Mexican Spanish (see Chapter 6.3.3). In all of these
cases the phonetic change is more advanced in high-frequency words.
This demonstrates not only that particular words can change at different rates, but also that sound change is conditioned by language
use. The representations for these words, furthermore, contain phonetic
information that would be excluded in principle in a phonemic
analysis.

Sociolinguistic studies have long acknowledged lexically specific
variation without having a satisfying mechanism for describing this

Doesn't seem so.

variation. Of course, mention of lexical items could be built into the variable rule. But in cases where the entire content of the lexicon is affected one way or another, such a notation obscures the distinction between lexicon and rule while trying to save the notion of rule. Pierrehumbert (1994a) argues that variability is not adequately described by rewrite rules and must be considered intrinsic to the grammar and representation rather than peripheral and derived.

Finally, it is important to note that no rule or constraint-based account can adequately account for the association between phonetic shape and token frequency. Hammond (1999) proposes to account for his finding that low-frequency words tend not to undergo rhythm changes in phrases by interspersing constraints specific to lexical items among the more general constraints of Optimality Theory. Pierrehumbert (1999) argues that this solution is undesirable because it provides no insight into the relationship between the low frequency of these items and their behavior with respect to rhythm. Only an approach that allows frequency of use to directly affect the lexical storage of items will provide the necessary explanations for the way that words are realized phonetically.

3.4.2   Change in the Locus of Contrast

In the previous section, we saw evidence for subphonemic features and gradience in the lexicon in cases of variation. In this section, we discuss cases in which two interdependent features together constitute a contrast. In such cases, phonemic and generative theories require that we choose only one feature as expressing the contrast. This choice is also arbitrary and often does not reflect the perceptual or linguistic reality. For example, it is well known that in English stressed monosyllables, a vowel is longer before a voiced consonant than before a voiceless one, as in [bɛt] versus [bɛːd] and [kɑp] versus [kɑːb]. Since the vowel length is predictable from the voicing of the consonant, it is not traditionally represented underlyingly, and thus no vowel length contrast is recognized for English.[4]

However, it is also well known that the length of the vowel constitutes an important perceptual cue in distinguishing words that end in voiced and voiceless obstruents (Denes 1955, Luce and Charles-Luce 1985, Port and Dalby 1982). Moreover, the actual difference in

---

[4] The discussion in this section is based on Hooper (1977).

duration between vowels before voiced and voiceless consonants is much greater in English than in other languages. Zimmerman and Sapon (1958) found that this length difference is four times greater in English than in other languages, and they suggested that vowel length in English may be phonemic. Chen (1970) obtained similar results comparing English vowel length before voiced and voiceless consonants with vowel length under the same conditions in French, Russian, Korean, and Norwegian. Hyman (1975:172) interpreted Chen's data, writing, 'It thus appears that English has extended this vowel-length difference beyond the normal range predictable from the phonetics.' The length difference in English is great enough to be contrastive, and it is used in a contrastive function to identify words. Thus on substantive grounds, it could be that the length difference is present in the lexical representations of English. Another closely related phenomena in English provides additional evidence that this is the case.

Consider vowel nasalization in English. It is a well-known fact of English that before a voiceless consonant, the actual phonetic form of orthographic VN is a nasalized vowel, with very little, if any nasal, consonant present, as in, *can't* [kæ̃t], *camp* [kæ̃p], and *bank* [bæ̃k] (Malécot 1960). The phonetic form of VN before a voiced consonant is a nasalized vowel plus a nasal consonant, as in *hand* [hæ̃nd]. Since the nasalized vowel occurs only before nasal consonants and voiceless consonants, and since the rules for the realization of VN in different contexts appear quite productive, there is no structural reason to postulate that English has lexical nasalized vowels, despite the surface contrast of *can't* [kæ̃t] versus *cat* [kæt].

However, there is evidence that speakers of English do treat such vowels as though they were contrastively nasalized. As in the case of vowel length, the presence or absence of the nasal consonant in words such as *ample* and *amble* is an important cue to correct word identification. Malécot (1960) found that when the nasal resonant was cut out of a word such as *amble*, subjects misidentified it as *ample* 76% of the time. This means that the distinction between V̄ and VN, though predictable, is used in a contrastive function much as the vowel length distinction is.

Moreover, children acquiring English often treat the nasalized vowel before a voiceless stop as though it were a phonemic nasal vowel. Children acquiring languages with phonemic nasal vowels, such as French, acquire oral vowels first and substitute oral vowels for nasal vowels. Interestingly enough, many children learning English as a first language treat the syllabic nuclei in words such as *can't* as though they contained nasalized vowels rather than VN sequences. These words are produced with an oral vowel and no nasalization in the syllable, in marked contrast to words ending in nasal consonants (e.g., *can*), or nasal plus voiced consonant (*hand*), which, in even the earliest forms, contain a nasal consonant. Thus these children treat words such as *can't* as though they contained phonemic nasalized vowels. Smith (1973:13–14) reports the following forms, which occurred from the earliest stages (age 2.2 to 2.8).

(1)   a.   dɛp   'stamp'   b.   mɛn   'mend'
          bʌp   'bump'   daun   'round'
          gik   'drink'   ɛn   'hand'
          dɛt   'tent'   bɛn   'band'
          ʌgu   'uncle'
          ɛbi   'empty'   c.   gin   'skin'
          gɛgu: 'thank you'   bu:n   'spoon'
                                          gi:m   'scream'
                                          wiŋ   'swing'

The same situation held in the earliest speech of my son:

(2)   a.   kæt   'can't'   b.   hæn   'hand'
          grɪk   'drink'
          dɛks   'thanks'   c.   fun   'spoon'
          fak   'spank'   ham   'home'
          fʌki   'funky'   ram   'lamb'
          fɛsɪt   'present'   wan   'one'
                                          čren   'train'

The forms in 1a and 2a contain no nasalization at all, while the b and c forms, which are contemporaneous, show that nasal consonants have been acquired, and that they occur finally, even at the stage when many other consonants do not occur in final position. Both children cited here allowed only nasal consonants and voiceless stops in final position.

Given the availability of nasal consonants, it seems clear that these children do not analyze words such as *can't*, *drink*, *thanks*, and so on, as containing vowel plus nasal consonant sequences, for if they did, the nasal consonant would surely show up. Rather they analyze these words as containing no nasal consonant, and they are not yet able to produce a nasalized vowel.

Another potential source of contrast occurs variably in casual speech, where a final voiced stop, /d/, after a nasal consonant may be devoiced, as in *and* [ænt], *second* [sɛkʌ̃nt] and *end* [ɛ̃nt]. This devoicing does not trigger the deletion of the nasal because it does not affect the length of the nucleus, which, as I will argue later on, is the relevant parameter here. Instead it produces a potential contrast between VN and a nasal vowel, critical evidence for phonemic status in some theories (see Vachek 1964).

The perceptual evidence, the child language evidence, and the casual speech evidence point to nasal vowels before a voiceless obstruent in English functioning contrastively even though the rules for producing them are still productive. This case, then, is another one in which contrastiveness and predictability are not mutually exclusive. The implications of such cases are clear: lexical representations may contain predictable phonological material.

3.4.3   Schemas Generalize Over Predictable Material

In the preceding section, I argued that vowel length and vowel nasalization are represented lexically in English. This does not mean that no generalizations are made concerning these phenomena. In fact, for stressed syllables, long vowels before voiced consonants, short vowels before voiceless ones, and absence of the nasal consonant before voiceless consonants are all very strong and productive patterns of English pronunciation that are easily extended to new or nonce words. Their representation in the lexicon does not preclude the formation of generalizations that can be applied productively. These generalizations can be stated in the form of schemas of varying degrees of generality or abstractness. In fact, the use of schemas, rather than feature-changing rules, allows us to generalize over both the vowel length and vowel nasalization cases to show that they are part of the same pattern of syllable rhymes in English monosyllables.

Measurements of syllable nuclei containing vowels, diphthongs, vowel plus liquid, and vowel plus nasal before voiced and voiceless obstruents show the same pattern: the vowel nucleus is longer before a voiced obstruent and shorter before a voiceless one. In the case of a nasal before an obstruent, the effect is apparent on the nasal consonant itself – it virtually disappears before a voiceless obstruent while remaining fully present before a voiced one (Chen 1970). It appears, then, that English monosyllabic rhymes come in two types: a long type that ends in a resonant (glide, liquid, or nasal) and may or may not be followed by a voiced obstruent, and a shortened type that is always followed by a voiceless obstruent. These rhyme types can be described in schemas, first of a very specific nature, and then also by very general schemas.

Assuming that V–resonant sequences (Vl, Vr, VN) can be considered nuclei, we may make the generalization that there are only two types of stressed monosyllabic rhymes in English: those with long nuclei, which are optionally followed by a voiced obstruent, and those with short nuclei, which are always followed by a voiceless obstruent. It is also the case that the voiced obstruent is typically shorter than the voiceless one, giving the temporal pattern described in 3 and illustrated in 4.

(3)   Approximate temporal patterns for the rhymes of stressed monosyllables, where the width of the column represents durational differences

    a. Long nucleus precedes voiced coda or no coda

Nucleus	(Coda)
V N	(voiced)
V : R :	(voiced)
V :	(voiced)

    b. Short nucleus precedes voiceless coda

Nucleus	Coda
Ṽ	voiceless
VR	voiceless
V	voiceless

(4)   Examples
    a. Ben, bend   b. bent
        burr, bird   Bert
        hell, held   hilt
        bed   bet

Declarative schemas are more appropriate for expressing these generalizations about the current synchronic stage of English, since they
allow us to generalize over nuclei of various types to arrive at only two
basic schemas for stressed rhymes of monosyllables (Hooper 1977).

The generative rules usually postulated for these patterns involve
two apparently distinct processes over which no generalization is
possible. One lengthens vowels before voiced consonants, and the
other would delete the nasal (after vowel nasalization) before voiceless consonants. The two rules move in opposite directions: one lengthens the nucleus, and the other shortens it. But the reason they are
formulated in opposite directions has nothing to do with the phonology of English. It has rather to do with assumptions about what phonemic representations should be like. It is assumed that phonemic
representations use unmarked feature combinations and rules to
derive the marked ones. Thus, it is assumed that since vowel length
is not phonemic in English, that English vowels are underlyingly
short, and that length is added. Similarly, since it is assumed that vowel
nasalization is not phonemic in English, underlyingly all vowels are
nonnasal, which means that a nasal consonant must be postulated
for phonemic representation.

These assumptions unfortunately steer us away from the wider
synchronic generalization about nucleus length, as given in 3, and
also from the possibility of a diachronic generalization about this
development. It is possible that the process taking place is a shortening of the nucleus due to the preglottalization of voiceless stops. The
retiming or anticipation of the glottal state change for voiceless stops
cuts short the preceding voiced segment – liquid, nasal, vowel, or glide,
while a following voiced obstruent or no following consonant at all
entails no change of glottal state and thus allows for the full articulation of the syllable. If this is the correct interpretation, then the schemas
in 3 are the appropriate expression of the generalization, as they explicitly relate the length of the vowel and the presence or absence of the
nasal consonant. Attributing the shortening to the voiceless consonant
also explains why syllables ending in vowels, liquids, or nasals are
also long.

To summarize this section, then, vowel length in English is predictable from the voicing of the final consonant, yet it greatly exceeds
the amount of lengthening found in other languages where it is predictable. It is also used as a perceptual cue to the identification of the
voicing of the final consonant. Similarly, a contrast between $\tilde{V}N$ and $\tilde{V}$

is the perceptual cue to the voicing of the following consonant, and children treat nasalized vowels as though they were phonemic. For these reasons, an analysis in which nucleus length and voicing of the final consonant are lexical features is proposed. This analysis captures the interdependence of these features and allows a generalization over short and long syllable rhymes. In addition, the analysis predicts future changes in English: final devoicing will leave the vowel length and nasal/nonnasal contrasts intact.

3.5   Usage-Based Categorization versus Phonemic Representation

Any theory that proposes that stored representations differ from actual tokens of use must wrestle with the problem of the nature of the stored representation. On the other hand, a theory such as that being presented here, which says that storage units are categorized tokens of use, must wrestle with the problem of the nature of categorization. In this section, we briefly mention some of the difficulties arising in structuralist theories that are avoided in the current theory. In the following section, we explore the question of the nature of categorization of tokens in the usage-based model.

3.5.1   Phonemic Representation

In positions of neutralization, especially where no alternation exists, the choice of an underlying representation in theories of full phonemic specification is arbitrary. In English words such as *sport*, *stack*, and *skin*, the voiceless stop following the /s/ is physically closer to [b, d, g] than to [pʰ, tʰ, kʰ], yet some would argue that the spelling conventions indicate that the cluster is conceptually voiceless. Since there are no particular consequences resulting from the choice of one phoneme over the other, the choice of representation is arbitrary.

Cases with an alternation are less arbitrary: one can argue that the word *writer* has an underlying /t/ on the basis of *write*. But words with no alternation mates, such as *butter* and *ladder*, still present a problem. If stored representations are written out in phonemes, either /t/ or /d/ must be chosen for these words.

Of course, no such problems arise if representations contain predictable features. The Voice Onset Timing (VOT) of clusters with /s/ are represented lexically. Since this timing relative to the onset of the

consonant is approximately the same as in other syllables beginning with voiceless consonants (Browman and Goldstein 1992), the /s/
cluster will be associated with other voiceless onsets, accounting for the
notion that the stop following /s/ is voiceless. Since the voice onset coincides with the release of the stop, the physical reality is that the stop is
similar to the 'voiced' stops of English.

With redundant specification, the flaps in *butter* and *ladder* are registered as flaps – they are neither /t/ nor /d/. However, they can be
related to other instances of alveolar stops because of their shared phonetic properties. In cases of alternation, both alternates are registered
in the lexicon and related to one another by lexical connections that
track both phonetic and semantic similarities.

A common practice, as I mentioned earlier, is to choose the
unmarked segment for the underlying representation. We saw in
Section 3.4.2 that this solution may also create problems. Choosing
short oral vowels for English phonemic representations has the effect
of forcing a single pattern to be generated by two distinct rules
that move in opposite directions, one that lengthens the syllable and
one that shortens it. Postulating stored representations that are essen-
tially identical to phonetic representations eliminates these arbitrary
choices and their sometimes deleterious effect on the proposed
grammar.

3.5.2 Phonetic Categorization

Recent research in phonetic categorization has begun to reveal much
about the way that phonetic tokens are perceived, categorized, and
stored. Early research emphasized the importance of the boundaries
between phonemic categories, which led to the exploration of the
phenomenon of categorical perception (Studdert-Kennedy et al. 1970).
It was found that listeners could discriminate stimuli across a category
boundary (say, the difference between [p] and [b]) much more
easily than they could discriminate different phonetic stimuli within a
category. This finding gave rise to the theory that listeners map the
acoustically relevant features onto discrete phonetic categories,
retaining information about the category identity, but losing the details
of acoustic form (Lahiri and Marslen-Wilson 1991). For example, both
the [ɑ] of *cot* and the [ɑː] of *cod* would be mapped onto the phoneme
/a/, and the fact that one vowel is short and the other long would
be lost.

Subsequent research, however, has revealed not only that listeners can discriminate stimuli within a phonetic category, but also that phonetic categories have a rich internal structure (Miller 1994). Experiments have shown that listeners can give consistent ratings of goodness of fit for phonetic stimuli within categories, which indicates that phonetic stimuli are categorized the way that other perceptual stimuli are – in terms of similarity to the more central members of categories. This type of categorization implies that details of phonetic stimuli are not necessarily lost in processing.

A further aspect of the internal structure of categories is that context can alter what is perceived as the best exemplar of a category. The contextual effects that have been studied and found significant are speaking rate, speaker, and the phonetic context. Thus, there is probably not just one prototype or central member of a phonemic category but several; the one that is activated depends upon factors of the context. This finding suggests that humans have a finely tuned perceptual system that is sensitive to contextual effects (Miller 1994).

Two models of mental representation of categorization are consistent with these findings. First, a prototype model of the sort proposed in Rosch (1978) would have the listener store an abstract summary description, or prototype, based on tokens actually experienced. Goodness-of-fit ratings would be based on similarity to this prototype. A second possibility is that the listener stores exemplars that are weighted for frequency (Nosofsky 1988). Goodness-of-fit ratings would then be based on similarity to the higher-frequency exemplars. These two alternatives both make very similar empirical predictions.

K. Johnson (1997) argues for an exemplar model of speech perception to account for the fact that hearers not only correctly identify words or utterances produced by different speakers (whose acoustic properties vary considerably), but also correctly identify the voice of different speakers they have heard before. In the exemplar model all perceived tokens are categorized and stored, creating categories that directly represent the variation encountered. This variation is used in speech processing. Johnson represents a set of exemplars as in Figure 3.1. The stack of ovals represents the set of all exemplars, and the lines radiating from these ovals associate them with auditory properties and other information, such as meaning or context of use.

An exemplar model requires practically unlimited memory. The evidence cited by Johnson suggests that memory for individual items is surprisingly vast. Experiments have shown that people recognize

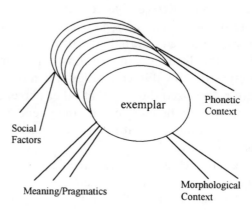

Figure 3.1. Exemplar representation and associations.

thousands of previously viewed pictures with surprising accuracy over very long periods of time. Memory for different instances of words is similarly strong and long-lasting (Palmeri et al. 1993, Schacter and Church 1992). Whatever the limitations on memory, there is certainly enough memory available to allow some version of an exemplar representation; that is, there is no necessity to sort exemplars into prototypes and discard the memory of the particular token. In fact, if tokens of experience were not stored in memory, at least for a while, no prototype could be formed, since categorization depends upon the comparison of multiple individual percepts. According to a possible variation on the exemplar model, tokens that are sufficiently similar are stored together, yielding a strengthened representation. At the same time, rarely used, nonsalient variants might fade from memory. These processes affecting exemplars could contribute to the impression that a prototype has been formed. Evidence for this modification of the exemplar model will be presented in Chapter 6.2.1. (See also Pierrehumbert 2001.)

Both the exemplar and the prototype alternatives differ considerably from the notion of an abstracted phoneme. In particular, these models are highly dependent upon the way phones are used in context. First, the frequency of a particular variant leads to its being considered closer to the prototype or the best exemplar. Second, the context in which variants are normally heard affects their categorization. Third, mental representations contain considerable detail about phonetic variants, including the specification of multiple acoustic features, not just those that determine phonemic contrast.

To describe this model in terms that phonologists traditionally deal with, we can say that phonemes are sets of phonetically similar variants, and that these variants, or allophones, are clustered in groups, such that what we analyze as allophones constitute salient contextually determined prototypes. In this model, in which contextually dependent variants constitute prototypes or sets of exemplars themselves, it is easy to see how new phonemes develop: a set of exemplars within a category gradually grows less dependent upon context, gradually changes phonetically so as not to be so similar to other members of the category, and eventually comes to appear in contexts where it was not formerly found or to otherwise contrast with sounds with which it was formerly in complementary distribution (see Janda 1999 for more on this process). For instance, a very stable set of variants for /t/ is found in Japanese: [ts] occurs before /u/ and [tʃ] occurs before /i/. This conditioning was formerly exceptionless, but now exceptions are appearing in English loanwords, where, for instance, *teen(ager)* is pronouned [tiin] rather than *[tʃiin], and *party* is pronounced [paati] rather than *[paatʃi] (Ito and Mester 1995:828). Thus, a contrast is set up between [ti] and [tʃi]. It is important to note that [tʃ] must have already had independent status before these words were borrowed; the borrowing simply revealed the change that had already taken place in the speakers' categorization of [t] and [tʃ].[5]

An important feature of this model of phonetic categorization is that the main criterion used is phonetic similarity, which is to say that determination of how to categorize a phonetic segment is based on its substantive properties, and not on its distribution. Phonetic tokens are classified as members of the same category if they are highly similar in their acoustic (and articulatory) properties. What is meant by highly similar? Of course, this is an empirical question, but a rough answer may be that allophonic differences at the level at which linguists note and transcribe them are distinct enough to constitute separate categories. Thus the difference in duration between American English stop [d] and flap [r] would be large enough to require a separate category for the flap. In contrast, the analogous difference between the stop [b] before a stressed vowel (as in *reborn*) and the shortened version of it before an unstressed vowel (as in *rubber*) might not be.

The findings reported here from experimental phonetics are consistent with the discovery of lexically specific variation (such as that found

---

[5] I am grateful to José Hualde for this example.

in *memory* versus *mammary*), the evidence for predictable features in the lexicon (i.e., vowel length and vowel nasalization in English), and the evidence for early interactions with morphology, which will be taken up in the next section. As we saw earlier, there can be phonetic categories associated with different contexts. It follows, then, that there can be phonetic categories associated with particular words; in other words, the lexical item itself can serve as the context. Members of the same phonetic category are related across words via lexical connections.

In a model in which the stored image of each word comprises a set of exemplars with a range of phonetic variation, the question arises as to why that each word in a language does not have a unique set of phonetic characteristics. Why is it that the words of a language do not take advantage of the whole universal phonetic repertoire but rather adhere to a highly restricted set of phonetic elements and sequences? An answer to this question is offered by Studdert-Kennedy (1987), who observes that when children begin to use the first words of their language, the range of phonetic elements that they utilize is in fact wide and unsystematic, as though they were treating each word as an independent holistic unit. An increase in vocabulary size, however, is facilitated, both from a production and storage point of view, by the reuse of the same elements in different words. Thus, the vocabulary explosion at approximately age three coincides with the emergence of a 'phonemic' analysis (see also Lindblom 1992).

In discussing the origins to language, Studdert-Kennedy (1998) further relates the analysis of the continuous speech stream in evolution into recurring units – the speech gestures – to the particulate principle, a principle of the physical universe. By this principle, any system that makes infinite use of finite means must break down into a small set of units that are capable of being recombined (Abler 1989). Applied to the finite set of gestural configurations that characterize any language, this means that there would be a strong tendency for speakers to reuse a single set of highly entrenched neuromotor patterns and to substitute members of this set for novel or less common configurations.

3.6   Phonetic Detail in the Lexicon – Variation and the Early Involvement of the Lexicon and Morphology in Change

We have now seen cases in which phonetic variation is lexically specific and cases in which certain predictable phonetic features can be used contrastively, especially if the magnitude of the feature (i.e., the extent of vowel length or the extent of vowel nasality) is great enough to be used perceptually to distinguish words. While it is generally accepted that phonological rules do often morphologize – that is, replace phonological conditioning with morphological conditioning (Dressler 1977, Klausenburger 1979, Tranel 1981, Vennemann 1972b), it is not usually recognized that this process of reanalysis can occur very early in the development of a phonological change. Some authors have stated that the restructuring in the phonology that leads to morphologization is triggered by opacity (Kiparsky 1971), while others have correctly pointed out that opacity cannot arise unless restructuring has already taken place (Booij 2000, Haiman 1995, Hooper 1976a, Janda 1999). Thus, restructuring is covert – the speakers change their analysis before the surface forms of the language change (Andersen 1973).

Consider as an example of the early interaction of phonological processes with morphological categories a traditional problem in German phonology, which concerns the status of the palatal fricative [ç]. In almost all contexts, the palatal is a predictable variant of the velar fricative, occurring after front vowels and after the consonants /r/, /l/, and /n/. However, the consistent realization of the diminutive suffix -chen contains the palatal fricative, even when the preceding noun ends in a back vowel, as in *Tauchen* 'small rope' and *Pfauchen* 'little peacock'. (These words form minimal or near-minimal pairs with the verbs *tauchen* 'to dive' and *fauchen* 'to hiss', which have the velar fricative.) Further, certain loanwords contain the palatal fricative in initial position or after a back vowel: *China* and *Photochemie*. The traditional solution to this problem (Leopold 1948, Moulton 1947) is to predict the [ç] from a boundary (or juncture). This is tantamount to claiming that the [ç] is part of certain morphemes and words, which in turn amounts to lexical status for [ç]. The consistent realization of -chen with a palatal, even after a back vowel, arose because this suffix originally had the form -ichīn, which contained a palatal vowel that conditioned palatalization of the velar fricative as well as umlaut (fronting of the stem vowel). The realization of this morpheme, then, was consistently palatal, and thus its lexical representation was palatal, even though at first the palatal was phonologically predictable. Since the palatal was always associated with this morpheme, it eventually came to occur in -chen even outside its original phonetic environment. Note that for the palatal in this morpheme to occur outside of a palatalizing environment, it had to already be represented as palatal in storage; thus, the representation as a palatal had to be established while the palatal was still predictable. Thus the morpholexical reanalysis of this suffix was not a response to the opacity created by the deletion of the initial vowel in *-ichiin*. Rather, the fact that the palatal remains after the deletion of its conditioning environment means that the palatal was already present in lexical representation.

Distinctive segments with restricted distribution are anomalous in theories with structural orientation, and attempts have therefore been made to render such segments nondistinctive by introducing them via rule. Hall (1989) and MacFarland and Pierrehumbert (1991) discuss the problem that German [ç] presents for Lexical Phonology. Since the appearance of [ç] depends upon morphological and lexical features, it would be introduced by a lexical rule. However, this would produce a violation of the constraint called Structure Preservation, which prohibits the introduction of nondistinctive features except at the postlexical level. This constraint expresses the generalization, which is usually valid, that morphologically and lexically conditioned alternations are alternations between phonemes or contrastive units. The problem with describing this tendency with a constraint is that it precludes any new feature that arises by phonological processes from becoming distinctive. Yet, clearly, phonological processes are the source of new contrastive features, and hence of new phonemes. The presence of new phonemes such as /ç/ in German shows that the tendency for morpholexical alternations to involve segments that are contrastive elsewhere cannot be captured by a strict synchronic constraint, but must be formulated rather as a strong diachronic tendency for phonetically conditioned variants to become contrastive and/or morphologically conditioned. For more discussion of the role of diachrony in determining this universal 'constraint,' see Chapter 8.6.

More recently, subtle interactions of morphology with allophonic or variable phonetic processes have come to light. As we will see in Chapter 6, morphological relations can impede or discourage the application of a process to a form. For instance, Steriade (2000) points out that American English flapping of [t] in words derived with *-istic* depends on whether the base word has a flap, even when the phonetic conditions for flapping are met. Thus *positivistic* (cf. *positive*) does not have a flap, while *fatalistic* (cf. *fatal*) does. This difference is presumably due to the formation of the *-istic* adjective directly from the base, maintaining the phonetic properties of the base – in this case, whether it has

Which?

a flap or not. Note that these derived adjectives are not very common. I would predict that, since flapping is productive in American English, if an adjective such as *positivistic* became very frequent, the [t] in question would start to reduce in duration and become a flap. Other similar examples are presented in Chapter 6.3, where it is argued that word-internal gestures occurring in alternating environments, such as the [t] in *positive* and *positivistic*, are slower to undergo change.

Another type of interaction of morphology with phonetic detail and variation concerns cases in which a sound within a grammatical morpheme (which is always of high frequency) is more reduced than are other instances of the same sound. Thus, the deletion of medial -*d*- or [ð] in Spanish occurred very early in the 2nd Person Plural suffix -*ades* and is currently occurring at a faster rate than in other lexical items in the Past Participle suffix -*ado*. The results of a study of this case are presented in Chapter 6.3.3.

Cases in which morphological status interacts with variable phonetic processes constitute important evidence against modularization. Phonetic implementation cannot be relegated to a derivative role in which it has no access to the lexical or morphological status of the elements upon which it works (as in Chomsky 1995). Rather linguistic organization and storage is based on experience with language where articulation, perception, meaning, and social import are all related intimately.

3.7   A Model for Sound Change

A usage-based theory postulates that change is inherent in the nature of language. Grammars are not static entities, but constantly in the process of change resulting from the way that language is used. Thus, a model of language must include the mechanisms by which change occurs as an integral part of its architecture. For that reason it is relevant – in fact, necessary – to provide an account of sound change in a model of usage-based phonology.

Generative models account for sound change through the addition of new rules to the grammar. Such rules are usually added at the end of the list of rules, very far 'downstream' from the lexicon and morphology and, in the beginning, are thought to have very little effect on the phonology, lexicon, or grammar. Sound change is seen as producing a minimal change. Lexical representations of affected words remain as they were before the rule was added, their phonetic shape changes due to the new rule, but otherwise everything remains the same.

In the usage-based model being explored here, memory representations are categorizations of tokens of use. Thus, if the tokens of use begin to change, the center of the category will also gradually change. The direct representation provided by phonetic categorization allows for gradual phonetic change in categories, as well as in particular lexical units.[6] We have already presented evidence that such change can be lexically specific, and that in some cases, high-frequency items tend to change faster than do low-frequency items. The model naturally provides an account of the pattern of lexical diffusion in which high-frequency items change more readily than low-frequency items (Pierrehumbert 2001). It involves at least the following three factors.

First, sound change, much of which is articulatorily motivated, occurs as articulation proceeds. Pagliuca and Mowrey (1987) and Browman and Goldstein (1992) divide gestural change into two types: retimings that cause overlap of gestures, and reductive changes that reduce the duration or magnitude of gestures (see Chapter 4.3). These changes occur in real time as language is used. Words and phrases that are used more often have more opportunities to undergo these changes, just as other types of motor skills that are used more often become more compressed and efficient (Anderson 1993, Boyland 1996, cf. Chapter 6.4).

Second, reduction also occurs within a discourse. Fowler and Housum (1987) have demonstrated that the second occurrence of the same word in the same discourse is shorter than the first occurrence. This tendency may be motivated by the fact that for the second occurrence of a word, the speaker can be less explicit phonetically because the context and the fact that the word is already primed make it easier for the hearer to access it. In addition, however, the speaker can actu-

---

[6] Given that tokens of use produced by the speaker or others can condition a shift in representation, we might ask why people don't change their dialect more easily when they are surrounded by another dialect. The incoming tokens differ from the stored image and should cause that image to shift. The answer has two parts. First, almost everyone does shift somewhat with prolonged exposure to a different dialect, but they often retain salient features of their original dialect, which makes it appear that they have not shifted. Second, phonetic shape is not just determined by memory representation and experience – it is also determined by the neural and motor patterns that have been laid down in childhood and reinforced by constant repetition. For many people, these entrenched patterns simply do not change very much without a concerted effort.

ally signal that the word is the same old word rather than a new one by reducing it. The result of this tendency is that words that occur more often in the same discourse may also be more frequent words and undergo more reduction.

Third, D'Introno and Sosa (1986) argue that familiar, and thus high-frequency, words tend to be used in familiar social settings, where there are fewer restrictions on reduction. Again, high-frequency words will undergo more reduction.

Given these factors (and perhaps others) and the idea that tokens of use are registered in memory, a high-frequency word is likely to be affected by changing phonetic patterns more easily than is a low-frequency word. That is, as particular tokens undergo on-line reduction, the stored representation shifts. More tokens of reduced variants will hasten the shift. As I noted earlier, this effect has been documented in several ongoing sound changes – for instance, American English *t/d* deletion, schwa deletion, and vowel shifts in San Francisco English.

Another relevant issue with respect to sound change and lexical representation is that sound changes cannot be undone. If sound change is viewed as rule addition, as in generative phonology, then underlying forms remain unchanged. The prediction is thus made that underlying forms would resurface if the sound change was halted or the rule became unproductive. However, no such change ever occurs (Cole and Hualde 1998, Janda 1999). Sound change has a permanent effect on the lexical representation of the words of a language (Bybee 1994, 2000b).

In a recent argument to this effect, Booij (2000) shows that Dutch vowel lengthening in open syllables, which resulted in long vowels such as those in 5 and, with further vowel quality changes, in alternations such as those in 6, later became unproductive. The lack of productivity is evidenced by the fact that after geminate consonants were degeminated, producing a new set of open syllables, the vowels in these syllables did not lengthen. Thus *wikke* 'vetch' became [vɪkə] and maintains its short vowel.

(5)   a. name   'name'   n[a:]me
      b. smake   'taste'   sm[a:]ke
      c. stave   'staff'   st[a:]ve
(6)   a. sch[i]p   'ship'   sch[e:]p-e   'ships'
      b. w[ɛ]g   'way'   w[e:]g-en   'ways'
      c. h[ɔ]l   'hole'   h[o:]l-en   'holes'

Even though the vowel lengthening process became unproductive, the long vowels in the forms in 5 and 6 do not shorten, and the alternations in 6 remain. This indicates that before the process lost its productivity, the forms it had affected were permanently changed in underlying form, including the plural forms listed in 6, which could presumably have been derived by rule from the singulars. This case is not at all unusual. The effects of sound change remain in the forms of a language until they are obliterated by subsequent changes, either further sound changes or those based on analogy with other forms. Once affected by sound change, old underlying forms never resurface.[7]

Postulating that sound change has an immediate and permanent effect on the lexicon also explains the continuity of changes taking place over a long period of time and their unidirectionality. For example, three common paths of reductive or assimilatory change are listed in 7:

(7) $t > d > ð > ø$
      $s > h > ø$
      $k' > k^j > c$

If stored items are changed gradually and the motivation for increased automation remains fairly constant, then the continuous nature and strict directionality of such changes is predicted. If sound change were 'rule addition,' there would be no explanation for why after 'adding' the 'rule', $d > ð / V\_\_V$, a language would go on to 'add' the 'rule', $d > ø / V\_\_V$.

3.8   Special Reduction of High-Frequency Words and Phrases

It is also interesting to consider how words and phrases undergo reduction in the more extreme cases of contraction and grammaticization. One might want to argue that such cases are not central to a model of phonological representation, but such an argument would be based on the false assumption that such cases are not common. I would argue that such cases are quite common, and that new instances are arising all the time. Not only does special reduction occur in greetings and discourse markers, but it is also always present during the grammaticization process. Phonological reduction creates grammatical markers that

---

[7] See Cole and Hualde (1998) for a reanalysis of some apparent cases to the contrary.

continue to be a locus of change due to high frequency. Thus, reductive change of this type fits squarely within phonological research. Consider the following list of items in English that have undergone or are undergoing special reduction:

(i)   forms of address: *Mrs., Miss*

(ii)   greetings and salutations: *hi, howdy, goodbye, tsup* (from *what's up*)

(iii)   contraction of the auxiliary with a pronominal subject: *I'll, I've, I'm, I'd, we'll, we've, we're, we'd,* and so on

(iv)   contraction of the auxiliary with negation: *doesn't, don't, won't, can't, isn't, aren't, wasn't, weren't, didn't, wouldn't, couldn't, shouldn't,* and so on

(v)   reduction of *don't* in *I don't know, I don't care,* and so on

(vi)   fusion of *to* in many phrases: *want to, have to, get to, got to, going to, supposed to*

(vii)   palatalization of [t] and [d] before *you: did you, don't you, can't you,* and so on

(viii)   reduction in compounds: *cupboard*

(ix)   reduction of adjectives preceding a noun: *ole* and *li'l*

(x)   other grammaticized words or phrases: *a/an, the, another, would've, should've, could've*

Considering that these special phrases are pervasive in the language as well as frequently used, their behavior constitutes a very important part of the on-line use of English. Thus a model of phonology should be able to account not only for their present form, but also for the very process by which phrases of this sort acquire their special phonological shapes.

The development of special phonological properties in high-frequency words and phrases entails two properties of language; first, that high levels of use lead to reduction and, second, that such reduction, as specific to these items, must be represented as part of their stored image. A further implication is that these frequent phrases (e.g., *I don't know*) are processed and stored as units. Of course, their component words (in this case, *I, don't,* and *know*) are also stored and related to the parts of the phrase, at least at first, by lexical connections. As use continues, however, further phonological reduction often obscures the relation between the original source words and the resulting fused phrase. In a parallel development, semantic and pragmatic change is also taking place, which also contributes to the obscuring of the identity of the component parts (Bybee and Scheibman 1999). Thus, misanalysis often occurs: *'ve* in *would've* is mistaken for *of* (Boyland 1996), *another* is misparsed as in *a whole nother*, and so on.

The important point is that such divergence of phonology and meaning could not occur unless the phrase already had its own lexical representation to which these special properties can be assigned. That is, a phrase or grammaticizing construction is registered as a processing unit in memory before any special changes occur; it is registered there by virtue of frequent repetition. Thus, the presence of units in the lexicon depends upon the frequency with which items occur and the frequency with which items occur together. These issues are discussed further in Chapter 6.4.

3.9 Conclusion

In this chapter, we have examined the evidence in favor of detailed and redundant specification of phonetic features in stored representations. We have seen that in certain cases of variation and change, specific lexical items can have their own ranges of variation that cannot be captured by a phonemic representation. We have also argued that certain pairs of interdependent features, such as vowel length and consonant voice and nasality and consonant voice, are necessarily present in stored representations. Evidence was also presented that morphologization takes place while phonological features are still predictable from the phonological context. Together, this evidence suggests that phonological representations are based on categorized tokens of use, and that linguistic percepts are organized and stored much as nonlinguistic percepts are organized and stored.

The representation of phonetic detail and range of variation associated with particular lexical items further entail a model of sound change that can account for both phonetic and lexical gradualness and for the effect of high token frequency on sound change. The same properties of this model also provide an account of the special reduction that occurs in very frequent words and phrases.

4

Phonological Processes, Phonological Patterns

4.1 Introduction

In Chapter 3, we saw evidence against the separation of contrastive and predictable features for lexical representation, in addition to evidence that variation can be lexically specific. To account for this evidence, I proposed that detailed phonetic tokens are categorized in the lexicon, and that regularities of phonological structure are expressed in schemas. This type of network model has no place for the notion of phonological rules in the sense of a series of operations that apply to abstract cognitive units to transform them into something more similar to phonetic output forms. This is not to say that the phenomena described by traditional phonological rules do not necessarily exist. What needs to be determined at this point is what aspects of the phenomena described by phonological rules are viable aspects of language behavior, and how they might be accommodated in such a model. Moreover, the many different types of patterns that generative phonological rules try to encompass are better understood as different types of generalizations, depending upon their association with the phonetics on the one hand versus the lexicon and morphology on the other.

One aspect of phonological behavior previously described by rules that is an undeniable fact about language behavior is the presence of certain articulatory patterns that are shared across speakers and that are transferred onto the production of novel words, loanwords, and early attempts by adults at a foreign language. In the usage-based model developed here, we can describe such articulatory regularities with schemas that generalize over learned patterns that are present in the language.

These phonological patterns are produced by a set of neuromotor production schemas that are reused and recombined in the process of articulation. Such schemas are not strict and static, but rather encompass a systematic range of variation keyed to the linguistic and social context. It is this variation in articulation that produces allophonic variants and the lexical variation we discussed in Chapter 3. This variation is due to on-line adjustments that take place in production and have as their motivation the increased fluency of the sequences of gestures. For the purposes of the following discussion, allophonic variation and phonetic variation tied to specific phonetic or social contexts will be attributed, as has been traditional, to phonetic processes, which will be narrowly defined as purely phonetically motivated modifications of articulation, occurring in real time, as for instance, in the case of casual speech variants, which usually represent sound change in progress.

Another sense in which the phonological patterns of a language are gradient is in terms of their frequency of occurrence in the lexicon of the language. Patterns of phonological structure (phonotactic patterns) are not strictly acceptable or unacceptable. Rather, judgments concerning the acceptability of articulatory patterns are based on experienced tokens: patterns that are not present are not learned and thus are generally judged to be unacceptable, while patterns with a high type frequency are rated as the most acceptable by speakers. These patterns also come into play in the adaptation of loanwords.

What is the substance of phonological patterns and phonological processes? In Chapter 3, we discussed perceptual evidence for the nature of stored representations. But stored representations must have an articulatory basis as well – in particular, a procedure for producing specific articulations. Clearly the motor-articulatory representation and the acoustic-perceptual representations are closely linked. While the nature of this link and its neural status is not yet understood, the fact that the two have such a close experiential association means that like other pieces of experience that co-occur, a strong neural link must necessarily be made.

The focus in this chapter will be on articulation viewed in terms of gestures or neuromotor events, as I will argue that articulation provides us with the best description and explanation for the regularities encountered in phonological patterns, casual speech modifications, the reduction of frequent phrases, and sound change in general. It has been argued that conceptualizing stretches of speech in terms of alphabetic units leads us away from understanding the true nature of the processes that create phonological regularities. Thus articulation will be examined in terms of the sequencing and coordination of muscular activity. Other types of units that seem to be useful to the understanding of phonology – segments and syllables – will be considered as emergent from the categorization of similar gestural patterns over stretches of speech.

4.2   Phonetic Etiology and Its Limits

Let us for the moment use the term 'alternation' to refer to any case in which a word or morpheme has more than one variant. Alternations can be of various types, ranging from the phonetically gradient variants of words such as *memory* or the flapping in *write* versus *writing* to the different forms that morphemes take in words such as *opaque* with final [k] and *opacity* with stem-final [s]. In early generative phonology all such alternations were described by phonological rules without any differentiation into types. Natural phonology of Stampe (1973) and Natural Generative Phonology of Vennemann (1971, 1972b) and Hooper (1976a) propose to distinguish alternations that have a true and consistent phonetic conditioning from those that are lexicalized or morphologized. Similarly, Kiparsky's (1982) Lexical Phonology divides rules into blocks based on their generality and the type of morphology they are involved with. The very general, phonetically conditioned alternations are referred to in Kiparsky's model as 'postlexical rules' and they apply across the board, whereas the morphologized or lexicalized alternations are handled by the lexical phonological rules. The difference between Kiparsky's proposal and the earlier proposal of Hooper and Vennemann is that while the rules of Lexical Phonology are acknowledged to be involved with the morphology, they are not taken to serve a morphological function, but rather are formulated as though they had a phonological function and motivation.

It is my view that alternations differ according to whether they are associated with the phonetics or with the morphology and lexicon, and that an important goal for phonological theory is to discover the status of any given alternation at any given time. This goal is consistent with the view of Optimality Theory that the constraints operating in a grammar have a functional etiology (see Hayes 1999). I argue, however, that the actual functional status of an alternation may not always be what it seems. The fact that alternations change their status over time, as we saw in Chapter 3, leads to a situation in which something that may seem to be fulfilling a phonological or phonetic function may in fact have changed, perhaps covertly, to a morphological function. I will discuss the predominant paths of change for alternations and suggest criteria for discovering the status of an alternation.

The vast majority of phonological alternations arise initially for phonetic reasons and in purely phonetic environments (but see Section 4.7.3 for some interesting exceptions). The etiology of incipient phonetic alternations is the increased automation of the neuromotor sequences of articulation (see Section 4.3). Therefore, phonetic processes as they first appear in a language tend to affect high-frequency and highly automated sequences and only later extend to the whole lexicon of words and phrases. Once they are generalized to the whole lexicon (as in American English nasalization of vowels before tautosyllabic nasal consonants and flapping of alveolar stops, or Spanish spirantization of voiced stops), they are sometimes described as automatic, meaning that as highly practiced components of the articulatory repertoire of native speakers, they tend to dominate a person's articulation, affecting the pronunciation of loanwords and resulting in a foreign accent during early attempts at another language.

Calling phonetic patterns automatic does not imply that they are not learned. Children must acquire the particular types and timing of articulatory gestures that are present in the words of their language. Evidence from child language shows that children master articulatory patterns by mastering particular words (Ferguson and Farwell 1975) and not in the across-the-board manner that would be predicted if articulatory patterns were universal and innate (as claimed, e.g., by Stampe 1973 and Prince and Smolensky 1997). The acquisition of phonology comes about through the gradual acquisition of more and more accurate phonetic detail in the production of the words and phrases of the language. Processes come to be automatic because they are highly practiced.

The phonetic processes of a language – that is, the recurrent neuromotor patterns of articulation – are language-specific and not universal. They differ across languages by virtue of the fine particulars of the gestures and by differences in relative timing. Thus, VOT patterns in Canadian French differ from both Canadian English and European French (Caramazza and Yeni-Komshian 1974), the extent of vowel lengthening before voiced obstruents differs in French, English, and other languages (Chen 1970), and the degree of coarticulation of adjacent stops across a word boundary is different in English and in

* But tendencies are universal.

Russian (Zsiga 2000). What is universal, however, is that vowels are
longer (and not shorter) before voiced obstruents, that consonants
coarticulate, and that voice onset times vary. In Section 4.4, we discuss
theories that propose that processes of change in articulation are not
specifically universal, but that the similarities among them are due to
certain universal mechanisms of automation that work on the given
gestural content of the language to create these processes.

One important way to distinguish a phonetic process from one that
has become fossilized in the morphology and lexicon of a language is
to investigate the degree of variability between the alternates. For
instance, the presence or absence of a schwa in the second syllable of
memory is not categorical but rather a gradient range; similarly, there
are many degrees of duration in the alveolar stop in *ladder* (Zue and
Laferriere 1979). On the other hand, the pronunciations of *opaque* and
opacity do not admit of any variants between [k] and [s], nor does the
voicing of the medial fricative in *houses* vary gradually between voiceless and voiced (though there is some variation in the sense that some
people pronounce this plural with a voiceless fricative). An interesting
contrast discovered by Zsiga (1995) is that the lexical palatalization
found in *confession* (compared to *confess*) is categorical, while the
productive phonetic palatalization in *confess your* is variable.[1]

Another criterion concerns the status of exceptions. Exceptions to
phonetic processes occur in low-frequency words, words perceived as
foreign or highly formal, and, in some cases, where morphological relations restrain ongoing change (see Chapter 6.3). In all of these cases,
with the repetition of the item, the change may eventually go through.
Thus it is said that words such as *veto* and *vita* are exceptions to English
flapping; yet for many speakers in contexts in which these items are
used frequently, flapping occurs. Thus, over a fairly short period of time
(within the lifetime of a speaker) these exceptions can fall. On the
other hand, the exceptions to alternations in the morpholexical domain
have a different status: even frequent repetition of the adjective *tricky*
will not cause it to succumb to Velar Softening and be pronounced with
a stem-final [s] rather than [k]. In fact, it is the nonalternating forms
that are usually viewed as regular, while the alternating ones are themselves the exceptions. For instance, the alternations in *house/houses*,
wife/wives, *leaf/leaves*, and so on, are exceptional and subject to elimination by the process of regularization.

---

[1] For more on palatalization across word boundaries in English, see Chapter 6.4.2.

A final criterion to distinguish phonetic processes from those alternations with morpholexical conditioning is the domain of application. Productive phonetic processes often apply across words in phrases, as when palatalization affects phrases such as *don't you*. But morpholexically conditioned alternations are part of 'word-level' phonology. Thus flapping occurs in phrases such as *hit 'im, about it*, or *at Anne's* but Velar Softening does not occur in phrases such as *opaque instance*. The way that word-level phonology develops from phonetic processes is discussed in Chapter 6, and the important exceptions to this generalization, exemplified by French liaison, are discussed in Chapter 7.

A significant tendency, though not a clear criterion, that distinguishes the two alternation types discussed here, has to do with the phonetic distance between the variants. Variants on a continuous range will tend be phonetically closer than those that are categorically discrete; compare the difference between a [d] and a flap with the difference between [k] and [s] (Hooper 1976a, Janda 1999, Stampe 1973). The source of this tendency is the fact that some phonetic accommodations continue to change, as when a palatal stop produced from a velar before a front vowel continues to change to [tʃ] and then to [ts] and [s] (as, for example, in Romance languages). However, not all phonetic variants continue to change, and not all features changes are specific to one type of alternation; thus, for example, a voicing alternation may be either phonetic or morpholexical. Nor do we have clear criteria for determining what would be phonetically close versus phonetically distant. As Steriade (2000) has pointed out, attempting to do so by distinguishing strictly between those features that are phonetic and those that are phonological is unsuccessful. However, the strong tendency that has led phonologists to try to make this distinction will be explained in Chapter 8 as a consequence of the morphologization process.

The major sources of word-level morphologically and lexically conditioned alternations are phonetic processes. There is a universal and almost inevitable diachronic trajectory of morphologization of phonetic processes (Dressler 1977, Hooper 1976a, Kiparsky 1971, Vennemann 1972b) as illustrated in 1.

(1)   phonetic process > morpholexical alternation

As explained in Chapter 3, this process of lexicalization and morphologization occurs very gradually and much earlier than generally supposed, producing the many transitional cases that blur the distinction between the two alternation types under discussion. Thus, rather than making an effort to find a discrete cutoff point between these types of alternations, it is more interesting to investigate the mechanisms by which this transition occurs. The proposal I made in Chapter 3, that the effects of sound change (or phonetic process) are registered in the lexical entries of words and phrases, provides a means by which phonetic distinctions gradually become associated with particular words and morphemes.

Further discussion of the morphologization process and of the nature of morphological generalizations is found in Chapter 5. In the current chapter, our focus of interest will be the types of generalizations that are purely phonological – phonetic processes and phonotactic generalizations. We will be interested in their sources and functions and the mechanisms that lead to their creation.

4.3   Articulatory Gestures

4.3.1   The Gestural Approach

Throughout the development of generative phonology, there has been a growing dissatisfaction with the restrictions imposed by alphabetic notation – the representation and, thus, the conceptualization of the domain of phonological phenomena as the segment. One response to this dissatisfaction is Autosegmental Phonology, which allows features to simultaneously associate with more than one segment (Goldsmith 1976, 1979). However, even in this approach, segments are still basic sequential units.

A more radical reformulation moves the focus away from segments entirely, by postulating that the basic unit for phonological description is the gesture. According to the theory being developed by Browman and Goldstein (1990, 1992, 1995), 'gestures are events that unfold during speech production and whose consequences can be observed in the movements of the speech articulators' (1992:156). A typical utterance is composed of multiple gestures overlapping or sequenced with respect to one another. An individual gesture is produced by groups of muscles that act in concert, sometimes ranging over more than one articulator. For instance, constricting lip aperture involves the action of the upper lip, the lower lip, and the jaw, but such a constriction is considered one gesture. Gestures can be specified in terms of the tract variables involved in their production. The tract variables identified by

Tract variable		Articulators involved
LP	lip protrusion	upper and lower lips, jaw
LA	lip aperture	upper and lower lips, jaw
TTCL	tongue tip constrict location	tongue tip, tongue body, jaw
TTCD	tongue tip constrict degree	tongue tip, tongue body, jaw
TBCL	tongue body constrict location	tongue body, jaw
TBCD	tongue body constrict degree	tongue body, jaw
VEL	velic aperture	velum
GLO	glottal aperture	glottis

Figure 4.1. Tract variables and associated articulators proposed by Browman and Goldstein.

Browman and Goldstein (1992:157) as relevant to the characterization of speech gestures are shown in Figure 4.1.

Though also viewing phonetic output as the result of coordinated muscular activity, Mowrey and Pagliuca (1995) argue that the gestures of articulatory phonology are not the relevant units for understanding phonological processes as manifest in casual speech and sound change, but that we must rather analyze the speech stream in terms of individual muscular events, their magnitude, and their relative timing. The vocal tract variables of Figure 4.1 are defined by spatial location – position of the articulator and degree of constriction achieved by it. For an articulator to achieve a target location, a number of individual muscles must work in concert. It is the impulses to these muscles that are the true primes for phonological processes, according to Mowrey and Pagliuca.

For the remainder of this section, however, we will not dwell on the differences between choosing the gestural event versus the individual muscle activity as the relevant unit of analysis. Instead, we will examine how the articulatory approach in general handles common phonological processes and the generalizations that can be made about these processes. We will examine the difference between a theory formulated at the level of gestures versus one formulated at the level of individual muscular impulses in Section 4.4.5.

There are a number of reasons to consider this articulatory approach to phonology compatible with usage-based theory. From a general theoretical perspective, gestural or articulatory phonology recognizes that speech is an activity – a spatiotemporal motor activity – and that phonological knowledge is procedural knowledge rather than static propositional knowledge. As procedural knowledge, phonology is subject to the same forces that modify other motor skills, and that affect their memory storage and access.

A practical advantage of the gestural analysis of phonological patterns is that it yields more insightful and more coherent descriptions of most phonological phenomena than a feature-and-segment analysis does. While linguists constantly bear in mind that the speech stream is continuous, our terminology is strongly biased towards thinking in terms of segments. Thus we speak in terms of insertion and deletion of segments and assimilation, which is sometimes thought of as one segment becoming more like another or taking on the features of another segment. None of these descriptive terms is particularly accurate. Moreover, approaching phonological processes in terms of muscular events may make it possible to develop a simple theory that makes crosslinguistic predictions about possible phonological processes.

4.3.2   Assimilation

Consider first the traditional conceptualization of assimilation, perhaps the most common of all phonological processes. As an illustration of a gestural rather than a segmental approach, Pagliuca and Mowrey (1987) discuss the palatalization of [s] before [i] as, for example, occurs in Japanese. A segmental characterization that represents the change as gradual might be given as 2.

(2)   si > sʲi > ʃi

The segmental representation that shows the [s] as first palatalized and then transformed into an alveopalatal would be described in distinctive features by saying that the value of [high] for [s] first changes from minus to plus. This would be explained on the basis of the [+high] specification for [i] spreading to the preceding segment. In the next step, the value for [anterior] is changed from plus to minus. The first step changes one feature of [s] to be the same as one feature of [i]. But the second step has no clear assimilatory explanation in the segment-based approach.

Many problems with this form of description could be pointed out, such as the fact that there is nothing to predict that it is the feature [high] that changes its value, rather than some other feature that differs between the two segments, such as [syllabic]. Nor is there any natural way to explain or predict the change in the feature [anterior]. Related to this lack of predictability is the more fundamental fact that a feature-and-segment analysis does not give a very accurate picture of what is really changing in a language with this process.

Pagliuca and Mowrey (1987) argue that it is not a feature or property of [s] that has changed to be more like [i], but rather that the formerly sequential gestures producing the [s] and the [i] have gradually been compressed so that first the transition between the [s] and the [i] is highly affected by the position of the tongue for [i]. A further and later development is that the two gestures come to overlap to such an extent that the whole articulation of the fricative is affected by the domed tongue gesture of the [i], increasing the area of the point of constriction. This analysis is confirmed in Zsiga (1995), whose electropalatographic data shows that in productive palatalization of [s + j] across word boundaries (as in *miss you*), the contact of the tongue with the palate is just what one would expect if the [s] and the [j] were articulated at the same time.

A consequence of this analysis is the view that this assimilation process is actually a temporal reduction: two previously sequential gestures are now simultaneous for at least part of their articulation. Other examples of assimilation that can be explained in this way include vowel nasalization, which takes place preferentially when a vowel is followed by a nasal consonant in the same syllable. In this case, the gesture that opens the velum for nasalization is anticipated; it is retimed to occur during the articulation of the vowel. The view of this change as a modification in timing makes it possible to relate articulatory processes of speech to modifications made in other well-rehearsed motor events, where repetition increases efficiency or fluency because sequences of events can be anticipated and one event can begin before the preceding one is totally completed.

4.3.3 Other Retiming Changes

Temporal factors are also involved in what has previously been viewed as the insertion and deletion of segments. Insertion of consonants is not very common, and when it does occur, it is clear that the articulatory gestures that compose the consonant were all present before the consonant appeared. An interesting diachronic example occurred in a set of Future tense verbs of Spanish, when the grammaticizing auxiliary *haber* suffixed to the infinitive form of the verb with which it

formed a construction. Subsequently, some high-frequency Second and
Third Conjugation verbs lost the vowel preceding the stressed suffix
and developed an excrescent [d] between the [n] of the root and [r] of
the erstwhile infinitive, as illustrated in 3:

(3)   venir + he > veniré > venré > vendré 'I will come'
      tener + he > teneré > tenré > tendré 'I will have'
      poner + he > poneré > ponré > pondré 'I will put'

Note first that it is a dental stop that develops here – in other words,
one at the same point of articulation as the surrounding consonants,
rather than a labial or velar. Secondly, it is voiced, as are the surrounding consonants. To explain [nr] developing into [ndr], a straight-
forward gestural analysis is possible. The velic opening corresponding
to the [n] is retimed such that the velum is reclosed before the stop
gesture at the alveolar ridge is complete. The result is a period of stop
closure without nasality, or, in other words, a [d]. Note that the loss
of the vowel in the auxiliary *haberé > habré* does not lead to an
'excrescent' [d].

4.3.4   Reductive Processes

Besides changes in the relative timing of gestures, there can also be
reduction in the magnitude of the gestures in casual speech or in sound
change. Such reduction in consonants usually falls into the class of
lenitions or weakenings. Mowrey and Pagliuca (1995) propose that the
traditional notion of consonant be viewed as a 'local articulatory
maximum' – that is, a temporal stretch at which a relatively large
number of muscular events coincide. In contrast, a vowel may be
viewed as a longer temporal stretch in which relatively few muscular
events take place.

The reduction of a consonant such as [p] along a path which is
crosslinguistically common (namely, [p] > [φ]/[f] > [h] > φ) can be
characterized as a successive decrease and loss of muscular activity.
The production of [p] requires muscular activity of both the upper
and lower lips acting to bring them together, as well as the activity
required to open the glottis. The production of [f] requires less
or no activity in the muscles of the upper lip, but continued activity
in the lower lip and glottis. [h] is produced with no activity in the
labial muscles at all, but requires the opening of the glottis. Total
deletion involves the loss of all the muscular events that were

associated with the original consonant (Mowrey and Pagliuca 1995: 81–83).

In addition to the reduction of a consonant to zero, another path of reduction for consonants yields a more sonorous or vowel-like consonant. Such changes are most notable in syllable-final position or postvocalic position. For example, the change of a syllable-final [l] to a back unrounded glide [ɰ] involves the loss of the tongue tip gesture. This change occurs in American English pronunciations of words such as *milk* as [mɪɰk].

Temporal reduction of a stop is another possibility. The English alveolar flap found in words such as *latter* and *ladder* is significantly shorter than the [t] or [d] that occurs preceding a stressed vowel (Zue and Laferriere 1979). The medial stops in *upper* and *trucker* are also shorter than their counterparts preceding the stress, but this difference is not as salient (Hoard 1971). In these cases, the change in the gesture is a temporal one: the duration of the stop closure is shortened.

The deletion of a consonant must involve both the loss of the gesture and a temporal compression, for as Pagliuca and Mowrey point out, the loss of a consonant in a string does not result in an articulatory gap. Thus, in most cases the substantive reduction (that is, the reduction in magnitude) of the gesture and the temporal reduction of surrounding gestures work together. The interaction of substantive and temporal reduction will be discussed further in Section 4.4.2.

Vowels reduce by lessening the magnitude of the gesture as well. In unstressed syllables, reduction can be manifest in various changes in the gestures, some of which may co-occur. Laxing of vowels usually refers to a decrease in muscular activity involving a lowered articulation for high vowels and more central articulation for peripheral vowels and even a shortening compared to vowels in stressed syllables. Centralization is the result of a lessening of the magnitude of gestures that move the articulators to peripheral positions. Shortening involves a loss of temporal duration of muscular activity. When reduction leads to complete deletion, both temporal and substantive reduction have occurred.[2]

---

[2] In Bybee et al. (1998), we found that the most common types of vowel reduction in a sample of 76 languages were described as laxing or weakening (9 cases) or centralization (9 cases). The same survey turned up 5 instances of reduction reported to be shortening, or temporal reduction.

4.3.5   Acoustic-Perceptual Aspects of Phonological Processes
and Change

Analyzing phonological processes in terms of gestures does not rule
out an acoustic-perceptual component to these processes. Any change
in gestures or their timing produces an acoustic-perceptual change.
In fact, for a gestural change to proceed and become conventionalized
as part of the language, its perceptual effects must be registered in
storage.

The remarkable degree to which speakers of the same dialect
achieve similarity in the details of their phonetic output attests to the
exquisite attunement of the perceptual system to fine detail. Therefore,
it is unlikely that hearers who have already acquired the phonetics
of their dialect would misperceive already acquired words to the extent
that that might cause a sound change. However, there are two roles
for perception in change. First, it is likely that in certain cases a change
can occur because children fail to perceive and acquire a relatively difficult phonetic configuration, such as front rounded vowels (see Section
4.4.4 for an example and discussion). Second, where contextual change
has already occurred for articulatory reasons, a perceptual reanalysis could extend a change that was already begun (Ohala 1981). For
instance, in a situation in which the vowel in a VN sequence is nasalized, if the nasal consonant is also weakening, then the nasalization
could be attributed to the vowel rather than to the consonant, thereby
contributing to a change toward having just a nasalized vowel with a
deleted consonant.

Furthermore, some cases of deletion are due to the overlapping of
gestures. Rather than simple reduction in magnitude, an overlapping
produces the acoustic effect of the gesture being hidden and, therefore,
perceived as deleted. For instance, the variable deletion of final [t] and
[d] in American English occurs most frequently in contexts where the
stop is both preceded and followed by a consonant. For example, the
phrase *perfect memory* provides a likely site for deletion. Browman and
Goldstein (1990) traced the articulatory gestures in this phrase to see
what happens to the coronal gesture of the /t/ of *perfect*, which was produced as a released [tʰ] when read from a list by the same speaker.
They found that in *perfect memory* the lingual gesture of the [t] was
present, but the preceding velar and following labial gesture overlapped the coronal one, obscuring it entirely. It would thus be perceived
as deleted, even though articulatorily it is still present.

This does not mean that *t/d* deletion is a myth, or that there is no variable process of *t/d* deletion. There is good evidence for a gradual process of shortening or reducing the lingual gesture following a consonant. In particular, after a nasal, [d] is very short and frequently deleted in certain high-frequency words, such as *and*, *hand*, and *second*. We can reasonably expect full deletion of [d] after [n] on the basis of previous changes in English: [b] has been lost after [m], as in *thumb* and *bomb*, and [g] has been lost after [ŋ], as in *ring* and *hang*. As the gesture shortens, the likelihood that it will be overlapped and thus acoustically obscured by surrounding gestures increases. Perceived deletion of this type can lead to actual deletion. If tokens with perceived deletion are frequent, a reorganization of exemplars will occur, with the eventual effect of the loss of the final [t] or [d] (Bybee 2000b).

The other interesting point about this example is that articulatory activity can remain even where it produces no acoustic effect. This underscores the gradualness of articulatory change and the continuity between one pronunciation and another. Mowrey and Pagliuca (1995) study the impulses to muscles during the articulation of casual speech variants of the phrase *I suppose that's true*. They find that even where the first vowel of *suppose* is not perceived, there is nonetheless some muscular activity, suggesting that the reduction and deletion of the vowel is extremely gradual, but that there comes a point at which the articulation involved in the vowel is so minimal that it is not perceived. Thus on the articulation end, speakers are controlling even more variation than can be perceived (see Labov 1994:349–370 on 'near-mergers'). This underscores the notion that in casual speech the choices are not 'vowel' or 'no vowel', but that in fact there are many intermediate gradations depending upon the phonetic, prosodic, and social situation.

4.3.6   Section Summary

In this section, we have reviewed gestural analyses of some common phonological processes, showing how they differ from feature-and-segment analyses, arguing that the gestural analysis corresponds more closely to the actual processes of change and thus offers additional insights into the mechanisms underlying phonological processes. A further argument that can be offered for gestural phonology is that it allows the unification of patterns that seem disparate in the feature-

and-segment analysis. In Section 4.4, I discuss certain generalizations that can be made about the nature of phonological processes and sound changes and, in Section 4.6, generalizations available in a gestural analysis of syllable structure.

4.4   Patterns of Change and Constraints on Processes

4.4.1   Temporal and Substantive Reduction

Many observers of sound change and casual speech processes have noticed the preponderance of weakening or reduction and assimilation in attested changes. This tendency suggests a hypothesis according to which regular sound change is entirely reductive or assimilatory, with the result that articulatory changes all move toward the compression and reduction of articulatory gestures.

A strong version of this hypothesis is put forward in Pagliuca and Mowrey (1987) and Mowrey and Pagliuca (1995), who propose that sound change is due to either substantive reduction or temporal reduction and, in most cases, both. Substantive reduction refers to the reduction in the magnitude of a muscular gesture, such as occurs in the change of a stop to a fricative (e.g., [d] > [ð]) or the centralization of a vowel to [ə]. Temporal reduction refers to the compression of gestures either by a single articulator, as when [si] changes to [ʃi], or by multiple independent articulators, as when VN becomes V̌N. The term 'temporal reduction' entails a reduction in the duration of the whole sequence of gestures. Pagliuca and Mowrey claim that constellations of gestures in a linguistic string tend to become shorter over time, as well as reduced in the amount of articulatory energy required for the production of the individual gestures.

The goal of Pagliuca and Mowrey's research is to demonstrate that apparent strengthenings and apparent acoustically motivated changes can be seen in gestural terms as instances of substantive or temporal reduction (see also Pagliuca 1982). As we saw above, certain apparent cases of 'strengthening', such as the apparent insertion of segments, can be viewed as the result of the relative retiming of gestures.

Browman and Goldstein (1990, 1992) put forward a very similar proposal. They hypothesize that all examples of casual speech alterations are the result of gestures having decreased magnitudes (both in space and in time) and increased temporal overlap. The only difference between the two proposals is that Browman and Goldstein are not so specific about whether they consider overlap to be due to temporal reduction. That is, Pagliuca and Mowrey explicitly claim that all temporal changes, including those creating overlap, are due to the compression of gestures, which results in an overall shortening of the temporal duration of the string, while Browman and Goldstein do not explicitly make this claim. Of course, these hypotheses are testable on spoken data, and further refinements will be possible when further data have been examined.

Browman and Goldstein (1990, 1992) restrict their hypothesis to casual speech alterations. This restriction has the advantage of defining an empirically verifiable sample of alterations. Mowrey and Pagliuca wish to address all sound change. In order to take this step, Mowrey and Pagliuca (1995) argue that the notion of sound change must be restricted to internally motivated changes (as opposed to changes due to language contact), to actually attested changes (as opposed to reconstructed ones), and to changes that are lexically regular. With these restrictions in place, it is not controversial to claim that the great majority of attested sound changes have an articulatory etiology and, in particular, involve assimilation (retiming) or reduction. The controversial issue is whether it is accurate to take the further step of proposing that all sound changes fall into one of these two categories.[3]

It is my view that this further step is of considerable theoretical interest and should definitely be attempted. First, it is always of interest to propose the strongest possible theory. Second, as we have already seen, certain cases of what would be viewed as addition of a consonant are not strengthenings, but rather adjustments in relative timing of gestures. Taking this strong position, then, is productive in that it forces a reexamination and a greater understanding of the nature of sound change. Finally, a unified view of articulatory modifications over time or over speech styles is likely to reveal that the general tendencies affecting speech production are the same as those affecting other instances of repeated motor behavior. With repetition, neuromotor routines become more compressed and more reduced.

---

[3] It is sometimes objected that a theory of sound change according to which all sound change is reductive would leave a language bereft of consonants and vowels, or at least that all articulations would be reduced to schwa. Such an objection ignores the fact that there are many sources of renewal of phonological material. For instance, Hopper (1994) shows in his paper on 'phonogenesis' that parts of old words and morphemes make up new portions of old eroding words.

4.4.2 The Interaction of Temporal and Substantive Reduction

Having identified temporal reduction and substantive reduction, we need to ask if these constitute two different types of processes, or whether they are related in some way. It appears that one relation between them does exist: many cases of one also involve the other (Mowrey and Pagliuca 1995). We have already noted that in cases of the complete deletion of a consonant or vowel, reduction in the magnitude of a gesture is involved, but at the same time there must also be temporal compression, because the deleted gesture leaves no gap in the phonetic string. Thus, deletion of a segment from a word involves a leftward compression of all the material in the word that follows the deleting element.

Moreover, Mowrey and Pagliuca (1995:76–78) point out that in cases of vowel nasalization, the nasal consonant often reduces and deletes. These may not be separate events, but rather one continuous event in which the opening of the velum is advanced in time while the occlusion associated with the nasal consonant gradually erodes. Other instances of change in which one element apparently conditions a change and then disappears would also involve both substantive and temporal reduction. Mowrey and Pagliuca conclude that such processes may involve 'substantive reduction of the majority of the articulations originally present and concomitant temporal reduction of remnant articulations' (1995:77–78). They also observe that substantive reduction must be involved in retiming, because most retiming is anticipatory and if reduction did not also occur, all the muscular activity in a word would, over time, end up bunched up at the left edge of the word!

4.4.3 Strengthenings

Two types of counterexamples to the strong claims about sound change made by Mowrey and Pagliuca need to be noted and discussed. First, we discuss some cases of apparent strengthenings that appear to be well attested. Then, in Section 4.4, we discuss the possibility of perceptually based changes and a proposal for distinguishing them from articulatorily based changes.

Recall that some apparent strengthenings, such as the insertion of an obstruent into certain sequences of consonants, have already been dealt with in Section 4.3.3. Diphthongization, which is viewed by some as a strengthening, can also be analyzed as a retiming since one can hypothesize that diphthongs are produced by sequencing vowel gestures that were formerly simultaneous. The crucial question would be whether the resulting diphthong has a greater temporal duration than the simple vowel from which it arose. Similarly, vowel lengthening needs to be studied in this context to determine whether over time a vowel can increase its length. (Recall that in Chapter 3.4.3, we saw that the vowel length difference in English before voiced and voiceless consonants is probably a case of vowel shortening rather than lengthening.)

In addition, Pagliuca and Mowrey (1987:462) suggest that affrication of voiceless stops, as occurred in the High German Consonant Shift ([p] > [pf] > [f], [t] > [ts] > [s], [k] > [kx] > [x]) is due to 'the erosion of stop closure integrity, which has, as an aerodynamic consequence, an increase in acoustic energy,' and that it is not a fortition, as some assume. Evidence that the general path of change that includes the stop-to-affricate step is a general lenition, or weakening, is that the subsequent step, which yields a fricative, is uncontroversially a weakening.

The distribution of weaker and stronger articulations suggests to some researchers an on-line strengthening. Fougeron and Keating (1997) found that consonants show more linguopalatal contact at the beginnings of utterances, phonological phrases, and phonological words. Since this difference is cumulative across the hierarchy of domains, they conclude that it is not due to a global weakening from the beginning of an utterance to the end, but rather to local strengthenings at the edges of prosodic domains. However, another possible conclusion is that the pattern is due to local weakenings internal to prosodic domains.

In my opinion, the real challenges to the reduction theory are the well-attested cases in Romance languages of the strengthening of a glide in syllable-initial position to a fricative, stop, or affricate. This change has occurred in several dialects of Latin America, yielding voiced or even voiceless fricatives or affricates in words such as *yo* 'I', *oye* 'listen', and *hielo* 'ice'. Lipski (1994) reports this pronunciation for parts of Mexico, Central America, Ecuador, Uruguay, and Argentina. A similar change is also in progress in parts of Spain.

The implication of such examples for the reduction theory depends upon certain facts about these changes that have not been explicitly examined to date. First, we would want to ask if such changes are motivated by the automation of gestures in production. One way to answer

*But marking-initial salience

this question is to examine the lexical diffusion patterns for such changes, asking whether the changes affect high-frequency words first (in which case automation of production would be involved), or whether they affect low-frequency words first. Second, if automation does seem to be involved, we would want to ask if the strengthening of the glide could be due to a temporal compression of existing gestures, or if some new mechanism is present. If automation is not involved, we would want to look for other, perhaps systemic, factors to explain this change. Finally, we might conclude that strengthening does take place under certain conditions.

4.4.4   Perceptually Motivated Changes

The second question raised by the reduction theory of sound change is whether it is possible for sound changes to have a perceptual rather than an articulatory motivation. We have already seen that any articulatory change has an acoustic/perceptual dimension (Section 4.3.5), but here we ask whether the motivation for a sound change can be purely perceptual, and how such a change would take place. As I said in discussing the proposals by Ohala (1981), it is unlikely that an adult who already knows the language would change a pronunciation because of 'mishearing' another speaker's pronunciation. However, it is possible that a child acquiring a first language might mishear or misanalyze a portion of the speech stream. Unfortunately, it is often difficult to distinguish an acoustic motivation from an articulatory one, since many changes that could have an acoustic motivation also involve the loss or retiming of a gesture. A further source of evidence, as yet not applied in such discussions, is the evidence from lexical diffusion. The difference between the mechanisms can be sorted out by examining the way in which the change affects the lexicon. If a misanalysis on the part of acquirers were the mechanism for a sound change, that change would have a very different means of implementation and pattern of lexical diffusion than a change whose cause was articulatory automation. Changes resulting from imperfect learning, such as overregularizations in morphology, affect the low-frequency forms of the language before the high-frequency forms, which tend to resist such changes (Hooper 1976b, Phillips 1984, 2001). Thus, information from lexical diffusion can inform us about the mechanism behind sound changes.

Consider an example discussed in Phillips (1984). The Old English diphthong *eo*, both long and short instances, monophthongized to /œ:/

and /œ/ in the eleventh and twelfth centuries. This front rounded vowel later lost its lip rounding and merged with /e:/ and /e/. Examples are *deop* > *deep*, *beon* > *be*, and *seon* > *see*. This change in progress is captured in the text *Ormulum* from about 1200 A.D. The author was interested in spelling reform and used two spellings for the reflexes of this Old English diphthong, *eo* and *e*, often representing the same word in two different ways. Phillips analyzed the spellings in this text and found that, among nouns and verbs, the less frequent words had more innovative spellings – that is, they showed unrounding of the vowel more often than the more frequent words did.

A possible interpretation of this pattern of lexical diffusion is that front rounded vowels are difficult to acquire for perceptual reasons. In a discrimination learning task, Gilbert and Wyman (1975) found that five-, six-, and seven-year-old English-speaking and French-speaking children had more trouble discriminating [œ] than any of the other three vowels tested, which were [ɛ], [a], and [o]. The most frequent confusion for nonnasalized vowels was between [œ] and [ɛ]. These findings suggest that the vowel [œ] may be difficult to acquire for perceptual reasons. We could therefore reason that a word with a front rounded vowel must be highly available in the input to be acquired correctly. Thus, the Old English pattern of lexical diffusion described by Phillips could be explained as the correct acquisition of /œ:/ and /œ/ in high-frequency nouns and verbs, but the failure to acquire the same vowels in words of low frequency.

An interesting twist in Phillips's results is that the preposition *betwenenn* 'between', the adverbs *sket* 'quickly' and *newenn* 'newly', and adjectives (except for numerals) display the opposite pattern. In this set, it is high-frequency words that show more innovative spellings. A mixed pattern of lexical diffusion suggests a mix of mechanisms. High-frequency words that are usually unstressed may undergo the change as a type of reduction – loss of lip rounding in unstressed position – while low-frequency words may undergo the change as learners fail to acquire the complex articulation.

This example suggests that a series of diachronic changes may have the effect of creating more complex segments by the increased overlap of gestures and then may resolve this complexity by further loss of gestures. The monophthongization of Old English *eo* to /œ/ was a retiming of gestures such that the lip-rounding gesture was anticipated and came to overlap the tongue-fronting gesture. The resulting vowel had a complex articulation that was not supported by other vowels in the

* Because spellers don't know to spell them.

language, as Middle English had no other front rounded vowels. If such vowels present an acquisition problem, their further change may come about through imperfect learning, in which case infrequent words will be affected before frequent words.

My general suggestion then, concerning establishing types of sound changes, is that lexical diffusion patterns can provide an additional and much-needed criterion for discovering both why and how sound changes take place. Hooper (1976b) and Phillips (1984, 2001) have suggested that changes with different motivations have different patterns of lexical diffusion. In Phillips's most recent formulation, changes resulting from articulatory reduction affect high-frequency words first, while changes resulting from an analysis based on other forms of the language affect low-frequency forms first (see Chapter 5 for further discussion of the second type of change).

4.4.5   Gestures or Individual Muscles?

As noted earlier, the frameworks proposed by Browman and Goldstein and by Mowrey and Pagliuca are very similar in that they look to articulation as a basis for unifying phonological processes and for representing words and phrases by incorporating the temporal relations of production. But there is a difference in the level of analysis proposed, which is in turn related to a difference in goals for each theory. Browman and Goldstein are searching for the appropriate unit of linguistic analysis that will account not just for phonological processes, but also for distinctiveness in the lexicon. For them, the appropriate unit is the gesture, which is an abstract characterization of an articulatory event, including its intrinsic temporal component. Gestures are abstractions away from tokens of articulatory events and only capture the distinctive features of such events. These abstract gestures, then, are comparable in level to phonemes, in that they are contrastive and may change in context. Mowrey and Pagliuca eschew this level of abstraction and, for their goal of accounting for articulatory evolution, they take each muscular event as a constituent unit of a word or phrase. Their theory does not include a proposal about lexical storage, nor does it provide an account of the fact that each word of a language is not made up of random combinations of muscular activity, but that instead each word utilizes the same constellations of muscular events. As we will see later on, their theory can be appropriately augmented to be more comprehensive. But for the moment, let us consider their argument that the gesture is not the appropriate unit of analysis for their purposes of accounting for the directionality and substance of sound change.

We have already observed that Browman and Goldstein's hypothesis about the nature of casual speech alterations and Mowrey and Pagliuca's hypothesis about the nature of sound change are virtually identical.[4] Mowrey and Pagliuca argue that their theory of change applies better at the level of the individual muscle than at the level of the gesture. The example they give involves the change of $[t^h] > [t̪^h] > [\theta]$, such as occurred in the First German Consonant Shift (Grimm's Law). In this change not only does the degree of constriction change (and that would be a reduction in the magnitude of a gesture), but so does the point of articulation. Mowrey and Pagliuca (1995:65) observe that a gestural analysis would require either an increase in magnitude of a gesture to move from an alveolar to an interdental point of articulation, or it would involve a transformation into a new gesture.

Mowrey and Pagliuca's account of this change focuses on the action of the styloglossus muscles, whose contraction both retracts and elevates the tongue, while other muscular activity serves to raise the tip and margins of the tongue toward the alveolar ridge. They argue that if the activity of the styloglossus gradually reduces, the effect would be for the tongue tip to retract and elevate less, reaching a constriction point first behind the teeth (yielding $[t̪^h]$) and then, with further reduction of styloglossus activity, a point between the teeth (yielding $[\theta]$). Thus, they argue that the cause of this lenition is the reduction of activity in one muscle, rather than in a whole constellation of muscles that would constitute a gesture. Unfortunately, the example they chose to argue their point is a reconstructed example which, as they correctly argue elsewhere, cannot be used as counterexample to theories of sound change since the starting points are not attested and might be incorrect.

Over the last three decades, a similar debate has taken place in many different forms. The central difficulty is that units or features that are designed to express phonemic contrast (segments and distinctive features, especially binary ones) do a poor job of describing what takes place in continuous phonological processes. The reason is that it is not

---

[4] I am fairly certain that each team arrived at their hypotheses independently.

= would be redundant

just the distinctive properties of the speech stream that are active in conditioning alterations that occur in fluent speech, but that in many cases, predictable aspects of the articulation are the causal factors in processes (Vennemann 1972a, and more recently, Kirchner 1997). Given the goal of Browman and Goldstein's theory – to obtain a unit of analysis that can account for contrast – the selection of a bundle of muscular events as the prime unit may be appropriate. However, for the task of predicting and explaining casual speech processes, sound change, and phonological processes, there are likely to be cases where a finer level of analysis is necessary.

4.5   Segments as Emergent Units

In network models, internal structure is emergent – it is based on the network of connections built up among stored units. The stored units are pronounceable linguistic forms – words or phrases stored as clusters of surface variants organized into clusters of related words. Browman and Goldstein (1991) suggest that phonological properties of lexical items are represented in gestural scores that characterize the activity of the vocal tract. It seems reasonable to suppose that an associated set of perceptual images would also be part of the representation.

   Units such as syllables and segments emerge from the inherent nature of the organization of gestures for articulation. Browman and Goldstein (1995:20) argue that 'syllable structure is a characteristic pattern of coordination among gestures.' Once the nature and timing of gestural coordination is described, in effect, syllabic structure has also been described. Several recent studies have also argued for the emergent nature of segments. Ohala (1992) argues that the temporal coordination of certain gestures enhances their acoustic effect and thus provides an evolutionary impetus for the development of segments. Studdert-Kennedy (1987, 1998) and Lindblom (1992) argue that it is the increase in the number of stored lexical items that leads children to organize gestures in such a way that consonants and vowels emerge.

   How do consonants and vowels emerge from gestural scores? A true one-to-one relationship between segments and part of the score is not to be expected, given the well-known problems with the notion of segment. However, what is present in the score are certain points of temporal coordination involving (for consonants) the achievement of the target, the beginning of movement away from the target, or, occasionally, the onset of movement toward the target (Browman and Goldstein 1995). These phasing points among the gestures of the independent articulators correspond in a very rough way to the areas in the speech stream that we tend to identify with alphabetic symbols designating consonants. Mowrey and Pagliuca observe that consonants represent articulatory maxima – that is, portions of the gestural score where muscular activity is concentrated. The more steady state portions of the score are identified as vowels. In this view, consonants and vowels are derived from gestural coordination.

Moreover, recurring sets of gestural phasing can be identified in independent words or phrases. Lindblom (1992) argues that anatomically and temporally identical control functions may be stored only once.[5] This means that parts of gestural scores of a language that are identical (or highly similar) will be linked to one another as representing the same motoric pattern. From such repeated sets of coordinated gestures, a 'segment' inventory can be derived. The reuse of the same sets of gestures in the same temporal configuration is necessary if a child (or a language) is to acquire a large vocabulary (Lindblom 1992, Studdert-Kennedy 1987, 1998).

The view that phonological representations are self-organizing means that units of analysis, such as segments and syllables, are emergent units and are permitted to have gradient properties. This view does not insist upon one unit of uniform size for describing all speech, but rather proposes that the organization of linguistic material into units depends entirely upon the substantive properties of that material.

4.6 Generalization over Syllable-Initial and Syllable-Final Position

One of the most common sites for modifications of consonants in phonological processes or sound change is syllable-final position. It is probably fair to say that the 'same' consonant almost never appears in both syllable-initial and syllable-final position without some modifications. Stops in syllable-final position often lack release features, such as a distinction between aspirated and unaspirated, as, for instance, in

---

[5] In the model developed here, it would be more appropriate to say that these control functions are associated with one another by lexical connections.

Dolakha Newari (Genetti 1994:33). Also, it is common for syllable-final obstruents to be voiceless, even if voicing is contrastive in syllable-initial position.

Browman and Goldstein (1992, 1995) have discovered a generalization regarding the difference between certain sonorant consonants in syllable-initial and syllable-final position. In syllable-initial position, the gestures involved in producing a consonant such as [n] or [l] are more synchronous than in syllable-final position, where the gestures are more spread out over time. Indeed, Browman and Goldstein (1992, 1995) report that multiple gestures following a vowel are phased such that the wider gesture – the one with lesser degree of constriction – comes earlier, yielding a structure in which the syllable nucleus has the widest opening and subsequent gestures are organized towards gradual closure. Studies of the relative phasing of syllable-final gestures leads to a unified description of the seemingly unrelated phonetic pattern of 'velarization' of [l] in syllable-final position and the nasalization of vowels before tautosyllabic nasal consonants. American English [l], both syllable-initial and syllable-final ('dark') [l], is produced with two gestures: one involving the tongue tip and one involving the tongue dorsum. For [l] before a vowel, the two gestures occur almost simultaneously, while after a vowel, the tongue dorsum gesture begins much earlier than the tongue tip gesture. In fact, for the postvocalic [l], the end of the retraction of the back of the tongue occurs only a little after the beginning of the raising of the tongue tip. The acoustic impression of a velarized or 'dark' [l] results from this retraction of the back of the tongue occurring before the tongue tip raises (Sproat and Fujimura 1993).

A similar difference in phasing accounts for the difference between syllable-initial and syllable-final nasals as well. For a prevocalic nasal consonant such as [m], the velum opening and labial closure are synchronous, with the end of the velum lowering coinciding with the end of the lip closure. For syllable-final [m], in contrast, the velum lowering occurs much earlier (resulting, of course, in a nasalized vowel), and the end of that gesture coincides with the beginning of the labial closing movement. Thus Browman and Goldstein suggest that a similarity in syllable structure across different consonants may be seen on the gestural level.

While I said in Section 4.5 that consonants and vowels may be viable substantive emergents from phonetic material, it is an empirical question whether consonants at the level of the phoneme are valid units. A serious question concerns whether, or to what extent, articulations that have been regarded as variants of a phoneme, such as syllable-initial and syllable-final [l] or [p], constitute the same unit. A traditional phonemic analysis regards the instances of [l] and [p] in *leap* and *peal* as the same in some important way. Yet phonetically, they show both similarities and differences, and over time, they tend to grow more dissimilar. Their difference is further underscored by the fact that speech errors rarely involve the transposition of a syllable-final and syllable-initial consonant. These facts suggest that a reasonable hypothesis about the minimal sequential units of phonological representation is that they include an inventory of syllable onsets, syllable nuclei, and syllable codas, but that the onsets and codas may not be unified into a single set of consonants. Certainly, based on the evidence just reviewed, the onsets represent local articulatory maxima to a much greater extent than the codas do.

This proposal would predict that a language could have a completely mutually exclusive set of syllable onsets and syllable codas. While such a situation may occur, it is normal for syllable-final consonants to be a subset of syllable-initial ones. This overlap can be attributed to the fact that syllable-final consonants typically arise from syllable-initial ones by vowel deletion. The diachronic trajectory of syllable-final consonants will be discussed further in Chapter 8. My goal in this section is merely to present the following suggestion. Since for consonants, some of the strongest evidence for a phoneme inventory is the recurrence of what appear to be the same consonants in different positions in the syllable, we need to examine this situation carefully to determine if the designation of a syllable-final consonant as the 'same' as its syllable-initial congener is warranted.

4.7 Phonotactics

4.7.1 Phonotactics and Phonological Processes

The separation of phonotactics from phonological rules in traditional theories is a consequence of separating the phonemic and the phonetic levels. Phonotactics are statements about possible sequences of phonemes, while rules derive phonetic representations. This distinction, however, is not always successfully maintained. Many cases have been noted in the literature of phonotactic constraints and phonological rules that cover the same generalizations. For instance, vowel harmony is usually a property of the phonemic representation of roots as well as a process necessary for the derivation of words since suffixes typically harmonize. In some languages (e.g., Spanish), all syllable-final nasals are homorganic with the following obstruent and this applies both morpheme-internally and across morpheme boundaries. A generative phonology of Spanish has to state a morpheme structure constraint on nasals as well as a phonological rule of nasal assimilation. In a theory that does not distinguish two levels of representation, this duplication does not occur (see Steriade 2000).

For cases such as these, it can be said that a single set of gestural patterns is utilized for the production of all words. In languages with vowel harmony, certain gestures of the tongue body and lips are held constant across words. In the case of Spanish nasal assimilation, only one gesture occurs across N$C sequences. In addition, if we use a gestural model and do not distinguish between phonotactic and allophonic patterns, we can capture some generalizations that were previously inaccessible. For instance, take the phonotactic facts of English that only voiceless phonemes occur after [s] (*spar*, *star*, and *scar*, but not **sbar*, **sdar*, or **sgar*), that these voiceless stops are unaspirated, and that syllable-initial voiceless stops are aspirated. All these facts have to do with the timing of the glottal opening and closing with respect to the execution of the supraglottal gestures. We only need to specify the possible gestural combinations for English, and all of these facts are accounted for.

Browman and Goldstein (1992) observe that in English, the peak glottal opening is synchronized to the midpoint of a fricative gesture, but to the end or release of a closure gesture. Thus for a sequence such as [sp], the peak glottal opening occurs during the [s] gesture and ends as the labial gesture of the [p] is released, producing an unaspirated stop. For a syllable-initial [p], on the other hand, the peak glottal opening occurs at the release of the labial closure, leaving a period of voicelessness after the release, which we know as aspiration. Thus a description of glottal and supraglottal gesture coordination provides us with a description of both 'phonotactic' and 'phonetic' facts.

4.7.2   Phonotactics as Emergent Generalizations

Classical descriptions of phonotactics have claimed that there is a three-way division of phoneme sequences into existing, possible, and impossible combinations. One can distinguish between accidental and systematic gaps in phonotactics by noting that English speakers know intuitively the difference between **blik* and **bnik* – namely, that *blik* is a possible English word because it violates no phonotactic constraints, but *bnik* is not possible because English has a constraint against syllable-initial clusters of [bn]. Subsequent experiments have revealed, however, that the intuitive knowledge of English speakers about phonotactics is much more detailed and subtle than this three-way distinction implies.

Fortunately, it is rather easy to construct nonce words that are more or less similar to existing words and to ask subjects to evaluate their degree of acceptability in their native language. In one of the earliest of such experiments, Greenberg and Jenkins (1964), asked subjects to evaluate 24 words as being close to English or far from English. The list included words that occur in English ([græs]) and ranged from words that differed from English words by only one phoneme ([klæb]) to words that differed in multiple ways ([mzöç]). The words were ranked by how many changes it would take to go from the nonce word to a real English word. The results of several variants of this experiment consistently showed that English speakers were able to judge accurately the degree to which the words differed from English words. These judgments could be made either by a comparison with the store of existing words or by estimating how many of the rules of English phonotactics were violated by the nonce form.

The Greenberg and Jenkins experiments suggest that acceptability may at least in part correspond to familiarity. The closer the nonce words were to English words, the more familiar and, thus, acceptable they seemed. Similarity is not the only measure of familiarity; patterns may also seem more familiar if they occur frequently in the lexicon. A series of recent experiments (Coleman 1996, Frisch et al. 2001, Pierrehumbert 1994a, Treiman et al. 2000, Vitevich et al. 1997) has explored the role of the type frequency or lexical frequency of phonotactic patterns, showing that, even among occurring patterns, subjects judge high-frequency sequences and patterns to be more acceptable than low-frequency sequences and patterns. Moreover, Hay et al. (to appear) show that lexical frequency affects perception and production, in addition to judgments of acceptability.

In a study of the effect of lexical frequency on well-formedness in English, Vitevitch et al. (1997) constructed sets of bisyllabic words from possible syllables that had a high probability of occurrence in the English lexicon and possible syllables that had a low probability of occurrence. The probability of occurrence was based on the frequency with which consonants occurred in syllable-initial and syllable-final position and the probability of co-occurrence of CV and VC sequences. An example of a high-probability (but nonoccurring) syllable is [kik], while a low-probability example is [giθ]. Sets of possible English two-syllable words were constructed out of two high-probability syllables, two low-probability syllables, and combinations of high–low and low–high syllables. In addition, some words had initial stress, and some had final stress. Subjects were asked to rate the nonce words on a scale of one to ten from 'good English word' to 'bad English word.'

The results showed that even though none of the words violated any English phonotactic constraints, significant distinctions were found according to whether the constituent syllables had a low or high probability of occurrence. The subjects rated the words containing high-probability syllables as much better English words than those containing low-probability syllables. For example [fʌl tʃʌn] was rated as a better English word than [ðaib dʒaiz]. In addition, the experiment revealed that words with initial stress were deemed more English-like than words with final stress. This result reflects the fact that more English words have initial than final stress, though it is important to remember that both are possible in English.

These results show, then, that speakers do not necessarily have a set of categorical constraints that distinguish possible from impossible English words, but rather that they are sensitive to probabilities of acceptable sequences. In other words, phonotactic knowledge is built up on the basis of the actually occurring words of English, not on the basis of abstract categorical rules extracted from these words.

In her study of medial consonant clusters in English words, Pierrehumbert (1994a) comes to a similar conclusion. Usually constraints on consonant clusters are described in terms of what is a possible syllable in a language, and it is assumed that, since words are comprised of syllables, these constraints also describe a well-formed word of the language. However, Pierrehumbert observes that for English at least, this is not necessarily the case. If all three-consonant sequences that are morpheme-medial consist of the coda of one syllable followed by the onset of the next syllable, then there should be over eighteen thousand possible three-consonant clusters found in English words. However, a dictionary count revealed only that 50 such clusters are found morpheme-medially.

The first factor Pierrehumbert takes into account in paring down the set of medial clusters to those that actually occur is that the combination of low-frequency onsets and codas produces clusters that are even more infrequent. Thus a stochastic syllable grammar would rule out a large number of theoretically possible clusters. Pierrehumbert reports that almost all of the 50 occurring three-consonant clusters were among the 200 most likely combinations. It appears, then, that to account for the actual shape of English words, it is necessary to take into account the frequency with which certain syllable onsets and codas occur in the lexicon.

Secondly, among the 200 most likely combinations of medial clusters, Pierrehumbert discovered that the gaps range from more systematic to more idiosyncratic. In a nonce word experiment in which subjects were asked to say whether a nonce word with a medial three-consonant cluster was 'most like a compound' or 'most suitable to be a part of the vocabulary of an English speaker of the twenty-first century,' the results showed that words with occurring clusters were more likely to be judged as 'suitable words' while the ones with non-occurring clusters were more likely to be judged as 'compounds.' Thus the subjects were able to distinguish between *cosprant* (which contains an occurring cluster) and *comkrant* (which does not). Since both words contain only possible syllables of English, the knowledge that one is more wordlike than the other is very likely based on a comparison of the nonce word to existing English words, rather than to abstract, categorical rules of syllable structure.

Once it is established that judgments about the acceptability of phonotactic sequences are based on the similarity between a word and the existing words of a language and on the frequency of the patterns in question, other issues arise concerning how the overall acceptability of a word is determined, as well as how similarity and frequency interact. Coleman and Pierrehumbert (1997) modeled the experimental results of Coleman (1996), in which it was found that some nonce words with nonoccurring sequences, such as /mɹuˈpeɪʃn/ were rated as better than nonce words with only occurring sequences, such as /ˈsplɛtɪsɑk/. Apparently the relatively high frequency of the -*ation* sequences in **mrupation* rendered it familiar, overriding the problem with the initial cluster. Coleman and Pierrehumbert found that while various methods of calculating the probability of a word yield significant results, the most successful method allows the well-formedness of lexically attested parts of words to ameliorate the unacceptability of the unattested or low-frequency parts, with the result that nonoccur-ring sequences are not necessarily ruled out.

Another question is whether similarity is more important than fre-quency, or vice versa. In accordance with the other results cited here, Frisch et al. (2001) show that the probability of patterns in the lexicon affects well-formedness, but they also demonstrate that judgments about a nonword can be influenced by a highly similar existing word. The presence of both similarity and frequency factors suggests a model in which subjects can compare nonce words to individual exemplars as well as to generalizations at various levels of abstractions.

The work cited here, then, confirms that judgments of acceptability or well-formedness are based on the experience of the language user. More familiar strings are viewed as more acceptable. Note that the frequency effect studied in these experiments is from type frequency, which determines productivity in the morphological domain (see Chapter 5) and the morphosyntactic domain (Bybee and Thompson 2000).

4.7.3   Phonological Generalizations with High Type Frequency as Sources of Change

Throughout this chapter, I have presented evidence for the hypothesis that sound change is phonetically (especially articulatorily) motivated, and that the source of new alternations are phonetically conditioned changes in articulation, which become lexicalized and morphologized. In this section, I will discuss some cases that do not readily fit this common pattern and argue that they come about by the extension of high type-frequency patterns at the expense of low type-frequency patterns.

Morin et al. (1990) investigate a very interesting case of an excep-tionless phonological generalization in Standard French that arose from the generalization of what was previously an alternation condi-tioned by the morphological category of plural. The generalization is that a word-final [ɔ] is tensed to [o]. Alternations which attest to the productivity of this pattern appear in cases of word formation, as for example, when *métropolitain* [metrɔpɔlitẽ] 'subway' is shortened to *métro* [metro] and *vélociped* [velɔsipɛd] 'bicycle' is shortened to *vélo* [velo]. Alternations also appear in pairs such as masculine *sot* [so] 'stupid' versus feminine *sotte* [sɔt]. Morin et al. argue that this pattern generalized from a rule that tensed vowels in the plurals of nouns and adjectives. First it generalized to affect nouns and adjectives, whether Singular or Plural, and later it generalized to adverbs.

The authors argue that the pattern of lexical diffusion of this change is not what one would expect if it were a phonetically motivated sound change. First, it affected the singulars of nouns and adjectives with [o] in the plural, before generalizing to invariable words. Second, the high-frequency adverb *trop* 'too much, too many' seems to be the last word to change (further information on frequency patterns in the lexical diffusion of this change are not available). High-frequency words are protected from analogical change, which is what a generalization from a morphophonological rule would be, whereas a sound change of articulatory etiology would affect high-frequency items first.

Another way in which this change differs from a sound change is that its context of application makes crucial reference to the end of the word. Productive phonetic processes tend to refer only to phonetic features, not to lexical-syntactic ones such as word boundary. (A discussion of the way changes conditioned by word boundaries develop can be found in Chapter 6.)

I suggest that this pattern is similar to a phonotactic generalization in that it places restrictions on the positioning of segments in words. We have just seen that phonotactic generalizations are based on frequency distributions in the existing lexicon. Subjects generally regard nonce words that use frequently occurring patterns as more nativelike than those that use rarer patterns, even if these do exist in the lexicon. If the lax vowel [ɔ] was relatively rare word-finally in the general lexicon, but the tense vowel [o] was frequent, speakers might have generalized that a final mid back rounded vowel must be tense, and then gradually have eliminated the exceptions to this generalization. An analogous situation might be those Spanish dialects in which an orthographic syllable-final *p* is pronounced as [k], as in [peksi] 'Pepsi' or [konsekto] 'concept'. A proposed explanation for this phenomenon is that [k] occurs much more frequently in syllable-final position than does [p]. Brown (1999a) shows that in approximately forty thousand words of conversation, there were only 13 different words with the internal sequences [pt] or [ps], as against 89 different words with the internal sequences [ks] and [kt]. For the case of French tensing of [ɔ], it would be interesting to know the ratio of final [o] to final [ɔ] in the lexicon before the change took place.

These examples show that it is possible for a phonological generalization to arise from frequency distributions in the lexicon rather than from pure coarticulation effects. However, the former type are much less frequent, since the conditions for coarticulation effects are always present in spoken language, but the particular imbalances in distributions in the lexicon that can lead to change occur less often.

4.8 Conclusion

In this chapter, we have seen some of the consequences of viewing speaking as a neuromotor activity in which words and phrases are routines for production and possibly perception. Both phonotactic and phonetic patterns are frequently repeated configurations of muscular gestures. These repeated sequences are subject to the tendencies that affect all repeated neuromotor activity, and these tendencies of compression and reduction in turn produce what linguists see as phonological processes or phonological change.

The traditional units of phonology are not necessarily basic to representation. Syllables can perhaps be viewed as organizational units for production, but the status of segments is still unclear. Particular vowels and consonants appear to emerge from gestural representation, but that does not mean that all words and phrases are exhaustively divisible into segments. In this chapter also, I have questioned whether syllable-initial and syllable-final versions of particular consonants can be regarded as members of the same category. We have also seen that knowledge of phonotactics is directly tied to experience with the words of one's language.

5

The Interaction of Phonology with Morphology

5.1 Introduction

A major focus of generative phonology has been on word-internal alternations – that is, cases in which a morpheme has phonological variants depending upon the word in which it appears (e.g., *divine, divinity*; *keep, kept*). Most of these alternations are morphologically and lexically conditioned, but the role of morphology and the lexicon has not been assessed directly in generative theory, as the assumption was made early on that the form and motivation for alternations involving the morphology and lexicon followed the same principles as those that were strictly phonological in nature. In fact, up to the present, generative frameworks (including Lexical Phonology) have paid very little attention to the nature of the morphological categories and lexical classes that govern morphophonological alternations. One goal of this chapter is to present evidence that the principles governing phonological patterns that reference morphology and lexicon are radically different in nature from those governing purely phonetically conditioned processes. The other goal is to review what is known about these lexical and morphological principles from the experimental, child language, and language change evidence.

The morphologization of phonological rules was discussed in Chapter 3.6, where it was argued that the involvement of phonological alternations with morphology occurs very early in the development of a phonological process, even while phonetic conditioning for the process is still present in the language. I also argued that there is an inexorable unidirectionality to the increasing morphological and lexical involvement in phonological alternations. This subsumes the claim that, with very few exceptions, phonetic processes creating

alternations become highly associated with morphology and lexicon
and the further claim that no reversal in direction occurs: alternations
that are conditioned by morphology do not change to become phonological processes. Thus with respect to the morphologization of phonological processes, there is a universal and unidirectional pathway of
change, from which we can derive certain synchronic predictions. For
further discussion, see Chapter 8.

5.2 Morphological versus Phonological Conditioning

The preference for morphological over phonological conditioning does
not stop once morphologization is complete, but rather can be seen at
various stages in the development of morphologically conditioned
alternations. The evidence shows that alternations associated with morphology are governed by a different set of principles than are true
phonological processes. We will see in this section the preference for
morphological conditioning over phonological conditioning, the tendency for phonologically similar alternations to be treated differently
according to morphological context, and the failure of morphologically
conditioned alternations to generalize to members of natural classes.
Later, in Sections 5.8 and 5.9, we will see that category structure in
morphologically conditioned patterns is product-oriented and based
on family resemblances, rather than source-oriented (derivational) and
based on discrete categories. Throughout this chapter, we will see
examples of how the interaction of phonology with morphology
increases over time and a set of phenomena that argues against a strict
modularization of phonology, grammar, and lexicon, as proposed in
generative theory.

5.2.1 The Preference for Morphological over
Phonological Conditioning

In Chapter 2, a network model was sketched (based on Bybee 1985),
which describes morphological relations among words as sets of
parallel semantic and phonological connections. That is, words such as
start, *started*, and *starting* are associated by phonological connections
linking their first five segments and semantic connections linking the
same portion of each word. Words such as *started*, *waited*, and *wanted*
are associated by phonological and semantic connections linking
[-ɨd]. These parallel semantic and phonological connections, then,

amount to morphological relations. They identify morphemes embedded in distinct words. It is important to note that in this process of assigning morphological structure, meaning is more important than phonological shape. We know this because homophones are not confused as being the 'same' morpheme, and because even widely divergent forms with the same stem meaning can still be identified as morphologically related. For instance, *went* is regarded as the Past Tense of *go*, even though there is no phonological relation between them. Apparently the strict meaning correspondence is sufficient to ensure that the words are considered to be in a morphological relationship that occurs for all other verbs. The meaning overrides the divergence of form.

This greater importance of meaning over form in the lexical network may explain why morphologization takes place. In an exemplar model, variation in phonetic form is keyed to properties of the context – phonetic, semantic, lexical, and social. The greater strength of semantic connections over phonetic ones may lead to the reanalysis in terms of semantic categories, yielding morphological conditioning.

Other evidence for the preference of morphological (meaningful) categories over phonological ones for the conditioning of alternations comes from some alternations found in Spanish paradigms. A number of common Spanish verbs exhibit an alternation in the Present Tense, such as that shown in 1 and 2, where the presence of a velar stop alternates with its absence.

(1)   salir 'to leave'

Present Indicative		**Present Subjunctive**	
salgo	salimos	salga	salgamos
sales	salís	salgas	salgáis
sale	salen	salga	salgan

(2)   crecer 'to grow'

Present Indicative		**Present Subjunctive**	
crez[k]o	crecemos	crez[k]a	crez[k]amos
creces	crecéis	crez[k]as	crez[k]áis
crece	crecen	crez[k]a	crez[k]an

It is possible to describe the distribution of the velar stop in two ways. With reference to a combination of phonological and morphological features, one can say that the velar appears before back vowels but not before front vowels in certain Second and Third Conjugation paradigms. With reference to morphological categories, one can say that the velar appears in 1st Singular Present Indicative and in the Present Subjunctive, but is absent elsewhere.

In a nonce probe task, Bybee and Pardo (1981) tried to determine how speakers analyzed these alternations. Subjects were presented with nonce verbs embedded in appropriate sentences. The nonce forms were similar to the verbs in 1 and 2, and the subjects were presented with two stem variants in two conditions:

Condition 1: The 1st Person Singular and 3rd Person Singular Present Indicative were presented (e.g., the nonce forms *palgo*, *pale*; *lezco*, *lece*). The subjects were then given a sentence that required a Present Subjunctive form.

Condition 2: The infinitive and the 1st Person Singular Present Indicative were presented (e.g., *palir*, *palgo*; *lecer*, *lezco*). The subjects were then given a sentence that required a 3rd Person Singular Present Indicative.

The goal was to determine if subjects would give forms based on the very similar existing forms with alternations in the same categories. The results were mixed. With some verbs, many of the responses conformed to existing patterns (55–65% of the responses, see Section 5.7), but with others, regularization was a common response, with the subjects making the verb into a First Conjugation verb, with a front vowel in the Subjunctive and a back vowel in the Indicative. Thus, in some cases, a 3rd Person Singular Indicative form was given with the velar and a back vowel (e.g., *palga* for 3rd Person Singular Present Indicative).

Because the results mixed velar and nonvelar with front and back vowels as well as with Indicative and Subjunctive for those nonce verbs that did not adopt a productive pattern, it was possible to test if there was any trend towards using the velar with a back vowel, as opposed to using the velar with the Subjunctive among these verbs. The results showed that the phonological features were combined almost randomly, with subjects using the velar before a front vowel in 52% of the cases, and before a back vowel in 48%. On the other hand, the percentage of velars used in the Subjunctive was much greater than that of velars used in the Indicative (65% vs. 42%). These results suggest no phonological association for the velar, but some association of the velar with the Subjunctive.

Other evidence for an association of the velar stop with the Subjunctive also appeared in the experiment. Some nonce items had no velar stops in either allomorph that was presented and yet some subjects formed Subjunctives with velars. The verbs in question were purposely constructed with phonological alternations that do not occur in Spanish. They were 1st Person Singular Present Indicative *lastro*, 3rd Person Singular Present Indicative *lase* and 1st Person Singular Present Indicative *seto*, 3rd Person Singular Present Indicative *sade*. For the first verb, the Subjunctive responses with velars were *lazca* (occurring twice) and *laga* (occurring once). For the second verb, the responses were *sezca* (once) and *saga* (twice). No other responses for these verbs had any consonants added that were not in the allomorphs presented.

It is important to note that for the existing Spanish verbs with velars in the 1st Person Singular Present and Present Subjunctive, the phonological criterion of velar before back vowel and no velar before front vowel works perfectly, and in some sense is simpler than the morphological description, since it does not seem possible to group the morphological environments into a natural class (but see Bybee 1985:68–74). Nonetheless, speakers of Spanish seem to have eschewed the phonological generalization, opting instead for a morphological one, supporting our proposed principle of the preference of morphological over phonological conditioning for alternations that are restricted lexically or morphologically. Whether this principle holds in all cases remains to be seen. The principle can only be tested experimentally or by observing child language or language change. It cannot be argued for on the basis of conceptual simplicity or elegance.

5.2.2 Divergence of Phonological Patterns in Different Morphological Contexts

Because phonological alternations have their source in regular sound change that occurs in phonetic environments, in a language with some morphological complexity, alternations from the same sound change could arise in various morphological categories. For instance, the voicing of intervocalic fricatives in Middle English created alternations in both nouns and verbs, as shown in 3, using forms from Present-Day English.

(3)
Nouns		**Verbs**	
Singular	**Plural**	**Infinitive**	**Past Participle**
leaf	leaves	leave	left
wife	wives		
knife	knives		
house	hou[z]es	lo[z]e	lost

In Middle English the final vowel was pronounced in Plural nouns and in the infinitive of verbs, giving an intervocalic environment. In the Singular form of the nouns, the fricative was word-final, and in the Past Participle it occurred before a voiceless stop. Neither of these environments conditioned the voicing of fricatives. In addition to these patterns, alternations were created in derived forms, such as *give, gift; live, life; thrive, thrift*, and so on.

All of these alternations have their source in the same general sound change, but they are all now morphologized. We know that the alternation between Singular and Plural nouns is morphologized – that is, conditioned by the morphological feature 'Plural' – because the homophonous possessive marker does not condition the voicing: it is *my wife's car*, not *my wive's car*. Another prominent feature of morphologized alternations is that they are lexically restricted. Only a small class of common nouns undergoes this alternation. Excluded are nouns such as *chief, horse*, and *class*. The alternation in verbs is even more restricted lexically, and very few verbs now show the alternation.

Although these alternations all had their source in the same regular sound change, once they became morphologized, they became independent of one another. The reason for this is that the association with the morphological categories dominates the phonological similarities, and the morphological categories involved here are independent of one another. Further changes in these alternations are governed by the morphological categories and are thus independent for noun and verb inflection and for derivation.

In the verbs, more leveling has occurred than in the nouns. Analogical leveling designates the loss of the alternation in related forms. When an alternation is lost, the member that survives is almost always the alternate that occurred in the more frequent or less marked form: the Singular of nouns or the Present Tense or base form of verbs (see Section 5.2.4). What happens in leveling is the same process as in regularization: a new regular form is created, using the more frequent form as the basis. Thus the Middle English Past Participle *bilefte* from *bilēven* has now been replaced with the regular form *believed*. Similarly, *heaved* has replaced *heft*, and *bereaved* is replacing *bereft*. In these cases, the voiced fricative is the member of the alternation that survives.

Compare this situation to that in nouns. Leveling or regularization is occurring in some American dialects, where young people are heard to say *houses* with a voiceless fricative. *Roofs* is listed as standard in most dictionaries. In the case of nouns, the Singular form serves as the basis for the new formation, which means that the voiceless fricative survives. Thus, the direction of leveling in phonological terms is opposite in nouns and verbs. Another difference is that the leveling in verbs appears to have occurred much earlier than the leveling in nouns. The alternation in nouns has been maintained fairly robustly until recently. Just consider the number of nouns that have the alternation: further examples are *thief, calf, half, wolf, bath, wreath, path.* Thus, even though a phonological account of the alternation between voiced and voiceless fricatives might propose to unite their nominal and verbal instantiations, the evidence from change shows that they are now independent of one another.

The residue of this sound change in derived words, such as *give, gift; thrive, thrift; hefty, heavy; staff, stave* is not at all likely to undergo leveling, because these words are no longer closely related to one another. The 'alternation' here has a very different status than it does in Singular and Plural nouns. In fact, it is probably not appropriate to even designate it as such, except in an etymological sense. An important difference between generative phonology and Optimality Theory, on the one hand, and the morphology-based theory on the other, is that in the former theories, the attempt is made to account for all instances of a phonological alternation with the same rule or constraint, thereby achieving descriptive economy, by some measures at least. The evidence, however, suggests a morphologically based account: once a phonological process becomes morphologized, if it occurs in different morphological contexts, its original coherence is fractured, and the alternations it originally created become independent of one another.

Another example of a morphologized alternation that exhibits different patterns of change under different morphological conditions is the mid vowel/diphthong alternation in Spanish. This alternation arose when the short mid vowels of Latin (ĕ and ŏ) were lowered to [ɛ] and [ɔ] in stressed syllables and then diphthongized to [je] and [we], respectively. In unstressed syllables, these Latin vowels remained [e] and [o]. Thus, in cases where a stem vowel from one of these sources is stressed in the presence of some suffixes, but not others, an alternation has arisen. It is apparent in the Present Tense of verbs, as shown in 4, and with derivational suffixes, as shown in 5.[1]

---

[1] The examples in 5 are taken from Eddington (1996).

(4)   **entender 'to understand'**   **volver 'to (re)turn'**
      Present Indicative

entiéndo	entendémos	vuélvo	volvémos
entiéndes		vuélves	
entiénde	entiénden	vuélve	vuélven

(5)

fuérte	'strong'	fortísimo	'very strong'
pimiénta	'pepper'	pimentéro	'pepper shaker'
puérta	'door'	portéro	'doorman'
conciérto	'concert'	concertísta	'performer'
buéno	'good'	bondad	'goodness'

The alternations illustrated in the verbs in 4 occur in a large number of verbs of First, Second, and Third Conjugation. However, not all verbs with a mid vowel in the stem have this alternation. Those derived from the Latin long mid vowels ($\bar{e}$ and $\bar{o}$) do not alternate (e.g., *comer* 'to eat', *beber* 'to drink'). We can conclude that the alternation is lexically restricted and possibly also morphologically conditioned, although the presence of stress is a valid predictor of the diphthong. It is also the case that verbs that have a diphthong in their stems in the Present Indicative Singular forms have monophthongs when that syllable is unstressed (there are only a few exceptions). Within the verbal paradigm, then, one could suppose that there could be a fairly general schema or rule covering this alternation.

However, nonce probe experiments that attempt to elicit this alternation in nonce verbs tend to be unsuccessful. For instance, Kernan and Blount (1966) used a nonce verb in the 3rd Person Singular Present Indicative, *suécha*, as a prompt for an expected Preterit form *sochó*, following this extremely common pattern of diphthong/mid vowel alternation. However, all of their subjects used the form *suechó* for the Preterit, not extending the alternation to the 'new' verb. In the experiment reported on in Bybee and Pardo (1981), we presented subjects with both a diphthong and mid vowel form of the same verb (e.g., *sochar, suecha*), and we still got diphthong responses in unstressed position in 23% of the cases.

Why don't Spanish speakers use this common alternation in nonce verbs more readily? The answer is that the diphthong/mid vowel pattern, like all other lexically specific patterns, is not a rule that is independent of the particular forms which it describes. It is simply a generalization over existing forms and not generally applicable in the way that a phonological process would be. Thus, it does not extend easily to other forms. It appears to be a property of certain existing verbal paradigms or stems, rather than a general rule.

In derivational forms, such as those in 5, the productivity of the alternation is also breaking down, but in this case whether the diphthong or mid vowel occurs in unstressed syllables seems to depend upon the particular derivational suffix used. In addition to the words shown in 5, those in 6, which have diphthongs in unstressed syllables, also occur.

(6)	fuérte	'strong'	fuertecíto	'diminutive of strong'
	ruéda	'wheel, tire'	ruedéro	'tire maker'
	piél	'fur'	pieléro	'fur dealer'
	huélga	'strike'	huelguísta	'striker'

Eddington (1996) elicited words formed with 10 different derivational suffixes from more than 50 native speakers, using real words and nonce words as prompts. The words used for prompts all contained stressed diphthongs, and the suffixes added all shifted the stress away from the diphthong. As we would predict, some responses contained diphthongs, and some contained mid vowels. The extent to which responses with mid vowels or diphthongs were favored seemed to depend upon the particular affix. Some, such as *-ero* and *-(i)dad*, occurred with mid vowels in approximately 70% of the responses. Others, such as *-ista*, and *-zuelo*, occurred with mid vowels in about half of the responses. A third group, including the productive diminutive *-(c)ito* and *-azo*, favored the diphthong, and only occurred with mid vowels in about 25% of the responses. These results suggest that the probability of the occurrence of the mid vowel or diphthong is related to the suffix used to form the word.[2] These derivational instances of the diphthong/mid vowel alternation differ from those found in the verb paradigms, since for verbs, whether the alternation occurs depends upon the stem, while for derivation it depends upon the suffix.

These two examples, then, illustrate a situation typical of morphologized alternation patterns. Once the alternation is associated with the morphology and with particular lexical items, it is analyzed independently in different morphological domains. Its association with particular categories, its productivity, and its directionality are all independently determined in each context. Thus attempts in generative phonology to reunite patterns that have been separated by morpho-

---

[2] The likelihood that the derived form will contain a diphthong or mid vowel is probably related to the number of existing words with each variant (see Section 5.6).

logical conditioning are not motivated and, in fact, miss the interesting interplay of the morphology with the phonological alternation. Similarly, even with language-specific ordering, the universal constraints of Optimality Theory are not specific enough to describe the lexically grounded behavior of morphologized alternations.

5.2.3   The Break-Up of Phonological Natural Classes in Morphologized Patterns

The previous examples have illustrated how an alternation pattern can be strongly associated with particular lexical stems and/or particular morphological categories. Once morphological conditioning becomes dominant, it follows that phonological principles, such as patterning based on natural classes, will no longer be applied in the same way as for phonetically conditioned processes. A striking example of the loss of reference to a phonological natural class turned up in the experiment reported in Bybee and Pardo (1981).

As mentioned in Section 5.2.2, the diphthongization of Latin ĕ, ŏ was parallel for the front and back vowels (see the examples in 4). For Third Conjugation verbs, the alternation also involves a high vowel in certain forms, as shown in 7.

(7)		**mentir 'to tell a lie'**	**dormir 'to sleep'**
	1st Person Singular Present Indicative	miénto	duérmo
	1st Person Singular Preterit Indicative	mentí	dormí
	3rd Person Singular Preterit Indicative	mintió	durmió

Despite the clear phonological parallelism in these paradigms, the subjects' responses to nonce verbs revealed that verbs with the front and back vowel alternations are not included in the same class. Nonce verbs with phonological similarity to *mentir* showed rather robust productivity, while verbs similar to *dormir* did not. For instance, the nonce verb *rentir*, presented in the infinitive, was given the 3rd Person Singular Preterit form *rintió* (rather than *rentió*, which requires no change in the stem) by 55% of the subjects, but the parallel prompt with a back vowel, *sornir*, only elicited a changed stem, *surnió*, in 1 out of 22 subjects. *Sornió* (with no stem change) was given as the Preterit of this verb by 20 subjects.

[handwritten: ✱ l is enough — Joseph]

Another difference between the front and back vowel verbs of this type was observed for diphthongization in the Present Indicative. A nonce verb *pertir* was put into the 3rd Person Singular Present as *piérte* by 18 out of 22 subjects (82%), while the parallel back vowel verb *norir* (constructed to be similar to the existing verb *morir* 'to die') was given a diphthong in 3rd Person Singular Present by only 9 of the subjects (41%).

The difference between the front and back vowel alternations in this case is not a phonological one, but rather a difference in the number of verbs exhibiting each alternation. The verbs with the front vowel alternation (*ié, e, i*) constitute a class of about 30 verbs having certain similarities in the phonological shape of their stems, which will be described in Section 5.9. In contrast, there are only 2 verbs with the parallel back vowel alternation, *dormir* 'to sleep' and *morir* 'to die'. Even though they are rather frequent verbs, two verbs is not enough to form a class (or a 'gang') that is productive (a fuller discussion of productivity is found in Section 5.6). In addition, it appears that despite the parallelism between the front vowel alternation pattern and the back vowel alternation pattern, no generalization is formed over the two. Apparently for phonological reasons, parallel changes in front and back vowels occur, but in morphological generalizations, front and back vowels are too different phonologically to be included in the same class.

[handwritten margin notes: frequency not verbs; No]

Another example of a once coherent set of phonological changes that are now fractured into diverse morphological and lexical alternates can be found among the vowel alternations resulting from the Great Vowel Shift of Early Modern English. One derivational context in which this alternation occurs is with nominalizations formed with the suffix *-ity*, which conditions a shortening of the stressed vowel in many words. Another is with certain nominalizations formed with *-tion* following a consonant. Thus pairs arise such as those in 8.

(8)   **Front vowels**   **Back vowels**

divine	[ay]	divinity	[ɪ]	profound	[aw]	profundity [ʌ]
serene	[iy]	serenity	[ɛ]	presume	[ju]/[u]	presumption [ʌ]
grave	[ey]	gravity	[æ]	commode	[ow]	commodity [ɔ]/[a]

Of the words exhibiting an alternation, there is greater regularity and a higher type frequency in the front vowel alternations than in the back vowel alternations. Thus, it is not surprising that Wang and Derwing (1994), in a nonce probe experiment designed to elicit words ending in *-ity* from nonce adjectives, found a difference between front and back vowels. The most common nominal responses for front vowels were [ɪ], [ɛ], and [æ], but the only back vowel commonly given as a response was [ɔ]. These responses reflect the high type frequency of nominalizations in *-ity* with these four vowels, but do not reflect the application of a general rule covering both front and back vowels in a parallel fashion.

It is true that since the Great Vowel Shift, the back vowel [ʊ], which would have originally alternated with [aw], has changed to [ʌ], as in *profundity*, but in the experimental results, the vowel favored to alternate with [aw] was [ɔ], not [ʌ]. The [ɔ] responses reflect the type frequency of words in *-ity* with [ɔ] (or [a] if the experiment had been done in the United States rather than Canada), such as *oddity, verbosity, generosity*, and so on.

[G]

A third example of the split of a natural class in morphological generalizations concerns the voicing in English noun Plurals shown in 3. Hualde (2000) points out that for nouns ending in *-th* [θ], the voicing alternation is somewhat productive. A large proportion of nouns with this final consonant undergo voicing (e.g., *mouth, path, bath, oath*), many vary among speakers (e.g., *wreath, moth, truth*), and very few have only nonalternating [θ] (e.g., *Sabbath*). On the other hand, there seems to be no tendency to extend the alternations between [f] and [v] or [s] and [z]. If anything, there is a tendency to regularize *houses* that leads to it being pronounced with a medial [s].

These examples suggest that phonetic similarity in the morphological domain has a different definition than in the articulatory domain. Interestingly, it seems to be both more specific, in the sense that generalizations are not made, for instance, over front and back vowels, but also, as we will see in Sections 5.8 and 5.9, more holistic in that longer sequences within words are compared to establish morphological classes or gangs.

5.2.4 The Basic/Derived Relation in Phonology and Morphology

Both phonological processes and morphologically conditioned patterns have some directionality, as captured by the notion of the input and output of a rule in generative phonology, or the underlying versus surface forms. To the extent that some notions of basic and derived forms are empirically valid, the application of this notion to morphology is very different from its application to phonology.

In the model developed here, underlying forms are not acted on by rules to produce surface forms synchronically, except in the sense that the pressures of articulation act in real time to create small modifications of stored forms. However, a sound change can be said to modify a sound existing at one period of time to produce a different sound at a later period of time. This is the directionality that is embodied in a generative phonological rule. Synchronically, this directionality can be discovered by examining the contexts in which variants occur. Thus, if fricatives are distributed such that they are voiced intervocalically, but voiceless elsewhere, we are justified in suggesting that the voiceless variant existed earlier and underwent voicing in a voiced context.

Once alternations become associated with the morphology, it is no longer the phonological criteria that determine directionality, but rather morphological criteria. But in what sense is there directionality in morphological alternations? A very robust source of evidence for a basic/derived relation in morphology comes from analogical leveling. A strong tendency in analogical leveling is for the variant that occurred in the unmarked or most frequent form to occur also in the less frequent or more marked forms (Bybee 1985, Mańczak 1980). For instance, in the forms in 9, an original alternation distinguishes a base form (on the left) from a more marked form (either the Plural of a noun, or the Past/Past Participle of a verb, on the right). The analogical formation uses the base form variant to produce a new marked form, not the reverse, which would mean using the marked form to produce a new basic one.

(9) | **Original forms** | | **Analogical formation** | **Nonoccurring forms** | |
| --- | --- | --- | --- | --- |
| roof | rooves | roofs | *roove | (Singular) |
| heave | heft | heaved | *hef | (Present) |
| weep | wept | weeped | *wep | (Present) |

The pattern of change exemplified here shows that the unmarked form is in some sense basic in its relation with the marked form. In Section 5.4, we will discuss more thoroughly the mechanism by which such changes take place and the formal modeling of the relationships among the forms. For the moment, I simply want to point out that morphological criteria differ from phonological criteria in this regard.

A contextual sound change occurring in a certain phonetic environment sets up an alternation, which is then reinterpreted as part of the morphology. With a change in conditioning environment comes a change in what is considered most basic. The result has been described as Rule Inversion by Vennemann (1972b). For instance, the [v] in *heave* was historically derived from an [f] by the intervocalic voicing process described earlier, but since the [v] occurs in the basic (Infinitive and Present) form of the verb, it becomes basic in a morphological sense and thus replaces the original [f] when a new form arises. In contrast, the same alternation in the noun paradigm does not change its directionality since the phonologically original sound happens, quite by accident, to occur in the Singular. Thus, while the original alternation occurred under phonetic conditions, the reanalysis is based on morphological relations and categories.

5.3 Lexical Storage of Complex Forms, Both Regular and Irregular

We have now discussed some of the ways that morphological information is associated with phonological alternations. We turn now to properties of a model that can accommodate these and other facts of morphology and their interaction with phonology. In this section, we discuss the storage of morphologically complex forms in memory. In subsequent sections, we turn to ways of modeling the relations among these forms and the effects of high and low frequency on both the storage and relations among forms.

In Chapter 2, I suggested that a usage-based model of storage of linguistic material would settle on words as the basic unit of storage, because words are the smallest units that are complete both phonologically and semantically, and that can be appropriately used in isolation. Note, however, that this only specifies the smallest unit of storage. In Chapter 6, we discuss the evidence for the storage of multiword sequences, such as phrases and constructions. In the present section, we will investigate the consequences of having multimorphemic words in the lexicon.

Also in Chapter 2, I pointed out that the model of storage being used here does not represent the lexicon like a dictionary – a long list of words and their properties – but rather as a complex network with multiple associations among words. Thus, any multimorphemic word or sequence is highly embedded in connections with other words containing at least one of the same morphemes. So verb forms such as *strike*, *struck*, and *striking* are highly connected with all other base forms, Past forms, and Participles, as are verbs such as *start*, *started*, and *starting*. What determines the forms that are actually in memory is usage: verb forms that are used frequently are stored in memory. Those that have not been used and those that are of very low frequency do not actually exist in memory, but if they are regular, they can easily be derived by using the associations in the network. That is, the fact that a word is classified as a verb automatically associates it with other verbs, which in turn have multiple closely associated forms.

For many years now, it has been clear from experimental results that irregular forms, such as English irregular Past Tense forms, are stored in memory in associative networks. Bybee and Moder (1983), replicated in Prasada and Pinker (1993), show that subjects' responses to the task of giving Past forms for nonce verbs is highly influenced by the form of existing Past Tense verbs (see Section 5.9 for further discussion). However, there is still disagreement over the representation of regular forms. In a proposal for a dual-processing model, Pinker, Marcus, and colleagues (Clahsen 1999, Clahsen and Rothweiler 1992, Marcus et al. 1992, Pinker 1991, Prasada and Pinker 1993) argue that there is a discrete distinction between regular and irregular forms: irregulars are stored in memory, but regulars are created by a symbolic rule. In contrast, the model developed in Bybee (1985, 1988a, 1995), along with the connectionist models (Rumelhart and McClelland 1986) and the analogical model (Skousen 1989, 1992), would claim that both regulars and irregulars are handled by the same storage and processing mechanisms. My proposal is that what determines whether a morphologically complex form is stored in memory is its frequency of use, not its classification as regular or irregular.

This debate is an excellent example of the difference between a structuralist theory and a usage-based or functionalist theory. The dual-processing model claims that differences in storage and access correspond to differences in the structure of forms: those that are structurally irregular are stored in memory, while those that are structurally regular are derived by rule. The usage-based model claims that the difference comes down to a difference derived from usage: the high-frequency forms have storage in memory and low-frequency forms do not, independent of their structural properties. In fact, the structural properties are also derived from usage, since the only way irregularity can be preserved is through sufficient frequency for memory storage. That is why low-frequency irregulars either regularize, or fall out of usage and disappear from the language.

The argument for using a symbolic rule to derive regular forms is that the regular pattern is extremely productive (in English at least) and does not seem to be influenced by existing local phonological patterning. The counterargument from the usage-based side is that productivity is strictly related to type frequency, and that the robust productivity and insensitivity to the lexicon of the English regular Past

* The opposite?

Tense formation is due to its overwhelmingly high type frequency. In languages in which the regular morphological patterns have lower type frequency, we find reduced productivity, but sensitivity to the lexicon (see Köpcke 1988 for German Plurals and Lobben 1991 for Hausa Plurals).

There is also positive evidence that high-frequency regular forms are stored in the lexicon just as irregulars are: namely, evidence for differential behavior of regulars based on frequency. I will cite several studies that reveal such differences. For other arguments, see Bybee (1995).

Stemberger and MacWhinney (1986, 1988) sought to elicit speech errors from subjects by asking them to form the Past Tense of regular English verbs as quickly as possible. The verbs under study all ended in /t/ or /d/, and 10 were of low frequency, and 10 of high frequency. Verbs ending in /t/ or /d/ were chosen because it had been found in earlier studies that speakers often make errors of no change on such verbs, producing, say, *wait* as a Past Tense (Bybee and Slobin 1982). Stemberger and MacWhinney found a significant association between token-frequency and the number of errors made by subjects in that more than twice as many errors were made on low-frequency verbs as on high-frequency ones. This finding suggests that even regular, morphologically complex forms are stored in memory and that frequency can affect the strength of their representations (see Section 5.6).

Alegre and Gordon (1999a) describe a lexical decision task that revealed word frequency effects for regular English Past Tense forms. Specifically, higher-frequency words were responded to more quickly than low-frequency words. Interestingly, Alegre and Gordon found significant frequency effects on reaction time for regularly inflected words with frequencies above 6 per million in Francis and Kučera (1982), but no frequency effects for words with frequencies below 6 per million. This finding supports the hypothesis that regular forms of higher frequencies are stored in the lexicon and can be accessed as whole words, and that they have differential representation based on frequency.

Hare et al. (2001) created a dictation task in which English-speaking subjects were asked to write a sentence using an orally presented word that represented two homophones, one a Past Tense form, some of which were regular and some irregular, and one a monomorphemic word (for example, *aloud* and *allowed*, or *spoke* as the Past of *speak* or as a noun). The results showed that the subjects tended significantly to select the homophone that was the most frequent, even when that form was a regular Past Tense form.

Evidence for frequency-sensitive memory

Not Lexicon?

Table 5.1. *The Effects of Word Frequency on* t/d *Deletion in Regular Past Tense Verbs (Non-Prevocalic Only)*

	Deletion	Non-Deletion	% Deletion
High frequency	44	67	39.6
Low frequency	11	47	18.9

χ^2: 5.00313, $df = 1$, $p < .05$

Sereno and Jongman (1997) used regularly inflected English nouns in a lexical decision task and found that it was the surface frequency of the form, whether the Singular or the Plural, that corresponded to how fast the subjects could identify it as a word of English. When the Singular was presented, nouns with high-frequency Singulars were responded to faster than those with low-frequency Singulars. When the Plural was presented, responses to nouns with low-frequency Plurals were slower even if the Singular was in the high-frequency group. Thus, the frequency of the particular inflected form was what influenced the speed of recognition.

Evidence from an entirely different research paradigm also supports the conclusion that regularly inflected words are listed in the lexicon. In a study of the lexical diffusion of the deletion of final /t/ and /d/ in English, I reported in Bybee (2000b) that there is a significant effect of frequency on *t/d* deletion for all words coded (2,000 words from running spoken text). In addition, considering just regular verbs with an *-ed* ending (either the Past Tense or Past Participle), and dividing these words into those with frequencies of greater than 35 per million in Francis and Kučera (1982) – the high-frequency group – and those with frequencies of less than 35 per million – the low-frequency group, the difference in the percentage of deletion was significant, as shown in Table 5.1. The tokens counted in Table 5.1 all occurred in non-prevocalic position (i.e., they occurred either before a consonant or a pause), as this is the phonetic context most favorable to deletion. Given that a sound change such as *t/d* deletion is gradual both phonetically and lexically and takes place incrementally as language is used (as argued in Chapter 3), the sound change will progress more quickly in high-frequency words than in low-frequency words. But these differential effects of sound change require that sound change is registered in the representation of words in storage.

Thus, if regularly inflected forms show differential effects of sound
change, they must be stored in memory. If the Past Tense morpheme
were added by a rule, there would be no way to derive a difference in
the progress of the sound change based on the frequency of the
Past Tense word form.

The evidence suggests that there are two ways of processing regular,
morphologically complex forms. One is through direct, whole word
access, and it occurs with higher-frequency forms. The other is through
accessing a base and adding appropriate affixes. Given a highly networked representation for morphological classes such as nouns and
verbs, these two avenues of access are not really very different, since
even low-frequency regulars are highly associated with other verbs that
have the appropriate forms stored in memory. The two methods are
more different, however, the more frequent the forms in question are,
because of the effect of frequency on representation, a matter to which
we will turn now.

5.4 Lexical Strength

In Bybee (1985) I proposed the notion of lexical strength to account
for certain diachronic tendencies of inflected words: the tendency for
more frequent forms of paradigms to resist regularizing change and,
when change is taking place, to serve as the basis of change. In addition, lexical strength can account for the fact that high-frequency paradigms maintain their irregularities, while lower-frequency paradigms
tend to regularize. These facts about change seem to correspond well
to the fact that high-frequency items are accessed more quickly than
low-frequency items in experimental situations.

A usage-based mechanism underlies the phenomena grouped
together here, since each time an item is accessed, its memory representation is strengthened. We have already suggested that in an exemplar model, each token of use adds an image to the representation.
Given that commonly used variants are weighted and can affect
judgments about the ranking of exemplars as characteristic or not
(Nosofsky 1988), it seems reasonable to suppose that identical or
very similar exemplars are mapped onto the same representation,
increasing its strength. Thus in an inflectional language such as
Spanish, a very commonly used verb form such as *pienso* 'I think' will
have a much stronger representation than the much less frequent
pensabas 'you were thinking'.

Not only does the increased lexical strength make the form easier to access, but this ease of access decreases the likelihood that the form will undergo change. Analogical or morphophonemic change that regularizes irregulars occurs when a more productive pattern is applied instead of accessing the irregular form. For instance, when the regular forms *weeped* or *creeped* are formed, it is because their irregular Past forms are so infrequent that they are difficult to access, and the regular pattern is applied instead. To English language users, *weeped* and *creeped* don't sound so bad because *wept* and *crept* do not have very strong representations. Compare an English speaker's reaction to *keeped* or *sleeped*. These sound much worse because the forms *kept* and *slept* are so much more frequent. Thus, the general pattern of regularization is for low-frequency irregulars to regularize first and for high-frequency irregulars to resist regularization. This regularization process is the same phenomenon I referred to as analogical leveling in Section 5.2.4. The term 'analogical leveling' describes the fact that a regularized form no longer has an alternation; the alternation has been 'leveled.' But the term, and the process it implies, is not an accurate statement of the mechanism underlying such a change. It is not the case that *wept* changes into *weeped* by changing its vowel; rather, a new form *weeped* is created (because *wept* is difficult to access), and the two forms exist side by side for a time.

The other way that lexical strength plays a role in regularization is in determining which form of a paradigm will be the one upon which the new form is based. I already mentioned in Section 5.2.4 that the unmarked form of the paradigm tends to serve as the new base for regularized forms. Thus, the base form *weep* is used to create a new Past, rather than the Past form *wept* being used to create a Present form *wep*. Similarly, the Singular of nouns serves as the basis of new Plurals, as when *cows* replaced *kine* as the Plural of *cow*.

There are currently two explanations for which forms survive in regularization. One relies on markedness theory as developed by Jakobson (1939, 1957, 1966). In this theory, all categories have the same internal structure: they consist of a binary choice between the presence versus the absence of a feature. The member of the category that lacks the feature is the unmarked member. In Jakobson's theory, Singular is the unmarked member of the category of number, Present is the unmarked member of the tense category, and so on. One can observe, then, that the base from which a new form is derived by regularization is the form of the unmarked member of the category. The unmarked member is also the one that can be expressed with a zero – that is, the absence of a marker that is nonetheless meaningful. (For example, in *I saw the dog*, the meaning is clearly one of Singular for *the dog* despite the absence of a Singular suffix.)

Jakobson's theory of markedness is a good example of a structuralist theory since it focuses on the structure of categories and proposes that all categories have the same structure, no matter what their content. Thus, phonological categories, too, are binary in his theory, and features are either present or absent in any phonological segment. For categories that seem to have three members (e.g., the category of person, which typically consists of first, second, and third person), the division is based on two binary oppositions: [+/– participant] and [+/– addressee] (Jakobson 1957).

Greenberg's (1966) study of crosslinguistic markedness relations reveals a strong correlation of markedness with token frequency: the unmarked members of categories are the more frequent members. This relation holds for the phonological, morphological, and lexical categories studied by Greenberg. Frequency could be regarded as a derivative correlate of the structural relation of markedness, except that frequency has been shown to override the structural relations. This means that frequency is probably a more basic factor, and that the structural relations posited by Jakobson are describing phenomena conditioned by frequency.

Cases in which local frequency relations override general markedness are discussed in Tiersma (1982). He cites examples of regularization (analogical leveling) in Frisian based on Plurals instead of Singulars in the case of nouns designating objects that frequently appear in groups of two or more, such as arms, geese, horns (of an animal), stockings, teeth, shavings, thorns, and tears. For instance, the alternation in *earm, jermen* 'arm, arms' is regularized in favor of the Plural as *jerm, jermen*, in contrast to a case like *poel, pwollen* 'pool, pools', which regularizes in favor of the Singular as *poel, poelen*. Tiersma points out that the irregular Plurals in English also designate entities that commonly occur in groups of two or more: *men, women, children, teeth, feet, oxen, geese, lice,* and *mice*. The phenomenon of local markedness, then, shows that frequency is a main determinant of markedness. See also Bybee 1985, Chapter 3 for more discussion of the properties of unmarked members of categories and how they arise.

Figure 5.1. The different relations in three sets of Singular-Plural forms.

With respect to morphological organization, lexical strength determines the nature of the relations among words sharing the same stem – that is, words of the same paradigm. The words of a paradigm have stronger representations if they are more frequent. It also follows that they are easier to access and thus may be part of the access route for the less frequent forms.

Different paradigms may have different structures, depending upon factors of usage and experience. Some verbs may be used more in the 1st Person, others in the 3rd; some nouns may be used more in the Singular, others in the Plural. For instance, three Singular-Plural pairs in English with different frequency relations might be represented as in Figure 5.1, where broken lines indicate shared features rather than identity of segments, and font size indicates relative lexical strength. For each of these paradigms, the likelihood and directionality of analogical change is different. The *house* paradigm is likely to restructure with a regular Plural, the *child* paradigm is likely to remain irregular just as it is, and the *louse* paradigm is losing, or has lost, its Singular form (since many people do not realize that *louse* is the Singular for *lice*). Of course, because of the way nouns are used in discourse, the Singular for most nouns is the most frequent and consequently has the greatest lexical strength. So for most nouns the relation as shown for *house* is applicable.

Note that the mechanisms operating to produce regular paradigms are inherent to the model described here. Lexical strength models the disparity between members of paradigms with high and low token frequency. Strong items are easier to access than weaker ones. Regularization occurs when the high-frequency form and the strongest morphological schema are easier to access than the lower-frequency irregular form. In models in which lexical entries are abstract base forms (as in generative phonology) or uniformly represented surface forms (as in some versions of Optimality Theory), an ad hoc mechanism for paradigm uniformity is required in the form of an independent constraint (Kiparsky 1971, Steriade 2000).

5.5   Paradigmatic Relations Expressed as Lexical Connections

Some forms of a paradigm are more closely related to one another than to other forms, depending upon the following factors: semantic similarity, phonological similarity, and the token frequency of the forms. In Section 5.2, I argued for the primacy of semantic relations over phonological ones by showing that there is a strong tendency for reanalysis to move from phonological conditioning factors to morphological conditioning. The same primacy of meaning over form is observed in the hierarchy of lexical connections: two forms will be considered more closely related if they share features of meaning than if they share features of form.

The degree of semantic relatedness is determined both by the number and the nature of shared features. As I argued in Bybee (1985), inflected forms of the same paradigm, which share the same stem and thus lexical meaning, are very closely related to one another, since inflectional affixes tend to make very small meaning contributions. However, even within inflectional categories, there are differences in the degree of relatedness via lexical connections. For instance, in verbal paradigms, forms inflected for different aspects are less closely related to one another than forms in the same aspect, but with different person/number inflection. The reason for this is that aspect has a greater effect on the meaning of the verb than does person/number agreement (Bybee 1985). Interestingly, this greater meaning difference is often reflected in a greater difference in form: stem changes in inflectional paradigms tend to parallel aspectual lines and rarely follow person/number lines across aspects (Bybee 1985).

Given these differences in degrees of semantic relatedness within paradigms, we can visualize paradigms as clusters of related forms, much as traditional paradigms are presented on paper in groups of person/number forms for each aspect, tense, and mood. Incorporating into this picture the fact that certain forms have greater lexical strength than others, we can represent a fragment of a typical Spanish paradigm as in Figure 5.2. Distance between forms corresponds to degree of relatedness, and the size of the form corresponds to its lexical strength. In this example, 3rd Person Singular forms are represented as the strongest, with other forms clustered around them, but 1st Person Singular forms are stronger than the 2nd Person or the Plural (see Bybee and Brewer 1980).

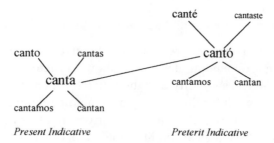

Figure 5.2. Relations among some forms of the Spanish verb *cantar* 'to sing'.

Different degrees of relatedness obtain among derivationally related forms. In fact, derivationally related forms tend to move away from one another semantically to a greater extent than inflectionally related forms do. Often the semantic distance is reflected in phonological differences among forms, as in *moon, month*; *heave, heavy*; *ease, disease*, but not always. Conversely, phonologically similar, derivationally related forms can be very different in meaning and use, as in *awe, awful*; *sweat, sweater*; *slip, slipper*. Derived words and their bases move away from each other semantically when they are used in different contexts. If they tend to be used in the same context, the relation remains clear, as in *erase, eraser*; *teach, teacher*; and *serene, serenity*. Inflected forms are less likely to move away from one another because they are usually applicable in the same contexts. For instance, a single event characterized at one point as *is singing* can be described later as *was singing, sang,* or *has sung*.

As a derived word comes to be used in contexts in which it is independent of its base, it might also grow more frequent. Its tokens of use will be associated with the new context, and it will at the same time gain in lexical strength, making it easier to access directly. Thus, increased lexical strength can lead to a lessening of lexical connections. This relation is discussed further in Section 5.7.

5.6   Lexical Classes: Productivity Due to Type Frequency

Productivity – the ability of a linguistic pattern to apply to new items – is one of the central properties of human language, since it is the property that allows a language to adapt to new circumstances. Productivity is a property of the human mind, as it is evident in both young children and adults. Productivity is gradient within languages: when there is more than one pattern for inflectional or derivational morphology or for syntactic constructions, it is often the case that one of those patterns is more productive than the others.

An important goal for linguistic theory, then, is to determine what factors make some patterns more productive than others. I will argue here that a factor of considerable importance is type frequency. The number of existing items that a pattern applies to bears a direct relation to the probability that it will affect new items (Bybee 1985, 1995, MacWhinney 1978).

First, it is important to note that token and type frequency do not have the same effect, and that type frequency is not just a derivative of token frequency. One clear example of the difference between token and type frequency, which I have also cited in Bybee (1985) and Bybee (1995), is from a study of utterances of French nursery school children by Guillaume (1927/1973). In French, verbs are distributed across different conjugation classes, with the largest number of verbs belonging to what is termed the First Conjugation (e.g., *chanter* 'to sing'). The other conjugation classes are not necessarily irregular, but they contain fewer verbs, most of which, however, are of relatively high token frequency. In French, for adults as well as children, First Conjugation is the most productive pattern for verbs. All of the children Guillaume studied overregularized verbs from other conjugation classes by making them First Conjugation. New verbs entering French are usually conjugated according to the pattern of the First Conjugation.

Table 5.2 shows a count of the verbs used by French nursery school children in spontaneous speech with one another.[3] It can be observed here that the token frequency of Third Conjugation is the highest, but that this large number of tokens represents only 29 types. On the other hand, while the token frequency of First Conjugation is lower than that of Third, these tokens are distributed over 124 types. Thus, if frequency affects productivity, it is type frequency that is the determinant, not token frequency. Other studies also conclude that type frequency is an important determinant of productivity (Baayen and Lieber 1991, Lobben 1991, Moder 1992, Wang and Derwing 1994). Wang and Derwing presented English-speaking subjects with nonce verbs and

---

[3] It is perhaps misleading for Guillaume to have grouped all Third Conjugation verbs together, as this group includes verbs of different conjugation patterns. However, the point remains that each of these verbs has a high token frequency and yet exerts no influence on less frequent forms.

Table 5.2. *Count of Verbs Used by French Nursery School Children During Play (Guillaume 1927/1973)*

	Number of Uses		Number of Verbs	
Conjugation Class	N	%	N	%
First (*chanter*)	1,060	36.2	124	76.0
Second (*finir*)	173	6.0	10	6.1
Third (*vendre*)	1,706	57.8	29	17.9

asked them to form the Past by changing the vowel of the verb. The association between the subjects' response vowels and the type frequency of those vowels in existing English Past tenses was significant, but the association with token frequency was not. For instance, the three most frequently given vowels in the experiment were /æ/, /ow/, and /ɔ/, which are among the four vowels with the highest type frequency in Past tense. The vowels with the highest token frequency in Past Tense verbs, on the other hand, are /ɛ/, /ɔ/ and /ey/.

Token frequency is not totally irrelevant to productivity, however. Very high token frequency has the effect of detracting from the productivity of morphological patterns. This effect will be discussed in Section 5.7.

What is the explanation for the effect that type frequency has on productivity? Several factors may play a role. From the point of view of acquisition, higher type frequency contributes to greater analyzability. Children first learn morphologically complex forms such as *went*, *broke*, *played*, and *spilled*, as single unanalyzed units. The repetition of the affix across multiple forms leads to the discovery that there is indeed an affix in those forms. This suggestion is supported by the findings of Marchman and Bates (1994) that the onset of overregularization errors in child language is related to increases in the size of vocabulary. The discovery of recurrent parts is more difficult, or does not occur at all, for affixes that attach to only a few forms, as in *oxen* and *children*. Second, the distribution of the affix across forms of medium and low frequency also aids in its identification, since such forms are more prone to analysis than forms that are used more often. Third, once identified and stored, the affix and associated schema gain in strength from use.

Since there can be degrees of productivity and a continuum of type frequencies for various patterns, a reasonable hypothesis is that the degree of productivity is determined (at least in part) by the number of items participating in a common pattern. Large classes will be highly productive, smaller ones less so. The question that then arises, of course, is how many items must exhibit the same behavior for a class to be established that shows some productivity. Is there a lower limit to classhood? This question is important because a purely analogical model, such as that proposed by Skousen (1989, 1992), hypothesizes that new formations are based on the single most similar item in the lexicon of existing words. This means that a class of one could be productive, given a new item that is more similar to it than to any other item in the lexicon.[4]

On the other hand, several researchers have noticed 'gang effects', which are productive generalizations based on resemblances to families of stored forms (Alegre and Gordon 1999b, Stemberger and MacWhinney 1988). In other words, gangs are classes of phonologically similar items that exhibit some productivity. A good example is the class exemplified by *string*, *strung*, which has been adding new members, such as *dig*, *dug*, and can be applied to nonce items, such as *spling* (giving *splang*) (Bybee and Moder 1983). In Section 5.9, I examine the notion of phonological similarity as applied to gangs, but for the moment it is interesting to consider how many items it takes to make a gang, or a class that shows productivity.

As our example, let us consider the Spanish verb alternation that was discussed in Section 5.2.1, the alternation of a velar stop with its absence in certain verbs of Second and Third Conjugation. The paradigms of interest are repeated here.

(10) salir 'to leave'

Present Indicative		**Present Subjunctive**	
salgo	salimos	salga	salgamos
sales	salís	salgas	salgais
sale	salen	salga	salgan

(11) crecer 'to grow'

Present Indicative		**Present Subjunctive**	
crez[k]o	crecemos	crez[k]a	crez[k]amos
creces	crecéis	crez[k]as	crez[k]áis
crece	crecen	crez[k]a	crez[k]an

---

[4] See Frisch et al. (2001) for evidence that a single word can in fact influence a highly similar nonce word.

Verbs with this alternation can be described as dividing into five subtypes, but experimental tests suggest that not all of these subtypes constitute a gang. These subtypes are:

(12) **Criterion**   **Examples**

Verb stem ends in *c*	crecer, crezco	'to grow'
Verb stem ends in a vowel	caer, caigo	'to fall'
Verb stem ends in *n*	poner, pongo	'to put'
Verb stem ends in *l*	salir, salgo	'to leave'
Verb stem in which *c* alternates with *g*	decir, digo	'to say'

These five subgroups have varying type frequencies.

1. Verbs ending in *c* are the largest group. An estimate of the number of items is made difficult by the fact that the class includes verbs formed with a common verbalizing suffix *-ecer*, all of which undergo the alternation. There are probably more than 300 verbs in this subclass.

2. Only six verbs have a stem ending in a vowel: *caer* 'to fall', *corroer* 'to corrode', *oir* 'to hear', *raer* 'to scrape', *roer* 'to gnaw', and *traer* 'to bring'. The unusual factor in this class is the absence of any other pattern for verbs with stems ending in *a* or *o*.

3. Three verb stems ending in *n* take the velar consonant, *tener* 'to have', *poner* 'to put', and *venir* 'to come'. These are three of the most frequent verbs in the language, and they appear with prefixes in about 50 derived words (e.g., *obtener* 'to obtain', *proponer* 'to propose', and *provenir* 'to originate').

4. Only two verb stems and one or two derivatives of each end in *l* and take the velar: *salir* 'to leave' and *valer* 'to be worth'. Both are very frequent verbs.

5. The fifth subtype also has two highly frequent verbs: *decir* 'to say, tell' and *hacer* 'to make, do'.

In the experiment, we presented subjects with two forms of the nonce verb, thereby illustrating the alternation (e.g., *lezco, lecer; faigo, faer; pale, palgo; rone, rongo*). Since subjects had a choice between two alternates, they had a 50–50 chance of selecting the one appropriate to the class. Productivity of the class would be indicated by responses appropriate to the class in more than 50% of the cases. Only the first two subclasses met this criterion. Appropriate in-class responses for the first two subclasses for both Indicative and Subjunctive forms were

64% and 56%, respectively. Responses for Subjunctive forms alone –
the forms with the velar – were 74% and 70%, respectively.

The productivity of the *crecer* class is predicted by its high type frequency. The *caer* class has only six members, but it is the only class that
provides a way to deal with verb stems ending *a* or *o*. The low type frequency and the phonological difficulty of adding a vowel suffix to a
stem ending in a vowel resulted in many more varied responses to the
request for an Indicative form for *faer* (where the in-class answer was
fae) than for any other item. However, the subjects' agreement rate on
a Subjunctive form of 74% indicates that a class of only six members
can constitute a gang. (For exact responses and further discussion, see
Bybee and Pardo 1981.)

On the other hand, nonce verbs ending in *n* had the lowest percentage of appropriate in-class responses (19%), indicating no productivity. Despite the fact that these three high-frequency verbs also
occur in many derivatives, it appears that the alternation is associated
directly with each verb and its derivatives, and that no generalization
is made over the three verbs. This finding follows from the effect that
high token frequency has on the ability of items to form gangs, which
is discussed in Section 5.7.

The two verbs ending in *l* also do not constitute a gang, eliciting in-
class responses only 28% of the time. Thus, we conclude that two and
three similar items cannot constitute a gang, especially if these items
are of high frequency.

Finally, we constructed nonce items to resemble *decir* and *hacer*. The
prompt items were *nice*, *nigo* and *proce*, *progo* (3rd Person Singular
and 1st Person Singular Present Indicative, respectively). For both
verbs, fewer than a third of the responses were modeled after *decir* or
hacer. These items all elicited the same number of in-class responses
even though the items *nice*, *nigo*, were designed to differ from *decir*
(*dice*, *digo*) by only one feature. Not only did this pattern show no particular productivity, but the nonce items constructed to be closer to one
of the real verbs did not elicit more in-class responses.

Several conclusions from the data present themselves. First, even
though we can describe the alternation of a velar with its absence with
a single rule, the items that exhibit the alternation do not all exhibit
equal productivity. One conclusion, then, is that Spanish speakers do
not categorize all of these verbs as belonging to the same class. Second,
the type frequency of each subclass is important to its productivity. The
class with the largest number of members is the most productive, but

a class with only six members also shows some productivity when the phonological shape of the nonce stem (having a stem ending in the vowels *o* and *a*) makes other patterns inapplicable to it. On the other end, potential classes with only two or three members do not constitute gangs. The minimum number of items needed to make a gang appears, then, to be greater than three.

The experimental data suggest that one or even two verbs are not enough to serve as a model for analogical change. However, a few examples are known of analogical changes that appear to be based on a pattern that occurs in a single paradigm. For example, in the First Person Singular, the Italian Passato Remoto of *stare* 'to be located' was *stetti* and for *dare* 'to give', it was *diedi*. The latter form changed to *detti*, presumably by analogy to the forms of a single verb, *stare*. Given the findings of Frisch et al. (2001), cited in Chapter 4.7.2, that high similarity to an existing word can render the phonotactics of a nonce word acceptable, it is perhaps possible that high phonological similarity to a unique form can condition an analogical reformation.

5.7   The Interaction of Lexical Strength and Lexical Connection

I have already mentioned several times that high lexical strength or frequency of a form weakens associations with other forms. The evidence that led to the proposal of this relation in Bybee (1985) comes from the diachronic change that creates suppletive paradigms. Although the term has been used more generally, in the original, strictest sense, a suppletive paradigm is one whose forms are based on roots that are not etymologically related. Examples among English verbs include *to be*, in which the forms *am*, *is*, and *are* are from one root, the forms *was* and *were* are from another, and the forms *be* and *been* from yet another. Another example is the verb *go* with its Past form *went*. Suppletion in inflectional paradigms only occurs in the most frequent paradigms. This fact suggests that it is the high frequency that gives a form the autonomy it needs to become independent of its etymological paradigm and join another. For instance, *went* was formerly the Past Tense of *wend* and had as part of its meaning 'to go turning'. Apparently, *went* increased in frequency, surpassing *wend*, and at the same time lost its meaning of 'turning' and came to mean only 'go + Past' (note the similarity to the 'bleaching' of meaning that occurs in grammaticization). From here, it could be interpreted as the Past of *go*, replacing the already suppletive Past of *go*.

This development and the much more common comparable development in derivationally related words reveals that morphologically complex words of high frequency achieve a certain autonomy from related forms. It suggests that words of high frequency are much less likely to form gangs than are words of lesser frequency. This hypothesis was investigated by Moder (1992) in several ways. First, Moder compared the type and token frequency of various classes of English Past Tense verbs. She found that if members of a class have high token frequency, this detracts from class productivity. For instance, she found that the *strung* class of verbs, which shows some productivity, has 13 members with a total token frequency according to Francis and Kučcera (1982) of 199. Another class, exemplified by *swept*, has 14 members with a total token frequency of 656. The latter class is much less productive than the *strung* class.

It might also be the case that high-frequency items that appear to belong to gangs do not in fact do so. Thus *begin*, which is the most frequent member of the class exemplified by *ring*, *rang*, *rung* may not actually be a member of that gang, or any other, because of its high frequency. In support of this idea, we can observe that no new members of this or the related *strung* class have two syllables or end in an *n*. To test this hypothesis, Moder (1992) conducted an experiment in which she primed subjects with high- and medium-frequency members of English irregular classes before presenting them with lists of nonce verbs resembling members of these classes. When primed with medium-frequency irregulars, subjects produced more nonce irregular Past Tense forms than when primed with high-frequency irregulars. Thus, while it might seem reasonable that high-frequency irregulars would be more available to serve as a model for nonce formations, the fact that they tend to be stored as autonomous and unanalyzed units actually makes them less available than more highly networked items.

Further evidence that lexical strength leads to greater autonomy can be seen in cases of functional or semantic change. Frequently used phrases such as *supposed to* or *I don't know* have become autonomous despite their regular relationship to other lexical items. *Be supposed to* was originally a passive construction derived regularly from *suppose*, a verb expressing a subject's mental state with respect to some proposition. The active form of this verb retains this original function, but the passive form has come to express obligation on the part of the passive subject with no agent expressed. In this usage, also, phonological reduction has occurred, giving [spostə]. *I don't know* is a regular phrase that has come into frequent use as a discourse marker; in which use it reduces to [aiɾ ɔ̃ɾə] (Bybee and Scheibman 1999). Both the phonological reduction and the change in function indicate that these phrases are autonomous from items containing related morphemes. An important determinant of this increased autonomy is frequency of use. These issues are discussed further in Chapter 6.

5.8   Product-Oriented Schemas

Generative rules express source-oriented generalizations. That is, they act on a specific input to change it in well-defined ways into an output of a certain form. Many, if not all, schemas are product-oriented rather than source-oriented. A product-oriented schema generalizes over forms of a specific category, but does not specify how to derive that category from some other. While the schema is templatic in nature, the speaker can be creative in deciding how to reshape a given form to fit the schema of the desired category.

A number of examples from child language data, experiments, and diachronic change illustrate the functioning of product-oriented schemas. Consider first the semiproductive class of English verbs exemplified by *string, strung*. A list of such verbs is given in Table 5.3. This class is one of the few Old English Strong Verb classes that has added new members in the last millenium. In the table, the verbs with asterisks beside them are the new members of the class.

Originally the members of this class all had a short *i* in the Present, short *a* in the Past, and short *u* in the Past Participle. One could describe this alternation by saying that *i* becomes *a* in the Past and *u* in the Participle. In other words, a source-oriented generalization was possible. However, as new members were added to the class, the Past and the Participle came to be expressed by the same form, and, more important for our purposes, no requirement that the Present form have *i* was enforced. Thus *strike* enters this class, and in some dialects *sneak* and *drag*, none of which have *i* in the Present.

If the Past were formed by a rule that changed *i* into *u* [ʌ], none of these forms would be possible. However, if the class is described by a product-oriented schema giving the shape of the Past form, but not specifying how that shape is attained, then these forms are possible class members.

A further interesting fact about this class, to be discussed in Section 5.9, is that the stems of all of its members end in a velar or a nasal con-

Table 5.3. *A Semiproductive Verb Class of English (Bybee and Moder 1983)*

	ɪ	æ	ʌ		ɪ	ʌ
-m	swim	swam	swum			
-n	begin	began	begun	-n	spin	spun
	run	ran	run		win	won
-ŋ	ring	rang	rung	-ŋ	cling	clung
	sing	sang	sung		fling	flung*
	spring	sprang	sprung		sling	slung*
					sting	stung*
					string	strung*
					swing	swung
					wring	wrung
					hang	hung*
					bring	brung**
-nk	drink	drank	drunk		slink	slunk
	shrink	shrank	shrunk			
	stink	stank	stunk			
				-k	strike	struck*
					stick	stuck*
					sneak	snuck**
					shake	shuck**
				-g	dig	dug*
					drag	drug**

* Not a Strong Verb in Old English, but made Strong by analogy, according to Jespersen (1942)
** Dialectal, not a Strong Verb in Old English

sonant. Apparently, the velar has become the most important defining feature of this class, because in the nonce experiment reported in Bybee and Moder (1983), a few subjects not only changed the vowel of the prompt to [ʌ] to form the Past, but also added a velar consonant. Thus, the stimulus form *vin* elicited *vung*, *smip* elicited *smuk*, *stid* elicited *stug*, and so on.

A better candidate for a source-oriented generalization would be an affixation process, such as that used to form the regular Past Tense in English. In most cases, the productive use of this schema appears to add /t/, /d/, or /ɨd/ to an input form, the base stem. However, there is some indication that even this fairly agglutinative affixation may be conceptualized as a product-oriented schema – that is, a schema that simply says, 'a Past verb ends in /t/, /d/, or /ɨd/,' rather than 'add /t/, /d/, or /ɨd/ to a verb to form the Past.'

As evidence, consider a prominent class of English irregulars, those that form the Past with a zero allomorph. This class is very stable, and it is noteworthy that it is not prone to regularization by children in the early stages of language development, even though it has the peculiar property of not changing the base to form the Past. Several researchers (Menn and MacWhinney 1984, Stemberger 1981) have argued that its stability is related to the fact that all the stems in this class end in /t/ or /d/. Thus it is possible for the child or adult language user to interpret these verbs as already fitting the schema for Past tense and not needing further affixation.

Parallel phenomena are found in other constructions in English and other languages (see Menn and MacWhinney 1984 and Stemberger 1981 for many examples). In fact, one of the main determinants of the distribution of zero allomorphs is phonological similarity between the stem and the segmental allomorph. In English, words such as *lightning* that end in *-ing* do not add the Progressive *-ing*. One says *It was thundering and lightning* and not **lightninging*. Derivational *-ly* for forming adverbs from adjectives does not attach to adjectives formed with *-ly*, such as *friendly*, which cannot form **friendlily*. In Spanish, the only nouns with a zero allomorph for Plural all end in *-es*, which is also the Plural marker. Thus, the days of the week *lunes* 'Monday', *martes* 'Tuesday', *miércoles* 'Wednesday', and so on, do not change for the Plural.

Product-oriented behavior shows up in nonce probe experiments quite readily (Bybee and Moder 1983, Köpcke 1988, Lobben 1991, Wang and Derwing 1994). Köpcke (1988) found that a common response to requests to pluralize the nonce German noun *Treika* was the form *Treiken*, using the suffix *-en*, but reshaping the noun to fit one of the German schemas for Plural [CVC *en*] rather than adding it to the noun directly. Wang and Derwing (1994) asked subjects to form new nominalizations with *-ity* on nonce adjectives in order to observe the vowel changes made. The results showed that certain vowels were favored with *-ity*, but that the choice of vowels did not depend upon the vowel of the base. The most common responses were /ɔ/, /ɪ/, and /æ/, but these vowels appeared in words whose nonce bases contained a wide variety of vowels. For instance, /ɪ/ was given as a response to bases with /ay/, as would be expected from, say, *divine*, *divinity*, but it was also a common response for bases with /ɛ/ and /ʌ/, moreover, /ɔ/ was a common response to bases with /aw/, /ow/, /uw/, /ʊ/, and /ɔy/, and /ɛ/ was a common response to bases with /iy/, as expected, but also to ones with /ɔ/! As mentioned in Section 5.2.3, Wang and Derwing found a significant correlation between the response vowels and the type frequency of these vowels in *-ity* words in the existing lexicon. The conclusion is that subjects are forming *-ity* words not by applying the vowel shift rule, but rather by attempting to create a word that is similar to existing words with this suffix.

Since the evidence for product-oriented schemas is quite robust, and since any morphological pattern that can be described by a source-oriented rule can also be described by a product-oriented one, it seems reasonable to ask if there are indeed any source-oriented schemas. These would be schemas that give explicit instructions for altering a certain well-defined input form by changing features or adding elements to create an output form. Wang and Derwing found some evidence of source-oriented behavior in their study (e.g., that [ɪ] was a common alternate for [ay]), but they conclude that these results are due to knowledge of English orthography.

The basic/derived relation as described above in Section 5.2.4 appears to express a source-oriented relationship: the most frequent, unmarked form is used to create (usually by the addition of an affix) a new derived or more marked form. But even this operation could be accomplished with a product-oriented schema. The directional aspect of the relation is accounted for by the asymmetry in frequency between the basic and derived form.

If there are no source-oriented schemas, one might ask why rules that change features work as well as they do, and why it is that so many morphological operations involve affixation, which is the addition of elements to a base form. The reason in both cases is diachronic. We have seen that alternations arise from phonological processes that do, in a diachronic sense, change features. In addition, morphology arises through grammaticization, by which a previously independent word develops gradually into a grammatical morpheme and can sometimes also become an affix. Because it was once an independent word, it appears as linguistic material added to a base. Synchronically, however, its cognitive representation could be as a product-oriented schema. Thus, we still await conclusive evidence for source-oriented schemas.

5.9 Phonological Similarity in Gangs

Research over the past decades has produced a fairly comprehensive body of knowledge about phonological natural classes and the notion of phonological similarity as utilized by phonological processes. Much less is known about phonological similarity as applied to morphologically or lexically conditioned categorizations. However, the facts discussed in Section 5.2.3 concerning the failure of morpholexical classes to exploit the phonological natural classes of front and back vowels suggests that phonological similarity is defined differently in this area than where true phonetic conditioning is concerned. In this section, we explore what is known about how phonological criteria figure in the formation of gangs of lexical items with similar morphological behavior.

Research results suggest that phonological similarity for morphological purposes is more holistic than for phonological processes (referencing more of the word than just contiguous segments), more specific (eschewing natural classes), and defined not by discrete categories, but by family resemblances or comparison to a best exemplar. These points can be exemplified by examining some cases of phonologically defined morpholexical classes. Consider first the *strung* class, whose members were displayed in Table 5.3. This class is semiproductive, attracting new members gradually over time. It is especially instructive to observe the shape of the new members. Many of those ending in -*ng* bear a striking resemblance to the few original verbs with this final consonant, such as *swing*, not just in the final consonant, but also in the fact that many of them have initial consonant clusters. In our nonce experiment, we found that subjects were more likely to assign a nonce verb to this class if it had a consonant cluster, especially one with an /s/ (Bybee and Moder 1983). The definition of the shape of verbs of this class, then, is holistic and involves properties of the whole word, not just the stem vowel or final consonants.

Second, observe that new members of this class, such as *strike*, *struck* and *sneak*, *snuck* could not have been formed by a proportional analogy of the form X is to Y as X_1 is to Y_1 because there was no existing form with the same base vowels as *strike* or *sneak*, and because no verbs in this class ended in *k*. Thus *strike* and *sneak* could not be chosen to be members of this class based on their Present forms, but a Past form in /ʌ/ does bear a resemblance to the existing Past forms. A generalization based on the Past forms in this way is a product-oriented schema, as we have already said. Another point to be made here is that while existing members all had a nasal or a velar nasal, apparently a final velar constitutes a close enough resemblance for class membership.

The description of the class as it stands today must say that all the verbs of this class end in either a nasal consonant or a velar consonant. Interestingly, the majority are defined by the intersection of these two features – that is, they end in *-ng* or *-nk*. Thus, we can say that the best exemplars of this class have both features, but that items that share at least one feature with the best exemplars can also be members of the class. This category structure is a family resemblance structure and shows that speakers categorize the phonological properties of words in the same manner that they categorize other natural and cultural objects.

A further aspect of the structure of this category must be noted. While originally the class included verbs ending in any nasal consonant, the new members do not include any ending in /m/ or /n/, but rather only velars, and a further innovation has been to add members with a velar that is not also nasal. This means that not only do the central member verbs have velar nasals, but the dominant feature has come to be velar rather than nasal.

The partial productivity of this class, then, is made possible by the phonological similarity of its members. Sets of verbs with similar vowel changes that do not share features of the stem are much less likely to form viable classes (or gangs). It has already been mentioned as well that many members of this class are not very frequent, which also contributes to their association with one another.

Classes with family resemblance structure that show some productivity can also be found in Spanish. As mentioned earlier, Third Conjugation verbs with mid vowels in the stem exhibit two alternation patterns, which are illustrated in 13.

(13)		**mentir 'to lie'**	**pedir 'to ask'**
		e - i - ie	**e - i**
Present Indicative	1s	miénto	pído
	2s	miéntes	pídes
	3s	miénte	píde
	1p	mentímos	pedímos
	2p, 3p	miénten	píden
Present Subjunctive		miénta, . . .	pída, . . .

Imperfect		mentía, . . .	pedía, . . .
Preterit Indicative	1s	mentí	pedí
	2s	mentíste	pedíste
	3s	mintió	pidió
	1p	mentímos	pedímos
	2p, 3p	mintiéron	pidiéron
Imperfect Subjunctive		mintiéra, . . .	pidiéra, . . .

In Bybee and Pardo (1981) we discovered a difference in productivity between these two patterns, with the *mentir* pattern showing more productivity than the *pedir* pattern. Nonce forms as in 14 elicited the expected responses in the 3rd Person Present Indicative (*pierte* and *riben*) more often for nonce forms fitting the *mentir* class in consonant structure, with 82% of the responses as *pierte*. Nonce forms resembling the *pedir* class elicited only 27% responses appropriate to that class (i.e., *riben*). There was also no tendency to use the *pedir* pattern for verbs structured like *mentir*, as shown by the absence of forms such as *pirte*, despite this nonce form's resemblance to a member of that class, *servir* 'to serve', which has 3rd Person Singular *sirve*.

(14) Form presented	pertir		(3p Pres Ind)	rebir	
Form elicited	pierte	18		riben	6
(3s Pres Ind)	pirte	0		rieben	5
	perte	1		reben	4
	other	3		other	7

What accounts for this difference in productivity? According to their type frequency, the *pedir* class should be more productive because it has 23 members, compared to 15 in the *mentir* class. The difference appears to be a tighter phonological structure for the *mentir* class, as shown in 15.

(15)		mentir	'to lie'		pedir	'to ask'
	/r/	herir	'to wound'	/d/	medir	'to measure'
		preferir	'to prefer'		pedir	'to ask'
		sugerir	'to suggest'		expedir	'to send'
		preterir	'to overlook'		impedir	'to prevent'
		conferir	'to confer'		despedir	'to throw'
		digerir	'to digest'		descomedir	'to berate'
		injerir	'to swallow'	/ñ/	ceñir	'to gird'
	/rt/	advertir	'to notice'		reñir	'to scold'
		divertir	'to amuse'		teñir	'to color'

/nt/	arrepentirse	'to repent'		constreñir	'to constrain'
	mentir	'to lie'	/t/	competir	'to compete'
	sentir	'to feel'		derretir	'to meet'
/rn/	cernir	'to sift'		repetir	'to repeat'
/rg/	erguir	'to raise'	/st/	embestir	'to attack'
/rb/	hervir	'to boil'		vestir	'to dress'
			/x/	elegir	'to choose'
				regir	'to rule'
			/g/	seguir	'to follow'
			/b/	concebir	'to conceive'
			/m/	gemir	'to moan'
			/nd/	rendir	'to conquer'
			/nč/	henchir	'to fill'
			/rb/	servir	'to serve'

The similarity among the verbs in the *mentir* class resides in the consonant structure medial to the verb. One could describe the structure of this class based on these medial consonants by saying that the resemblance emanates from the members with -*r*-, which have the largest number of types, and extends to -*rt*-, which then forms similarities with both -*nt*- and with other combinations of -*rC*-, as shown in Figure 5.3. Not shown in this figure, but undoubtedly important, is the fact that the vowels preceding and following the consonant group are also the same across the verbs.

No such set of resemblances is apparent in the less productive class. Thus the accidental resemblance of a set of forms to one another can trigger the formation of a gang and the resultant partial productivity of the class.

A third example of a morpholexical class with a family resemblance structure is a set of medium- to high-frequency verbs in Spanish with very irregular Preterit forms, as illustrated in Table 5.4.

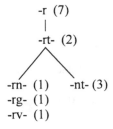

Figure 5.3. Family resemblance structure for the *mentir* class.

These Strong Preterits are characterized by stress on the penultimate or stem vowel rather than on the suffix vowel as in regulars. Most of them have a high vowel in the stem, and some change the final consonant of the stem. There is no good way to write generative rules that would derive these Preterits from the stem as it occurs in the infinitive and elsewhere in the paradigm. However, as Zager (1980) points out for this class in Old Spanish, when viewed as a product-oriented class, an interesting family resemblance structure emerges. This is shown in Table 5.5, where forms across the horizontal plane show decreasing

Table 5.4. *Examples of Strong Preterits in Spanish Compared to Regulars*

Infinitive	Regular Preterit (1s)	Gloss	Infinitive	Strong Preterit (1s)	Gloss
cantar	canté	'sing'	tener	tuve	'have'
comer	comí	'eat'	estar	estuve	'be'
vivir	viví	'live'	hacer	hice	'make/do'
			querer	quise	'like/want'
			poder	pude	'be able'
			poner	puse	'put/place'
			venir	vine	'come'

Table 5.5. *Family Resemblance Structure for Strong Preterits in Spanish (First Person Singular)*

	-β-	-s-	-x-	-p-	-d-	-n-
-u-	tuve estuve anduve hube	puse	conduje	supe cupe	pude	
-i-		hice quise	dije			vine
-a-			traje			

similarity in the medial consonant to the four central forms with [uβe] and the vertical plane shows decreasing similarity in the vowel.

This class was much more active in attracting new members in the Old Spanish period, and the variation seen during that period supports the proposal that the class was organized around a set of best exemplars. To cite just one example of a variant that still exists in many dialects, the Weak Preterit for *traer*, which is *traje* in the standard language, is *truje*, a form with the vowel that occurs in the majority of members of the class. Note that the Preterit of this verb originally had -*a*- throughout its paradigm. The innovative form *truje* thus resembles the other Preterits in the class more than it resembles its own base.[5]

Another property of phonological similarity as applied to gangs or to morpholexical classes is that more specific schemas take preference over more general ones (see Langacker 2000, Aske 1990; cf. the Elsewhere Principle of Kiparsky 1973). Langacker (2000) points out that this principle follows from the fact that more specific schemas describe forms with a greater number of shared features. For instance, Bybee and Pardo (1981) found no productivity for a class based on the three high-frequency verbs *tener, venir,* and *poner.* That is, subjects did not use the velar alternation with nonce verb stems ending in /n/. However, each of these verbs enters into a number of derivations with prefixes, all of which have the same alternations as the base verbs, even though some are semantically opaque. Some examples are *devenir* 'to become', *prevenir* 'to get ready, prepare', *proponer* 'to propose, suggest', *deponer* 'to remove from office', *detener* 'to stop, halt', and *obtener* 'to obtain'. While -*tener,* -*venir,* and -*poner* may not be morphemes in these words in the sense that they are meaningful parts, the derived words from each stem may form a gang based on their considerable phonological similarity. Their membership in the gang explains why they maintain the irregularities in the stem. Thus, in this case very specific gangs, based on each verb stem, may be formed, but no general overarching gang, is formed for stems ending in /n/.

5.10 Conclusion

In this chapter I have discussed and illustrated a few simple principles of lexical organization and processing that account for a large number

---

[5] A similar example can be found in Magni (to appear), where the development of the Latin Perfect into the Italian Passato Remoto is described in terms of product-oriented classes with a family resemblance structure.

of phonological phenomena associated with morphological categories and morpholexical classes. Three of these principles are directly related to frequency, and three of them govern the conceptual organization of morphological categories and lexical classes. The three principles based on frequency are:

1. Items with high token frequency have greater lexical strength and therefore resist morphological or analogical change, serve as the basis for change, and have greater autonomy.
2. Patterns with high type frequency are more productive than patterns with low type frequency.
3. As high token frequency leads to greater autonomy, items with high token frequency have weaker connections to related forms and thus are more likely to become independent and less likely to contribute to the formation of productive classes.

The three principles that govern the nature of the morphological categories and classes are:

1. Associations via meaningful features take precedence over associations via features of form.
2. Schemas are product-oriented.
3. The morpholexical classes that schemas apply to have a family resemblance structure.

I hope to have demonstrated in this chapter that morphological and lexical principles differ from phonetic principles, but that the intermingling of phonology, lexicon, and morphology runs both wide and deep in natural language.

6

The Units of Storage and Access: Morphemes, Words, and Phrases

6.1 Introduction

In this chapter, I address the nature of the units of lexical storage and explore the phonological evidence for the manner of representation of morphemes, words, phrases, and constructions. The focus of this chapter is to demonstrate that the model of lexical representation presented in this book – in which words are represented in the lexicon as a range of phonetic variation – leads us to an explanation for the predominance of alternations within words rather than across word boundaries and helps us explain some of the properties of word boundaries, such as the tendency for a final word boundary to act like a consonant. Section 6.2 begins by exploring the phonological properties of words, using evidence from words that vary in context to motivate a hypothesis about the manner in which the diverse exemplars of individual words are organized and reorganized. Since alternations between variants of words tend to occur at word boundaries, we also explore the properties of word boundaries and explain why a final word boundary usually acts like a consonant. In Section 6.3, we examine the evidence from sound change in progress for the lexical connections made among different instances of word-internal morphemes. The importance of alternating versus nonalternating environments for the progress of a sound change is explored with respect to both words and morphemes.

The discussion then moves on to the representation of larger stretches of speech. In Section 6.4, I argue that frequent phrases and constructions behave like words phonologically, since phonological processes which are otherwise restricted to word-internal position apply internally to such chunks. Here we find that the token frequency of a sequence is an important determinant of phonological reduction, and we explore both simple token frequency effects and the effect of other measures of probability. The evidence examined here suggests that high-frequency strings of words are stored and accessed as single units. Further evidence to this effect is presented in Chapter 7, which concerns the contexts for the loss and maintenance of French liaison.

6.2   Phonological Representations of Words

6.2.1   Words Tend to Have a Single Range of Variation

In Chapter 3, we discussed evidence from sound change for possible models for the memory representation of words. I argued that since sound change affects words gradually and at a rate dependent upon frequency of use, and since specific words have specific ranges of variation, lexical representations of words must be a compilation of the language user's experience with the word. In the exemplar model of representation, all perceived tokens of a word are categorized and stored with information about their contexts of occurrence. The phonological category for a word thus directly represents all the variation encountered. Another possibility is a prototype model, in which an abstract summary description is derived and stored for each word, based on the tokens actually experienced, which are discarded after the prototype is formed. In many cases, the predictions made by these two models are the same. However, a consideration of the way that words behave when undergoing changes conditioned by contiguous words in the speech stream suggests a model somewhere between these two proposals, a modified exemplar model.

Words have phonetic variants of diverse types. There may be differences between a word in casual versus formal speech. For instance, *family* may have two or three syllables depending upon speech style. Another common source of variation in a word depends upon the phonetic context provided by surrounding words. Thus in many dialects of Spanish, an /s/ before another consonant loses its coronal articulation and reduces to [h], or it deletes entirely. This reduction occurs for both medial and word-final /s/, as long as a consonant follows. Thus a word such as the copula *es* 'is' will be pronounced as [es] before a vowel, but as [e^h] before a consonant.

In an exemplar model, tokens of each variant are stored along with contextual information, which in this case concerns whether the following segment is a consonant or a vowel. If such memory representations are strong and stable, no further change could be expected to occur. However, the strong propensity for a further change in such cases suggests that a simple storage of exemplars is not an accurate reflection of how memory for the phonetic shape of words is structured. Rather, it appears that contextual variants of words are not stable, but that some reorganization of variants and perhaps loss of strict contextual information occurs. The tendency in a case such as the reduction of final /s/ in Spanish is for the /s/ to eventually disappear in all contexts, leaving no phonetic variants of the word that depend upon the initial segment of the next word. Let us see how such a change occurs in order to understand what type of storage model would be appropriate to account for this case.

Most dialects of Spanish in which the reduction of preconsonantal (or syllable-final) /s/ is occurring show considerable variation. In the following tables and examples, this range of variation will be reduced to only three phonetic categories, labeled [s], [h] (called 'aspiration' in the literature), and ø. The examples in 1 illustrate the variation found in connection with /s/ in the different phonological environments where /s/ deletes or aspirates in Latin American Spanish (Terrell 1978). Nonphonological factors involved in this variation include the sex and age of the speaker, lexical factors, speaking rate, and register.[1]

(1)   a. __C: word-internally before a C
           feli*h*mente   'happily'
           e*h*tilo   'style'
           denti*s*ta   'dentist'
    b. __##C: word-finally before a C
           o se traen animale*h* finos   'or fine animals are brought'
           haya mucho*s* temas   'there are many themes'
           su*ø* detalle*h*   'his details'
    c. __##V: word-finally before a V
           y mientra*h* esa sonoridad así   'and during this voicing thus'
           no va*s* a encontrar   'you are not going to find'
    d. __//: before a pause
           en momento*s* // libre*h* //   'in moments, free'

Tables 6.1 and 6.2 show the rate of aspiration and deletion in different contexts in two dialects of American Spanish, those of Argentina

---

[1] This discussion is based on Hooper (1981) and Bybee (2000a).

Table 6.1. *The Variable Reduction of /s/ in Argentinian Spanish (Terrell 1978, Hooper 1981)*

	[s]	[h]	[Ø]	N
—C	12%	80%	8%	4,150
—##C	11%	69%	20%	5,475
—##V	88%	7%	5%	2,649
—//	78%	11%	11%	2,407

Table 6.2. *The Variable Reduction of /s/ in Cuban Spanish (Terrell 1977, 1979, Hooper 1981)*

	[s]	[h]	[Ø]	N
—C	3%	97%	0%	1,714
—##C	2%	75%	23%	3,265
—##V	18%	48%	34%	1,300
—//	61%	13%	26%	1,776

and of Cuba. These tables generalize over thousands of tokens produced by dozens of subjects and obscure some important factors, including some lexical factors (see Bybee 2000a). For present purposes, however, let us focus on one difference between the two dialects. The Argentinian dialect can be considered to be at an early stage in the implementation of this change relative to the Cuban dialect. The important point to note about Argentinian Spanish is that at this stage, the word boundary appears to have little effect. Looking at the first column of Table 6.1, we see that the maintenance of /s/ is largely predictable from the phonetic environment. Before a C the maintenance of /s/ is at 11–12%, with no significant difference between word-internal and word-final /s/. The maintenance rate at the end of a word before a V (__##V) is 88%, since a following vowel does not constitute the appropriate environment for the change. No figures for a word-internal /s/ before a vowel are given because the /s/ is always maintained in this environment. Note that the maintenance of /s/ before a pause (//) is also high, suggesting that part of the reduction perceived by hearers results from the masking of the alveolar features of /s/ by the following consonant.

The main variants for words ending in /s/ in Argentinian Spanish are [s] and [h]. Total absence of a final consonant is less frequent, though it does occur. For the stored representation of such words, then, there is a set of exemplars with [s] designated as occurring before a vowel in the following word and before a pause, and with [h] designated as occurring before a consonant in the following word, as well as a small set of exemplars with no final consonant, occurring mostly before other consonants. Such a situation could presumably remain stable over a long period of time if the exemplars and their contexts are stable parts of memory. However, developments in a dialect in which the change is a little more advanced suggest some considerable reorganization of exemplars.

The fact that the maintenance rate of /s/ in Cuban Spanish is only 2–3% before a consonant indicates that this dialect is in a more advanced stage of the change. Again, the presence of a word boundary makes little difference when a consonant follows the /s/. A general increase in rates of aspiration and deletion also suggests that the change has progressed phonetically. In addition, a major restructuring of contexts for [h] suggests that the exemplars for words have undergone some reorganization. Note that a major difference between Argentinian and Cuban Spanish is in the use of /s/ at the end of a word before a vowel. In Cuban Spanish, aspiration and deletion are more common in this context, with the maintenance of /s/ down from 88% in Argentine to 18% in Cuban, even though it is not the appropriate phonetic context for the change, and no such change is taking place with word-internal /s/ before a vowel. Variants with [h], then, are occurring in the 'wrong' context.

What would cause a phonetic change to occur outside of its phonetic environment? If representations are sets of exemplars with their context specified, then we would not expect an exemplar to occur in the 'wrong' environment. But if the representation of a word organizes the exemplars such that infrequent or marginal instances are lost and central, but frequent ones are kept and strengthened, then for words of medium to low frequency, more frequent exemplar types might replace less frequent ones. (For words of high frequency, most exemplar types would be common enough to be kept, resulting in more stable variants for high-frequency words in certain contexts. See the discussion in Chapter 7.) In the case of Cuban Spanish, then, it appears that the variants with final [h] have become more central than variants with final [s], and that these more central variants are now occurring, at least variably, in all contexts.

What factor makes the variants with [h] more central? One possibility is their frequency. Since in Spanish, two out of three words in running text begin with a consonant, the variants with [h] are more common than those with [s] once [h] becomes the regular variant before consonants. Table 6.3 shows the percentages of word-final /s/ that occur before a consonant, vowel, or pause in the same corpora as reported on in Tables 6.1 and 6.2.

The stabilization of a single variant for a word suggests that representations are exemplar-based, but that all exemplars are not equally accessible. Highly similar exemplars are mapped onto the same representation, strengthening the phonetic features that occur most often. The representation of each word is a range of variation built up from exemplars that have been experienced, with the most frequently occurring properties representing the center of the range of variation. These more central representations are more accessible and may replace the more marginal ones.

Words manifest many phonetic variants due to the context in which they are used. Position in the phrase, contiguous segments and prosodic features, and even the frequency of surrounding words may influence their exact phonetic realization. These on-line adjustments create a continuous range of variation of the sort described in Chapter 4 as the result of phonetic processes. In the present case, and in other cases which come to be regarded as sound changes, some of the variants are extended phonetically and conventionalized or lexicalized, so that a word may be described as having two major, discrete variants. It is possible at that point that the representation of a word may have

Table 6.3. *Percentage of Occurrence of Word-Final /s/ before a Consonant, Vowel, and Pause in Two Dialects of Spanish*

	Argentinian	Cuban
—C	52.0%	51.5%
—V	25.1%	20.5%
—//	22.9%	28.0%

not one continuous range of variation, but rather two focal variants that are more discrete and occur in different contexts. For example, the word *más* 'more' might occur as [mah] before a consonant and variably before a vowel, but as [mas] in the phrase *más o menos* 'more or less'.

However, such situations are not often stable. What we see is a tendency for words to keep only a small range of variation, which precludes them from developing lexicalized alternations for different contexts, unless they are of very high frequency. The effect of this tendency is for lexicalized alternations across word boundaries to be rather rare. The way in which they do develop and are maintained will be discussed in Section 6.4 and in Chapter 7. In contrast, lexicalized alternations between morphemes within words are much more common, giving rise to the many cases ascribed to 'word-level' phonology. The reason that alternations between morphemes arise is that the different contexts in which they occur are individual words, each of which has its own representation where the alternates can be recorded and maintained. Thus, the fact that lexical alternations are much more common within words than across word boundaries is explained by the proposal that words are listed in the lexicon. In a model that lists morphemes instead of words, there is no explanation for the different effects of morpheme boundaries versus word boundaries.

6.2.2   Word Boundary Phenomena

The example just discussed, which I believe to be representative of word boundary phenomena, helps us to consider the question of how word boundaries influence phonological behavior. What a word boundary indicates is a location in which a portion of a word comes in contact with a variety of phonetic contexts, or an alternating environment (Timberlake 1978). Gestural configurations within words have a constant, or uniform, context, but at the edges of words, gestures interface with a variety of other gestures.

Typically, word boundary phenomena originate from phonetic conditioning that is not restricted, and that applies both word-internally and between words (Kaisse 1985:15, Hayes 1990:105). The changes caused by the phonetic processes may not create alternations within words, as when word-internal Spanish /s/ aspirates and deletes before a consonant, but across word boundaries alternations may arise, at least for a time, because the environment alternates. So even though there appear to be cases where alternations occur at word boundaries but not elsewhere, I predict that they develop from processes that were more generally phonetically conditioned, and that occurred elsewhere if the right conditions were met. For example, the French liaison alternations to be discussed in Chapter 7, which developed from a word-final deletion process, was just a specific instance of a syllable-final deletion of consonants that took place within words as well.

Certain word boundary phenomena are from the beginning restricted to certain phrases or constructions. Some examples of this type will be discussed in Section 6.4 – namely, palatalization in phrases such as *did you*, *would you*, and so on, and the reduction of *don't* in phrases such as *I don't know*. I will argue that these special processes occur only in high-frequency phrases which are in fact behaving like words. Moreover, the processes observed to apply in these cases are the same processes as those that apply within words (though perhaps in a different stage of development). For instance, palatalization in *that you* is comparable to palatalization in *picture*, and the vowel reduction and flapping of *I dunno* is comparable to reduction to schwa and flapping in many English words.

6.3   Morphemes within Words

6.3.1   Alternations Develop in Morphemes

Lexical alternations conditioned across word boundaries are uncommon and unstable, while alternations within words are very common and much more stable. I attribute this fact to the tendency to have a single representation per word in the lexicon. Thus, the same morpheme occurring in different words may develop discrete variants, but the same word occurring in different contexts is less likely to develop such variants.

In Chapter 5, I discussed the fact that word-level alternations develop from phonetically conditioned processes. For instance, the Old English masculine noun *hlāf*, *hlāfas* (nominative, accusative Singular and Plural of 'loaf') had developed stem alternations from the intervocalic voicing of fricatives beginning in pre–Old English, but not reflected orthographically until the Middle English period, giving the Singular/Plural pair *lōf*, *lōves*. Given that sound change occurs gradu-

ally and affects the lexical representation of words incrementally, the
fact that the Singular and Plural differentiate is due to the occurrence
of the sound change in the Plural, but not in the Singular. Also, in the
Spanish case discussed in Section 6.2.1, where alternates occur in different words, as in the case of the noun *voz* [boh] and its plural *voces*
[boseh], an alternation has been established. This situation contrasts
with the cases where a sound change produces variants of the same
word, which are not, in the end, represented lexically and do not
produce a stable alternation.

This proposal gives words and morphemes a very different status.
While the variants of words form a single category and tend toward
uniformity, morphemes apparently behave independently in the different contexts in which they occur. However, there is evidence that
the different occurrences of morphemes are not completely independent of one another, only that their behavior, especially under conditions of ongoing sound change, differs from that of words. The behavior
of morphemes undergoing sound change gives us further evidence
about the status of morphemes in the lexicon.

6.3.2   Morphemes in Alternating Environments

Timberlake (1978) has presented cases where it appears that a change
can be retarded, even in its phonetic environment, if it occurs in a morpheme with alternates that appear in other phonetic environments.[2]
Timberlake refers to such morphemes as occurring in 'alternating environments'. Morphemes that always occur in the same phonetic environment are said to occur in 'uniform environments'. In the cases just
discussed, word-final /s/ in Spanish occurs in an alternating environment, while word-medial /s/ in most words is in a uniform environment.
The /f/ in *hlāf, hlāfas* is in an alternating environment, being in some
cases word-final and in other cases prevocalic.

In Timberlake's examples, a sound change progresses more slowly
in a morpheme that occurs in an alternating environment. Consider the
following examples from the Mazowian dialect of Polish (Timberlake
1978: 313–314). Transcriptions are from Timberlake and his sources.
In 2, root-internal velars are always more or less palatalized before /i/
(the symbol [ⁱ] indicates full palatalization and ['] indicates partial
palatalization):

---

[2] The discussion in this section is based on Bybee (2000a).

(2) kʲij   'stick'
     skʲiba   'ridge'
     gʲipsu   'gypsum'
     k'ılômetr   'kilometer'
     g'ıńe   'bends'

In alternating environments, represented here by the position before a suffix, stops are palatalized before /i/ in only about half of the recorded examples, as shown in 3:

(3) prog'ı   'hearths'   cf. progu (Gen. Sg.)
     drog'ı   'roads'   cf. droga (Nom. Sg.)
     burak'ı   'beets'
     jarmak'ı   'fairs'
     morg'ı   'acres'
     rog'ı   'horns'
     gruskı   'pears'
     kackı   'ducks'
     zmarsckı   'wrinkles'
     drugı   'other'
     robakı   'worms'

When the velar is stem-final, it sometimes occurs in a palatalizing context and sometimes not. This is the reason, according to Timberlake, that the palatalization process is retarded even when the conditioning is present.

A very minimal effect of this kind is seen in the Spanish case, where there is a very small difference (only 1%) between the percentage of [h] before a vowel word-internally and across word boundaries (see Tables 6.1 and 6.2). The major effect found in change across a word boundary is the appearance of the changed segment outside of its phonetic environment, an effect that we do not observe within words until the alternation is morphologized and analogical change begins to take place.

The effect reported by Timberlake is interesting because it gives us some positive evidence for the functioning of morphemic units in lexical storage. Let us now consider a possible account of it in the model being proposed here. Note first that Timberlake observes that this effect is not the result of morpheme boundaries, as he has also discovered examples of the effect internal to morphemes. I have argued that the level ordering of Lexical Phonology cannot account for all the

Table 6.4. *Rate of Deletion for Regular Past Tense Compared to All Other Words of Comparable Frequency (403 Tokens or Fewer)*

	Percentage of Deletion
All words	45.8%
-ed verbs	22.6%

cases that Timberlake presents; in fact, it makes the wrong predictions in some cases (Bybee 2000a). I propose instead that the effect is the result of lexical connections among distinct instances of the same morpheme in the lexicon. If paradigmatically related words are grouped together in storage and if their identical parts are mapped onto one another, then the beginnings of variation due to a gradual sound change broadens the phonetic range of exemplars. Before the alternation is firmly established, such that different forms of the same paradigm have distinct allomorphs, variants that are not in the context for the change might exert some influence over those that are, with exactly the observed effect of keeping the center of the variation more conservative than it would be in a uniform environment.

So far, the examples we have discussed involve alternations in stems. The same effect can be observed with affixes. Affixes, such as English Past Tense /t/ or /d/, are in an alternating environment, because they may occur after vowels, as in *played* or *tried*, or after consonants, as in *walked* or *learned*. The suffix is only in a context for deletion when it is preceded and followed by a consonant. A monomorphemic word also has an alternating following environment, but its preceding environment is uniform. It could be for this reason that Past Tense /t/ and /d/ delete less often than do /t/ or /d/ in monomorphemic words, as shown in Table 6.4 (data from Bybee 2000b).[3]

Regular Past Tense verbs in the corpus did not cover as broad a range of frequencies as other words. The highest-frequency regular

---

[3] These data include only cases where a consonant precedes the final /t/ or /d/. An interesting fact about morphemic /t/ and /d/ in the corpus studied is that it precedes a vowel in the next word more often than does nonmorphemic /t/ or /d/. Thus, in a probabilistic sense the environment after the word boundary is not the same for morphemic and nonmorphemic /t/ and /d/, which may account for the difference in their deletion rates.

Past Tense form was 403 per million according to Francis and Kučera (1982). Therefore, in Table 6.4, deletion in regular Past forms is compared only to deletion in other words with a frequency of 403 per million or less.

6.3.3 Uniform Environments

As might be expected, sound changes taking place in uniform environments and within morphemes seem to occur at an accelerated pace of change. The deletion of Spanish /d/, which is allophonically [ð], is much more advanced in the Present Participle -*ado* than in other contexts (excepting high-frequency words, such as *lado* 'side') (D'Introno and Sosa 1986). Similarly, a very early instance of the loss of intervocalic /d/ occurred in the 2nd Person Plural morpheme -*ades*, which became -*ais* in Old Spanish. At first, it might appear that such cases give evidence for a single representation for these morphemes, since their high frequency accelerates change. However, an examination of the rates of change in different contexts for this ongoing change also shows that the suffix is stored as a part of whole words. In the following, we present data on this case in some detail.[4]

The data presented here are based on 751 tokens with medial, orthographic *d* taken from interviews with native speakers of New Mexican Spanish. The recordings are part of a project in which samples of native New Mexican Spanish from speakers in all parts of the state were collected (Bills 1997). All instances of medial *d* were coded as having [ð] present or absent. For the speakers in the study, the overall rate of deletion of *d* was 22.6%. But for different conditions, depending both on morphology and word frequency, the rate varies from less than 10% to more than 60%. As just mentioned, the highest rate of deletion is found in the Past Participle suffix -*ado*. In the following, we will determine whether this effect is due to frequency, phonetic environment, or the fact that -*ado* is a morpheme.

First, let us verify that there is an overall frequency effect in the lexical occurrences of medial *d*. Table 6.5 shows the rate of deletion for high- and low-frequency words. Token frequencies are based on the counts published in Juilland and Chang-Rodriguez (1964). For the

[4] I am grateful to Dawn Nordquist for coding the data presented here, to Rena Torres-Cacoullos for checking a portion of the codings for reliability, and to both of them for assisting with the statistical analysis.

Table 6.5. *Rate of Deletion According to Token*
Frequency for All Non–Past Participle Tokens of
Medial d

	Low Frequency		High Frequency	
	N	%	N	%
Retention	298	90	209	76
Deletion	34	10	67	24

$\chi^2 = 21.43; df = 1; p < .001$

figures in Table 6.5, the tokens are divided into two groups of approximately the same size – the low-frequency tokens have a frequency of
123 or less, and the high-frequency tokens a frequency of 124 or more
(up to 1,040 in the corpus).

As with the cases discussed in Chapter 3, we observe that this sound
change is further advanced in high-frequency words than in low-
frequency words.

Next, consider the rate of deletion in Past Participle forms. The Past
Participle suffix can be analyzed as having two allomorphs: one for First
Conjugation, *-ado*, and the other for Second and Third Conjugations,
-ido.[5] The rate of deletion for the First Conjugation suffix (58%) is
higher than the overall rate of 22.6%. The figures in Table 6.6 include
Past Participles used in verb forms, such as the various forms of the
Perfect, and when used as adjectives and nouns. Interestingly, the rate
of deletion for the First Conjugation allomorph is higher than for the
non-First Conjugations.

D'Introno and Sosa (1986) studied the deletion of *d* in the speech
of 36 adults from Caracas, Venezuela, and found the highest rate of
deletion in the environment *a__o*. This was also the most frequent
phonological context for the occurrence of *d*. One issue to consider,
then, especially in light of the fact that the allomorph *-ido* does not

---

[5] One could analyze *-do* as the Past Participle and the vowel as indicating the conjugation
class. Since in the model being used here, morphemes are not separated out of words,
but are the results of multiple lexical connections, we are not required to choose one or
the other analysis. In the text, I will cite *-ado* and *-ido*, as though they were different
allomorphs.

Table 6.6. *Rate of Deletion in the Past Participle Suffix*

	First Conjugation: -ado(s), -ada(s)		Second/Third Conjugation: -ido(s), -ida(s)	
	N	%	N	%
Retention	38	42	30	71.4
Deletion	53	58	12	28.6

have the same high rate of deletion, is whether it is the phonological context itself, its frequency, or the morphological status of Past Participle that conditions the higher rate of deletion. The phonological argument would be that the more open jaw position for the preceding /a/ pulls the tongue tip away from the dental area, encouraging the loss of frication. The frequency argument might be that the frequency of the gestural sequence that produces *-ado* leads to greater reduction through greater automation. I know of no studies that investigate whether the frequency of phonetic sequences might increase their likelihood of reduction. In the D'Introno and Sosa study, the sequence *-ado* occurred 2,163 times, and the sequence *-ido* occurred 782 times; deletion in *-ado* occurred in 19% of the tokens and in *-ido* in 4.5% of the tokens. The possibility that the frequency of phonetic sequences regardless of what word or morpheme they occur in might condition reduction needs to be borne in mind and investigated in future studies. In the current case, it is impossible to disentangle the frequency of the phonetic sequence from the fact that it constitutes a frequent suffix, so we will only be able to investigate the relative contributions of morphology and phonology in these data.

To see if the higher rate of deletion in *-ado* Past Participles is due to phonological or morphological factors, we compared the overall deletion/retention rate after /a/ and /i/ to the rate for Past Participles with these vowels. The results are given in Tables 6.7 and 6.8.

From these tables, it is clear that the higher rate of deletion in the PPs is not a purely phonetic effect. There is a highly significant difference between the rates of deletion following *-a* and in the Past Participle *-ado* and a similarly significant difference between the deletion rate following *-i* and the rate in the Past Participle *-ido*.

Table 6.7. *Rate of Deletion in the First Conjugation Past Participle Suffix vs. /d/ Following /a/ Overall*

	First Conjugation: -ado(s), -ada(s)		All Instances of /d/ Following /a/	
	N	%	N	%
Retention	38	42	128	59
Deletion	53	58	89	41

$\chi^2 = 7.815$; $df = 3$; $p = .0002$

Table 6.8. *Rate of Deletion in the Second and Third Conjugation Past Participle Suffix vs. /d/ Following /i/ Overall*

	Second/Third Conjugation: -ido(s), -ida(s)		All Instances of /d/ Following /i/	
	N	%	N	%
Retention	30	71	129	91
Deletion	12	29	13	9

$\chi^2 = 11.345$; $df = 3$; $p = .0002$

One explanation for this morphological effect would be to attribute it to the token frequency of the suffix. With 91 occurrences of Past Participle *-ado* and 52 occurrences of Past Participle *-ido*, the Past Participle is the most frequently occurring meaningful element containing medial /d/ in the corpus. In the discussion of lexical diffusion in Chapter 3 and in the literature in general, it is word frequency that is considered relevant to the diffusion of a sound change, not morpheme frequency. But it is possible that since *-ado* presents a uniform and favorable environment for deletion, and since all occurrences of the *-ado* Past Participle are connected to one another via lexical connections, the change can proceed faster in this suffix than elsewhere.

We might even consider claiming that if a sound change can occur preferentially in a suffix, it is evidence for the independent status of the suffix, and further argue that the lexicon contains a list of

Table 6.9. *Deletion/Retention Rates for High-
and Low-Frequency First Conjugation Past
Participles*

	High frequency		Low frequency	
	N	%	N	%
Retention	20	36	18	50
Deletion	35	64	18	50

$\chi^2 = 1.68; df = 1; p > .10$

morphemes, rather than of words, as we have thus far proposed. However, additional examination of the data suggests problems with this position. Evidence that the Past Participle suffix is not independent, but occurs in words, emerges from the effect of word frequency on deletion in the Past Participle suffix. In the First Conjugation, high-frequency Past Participles have a higher rate of deletion than do low-frequency Past Participles, as shown in Table 6.9. High-frequency Past Participles are those listed in the Juilland and Chang-Rodriguez frequency count, and low-frequency Past Participles are those that did not occur in that database.

While these figures do not attain statistical significance (likely due to the small numbers of items), they correspond to the findings presented in Bybee (2000b) and in Table 5.1 in Chapter 5 concerning *t/d* deletion in the English Past Tense: deletion occurs more in high-frequency than in low-frequency Past Tense verbs. In both of these cases, then, sound change is affecting the whole word – the verb stem and the regular inflectional ending together – as the rate of deletion corresponds to the frequency of the whole word.

Focusing just on the Spanish case again, we have an effect of the morpheme *-ado*, as well as an effect of the frequency of the words that *-ado* occurs in. This suggests that the Past Participles are represented as whole words, but that the different instances of *-ado* are associated with one another and can have an effect on one another, much as we suggested for the words that present an alternating environment. In that case, the appearance of the morpheme in an alternating environment slows the change down. In this case, the environment for the change is uniformly present, a fact that apparently speeds the change

up. It is also possible that the lexical connections between -*ado* and
-*ido* are responsible for the higher rate of deletion in -*ido* than in other
instances of /d/ following /i/.

This study of medial *d* in Spanish was undertaken in order to try to
understand the effects of the presence of /d/ in words and affixes on
the progress of the deletion. A word frequency effect was found, as predicted by the theory of gradual lexical diffusion. In addition, a morphological effect was found for /d/ in Past Participles that was stronger
in First Conjugation than in non-First Conjugation Past Participles.
Other factors that might have been of interest could not be investigated. There was no word frequency effect among the -*ido* Past Participles. The possibility of explaining the effect of First Conjugation as
the result of its higher type frequency was thwarted by the fact that the
type-to-token ratio for both First and non-First Conjugation was
approximately equal in the corpus. This study, then, needs to be supplemented by other studies of sound change in progress that affects
words, affixes, and other grammatical morphemes.

6.3.4   Alternating Environments That Block Change

In the examples of alternating environments within words that have
been studied so far, here and in Timberlake (1978), it appears that the
sound change and creation of an alternation eventually goes through,
albeit at a slower rate than in uniform environments. It is possible,
however, that the alternating environment might block a change, when
the environment for the change is a less frequently occurring one
in a paradigm. The following examples appear to be cases of such a
blockage.

6.3.4.1   The Weakening of /f/ to /h/ in Spanish

In the written Spanish of the fifteenth and sixteenth centuries, initial *f*
came to be represented as *h*, although it is likely that the change in the
spoken language began much earlier (Menéndez-Pidal 1968:123). Thus
Latin *fabulare* > Spanish *hablar* 'to speak'; Latin *facere* > Spanish *hacer*
'to make, do'. One environment in which the change generally did not
occur was before the diphthong /we/. Thus the /f/ is maintained in *fuego*
'fire', *fuente* 'fountain', *fuerte* 'strong', and in other words in which the
labiality of the /f/ was reinforced by the /w/. Because some verbs have
an alternation between /o/ and /we/ in their stems, an initial /f/ may

Table 6.10. *The Forms of Two Spanish Verbs*
with ue *and with* o

	Number of Occurrences of	
	ue	*o*
forçar	31	12
folgar	6	21

$\chi^2 = 16.53; df = 1; p < .001$

occur in an alternating environment. Two common verbs of this type
are Old Spanish *folgar* 'to be idle' and *forçar* 'to force'. In the first of
these verbs, the /f/ changed to /h/, giving Modern Spanish *holgar*, but
in the second, the /f/ remains, giving Modern Spanish *forzar*. Since both
verbs had an alternating environment, why did one undergo change,
while the other resisted it?

Brown (1999b) studied the instances of orthographic *f* and *h* in a fif-
teenth-century Spanish text, *La Celestina*, and found that this distinction between the two verbs had already arisen. The forms of *forçar*
occurred in all 43 instances with *f*, while *holgar* appeared 27 times with
h and once with *f*. The usage of the various forms of these verbs
explains why. In this text, the forms of *forçar* with the diphthong, the
phonetic environment that preserved the *f*, occurred much more often
than the forms with /o/; the opposite situation obtained for *holgar*, as
shown in Table 6.10.

Since *forçar* happened to occur more often in forms with the diphthong, the /f/ was preserved in this verb; since *holgar* was used more
often with the /o/, the /f/ changed to /h/ in this verb.[6]

6.3.4.2   Palatalization in Latin Verbs

A regular phonetic development in spoken Latin was the palatalization of /k/ and /g/ before front vowels and glides. This sound change
produced some of the alternations in Spanish Second and Third Con-

---

[6] Other words that might affect these words are the related nouns *fuerza* 'force' and
holganza 'leisure'.

jugation verbs that we discussed in Chapter 5.5.3. For instance the
Latin verb *dīcere* 'to say, tell' has its stem-final /k/ before a front vowel
in most of the paradigm and occurs before a back vowel only in the 1st
Person Singular Present Indicative and in the Present Subjunctive, as
shown in 4.

(4)   Latin *dīcere* 'to say, tell'

Present Indicative		**Present Subjunctive**	
dīco	dīcimus	dīcam	dīcāmus
dīcis	dīcistis	dīcas	dīcātis
dīcit	dīcunt	dīcat	dīcant
Imperfect Indicative:		dīcēbat	
Future:		dīcet	

When the /k/ palatalized, an alternation was established in this
paradigm, which still remains in Spanish today, as shown in 5, where
the orthographic *c* represents [θ] in peninsular Spanish and [s] in
American dialects.

(5)   Spanish *decir* 'to say, to tell'

Present Indicative		**Present Subjunctive**	
digo	decimos	diga	digamos
dices	dicís	digas	digáis
dice	dicen	diga	digan
Imperfect:	decía, and so on		

In First Conjugation verbs, the phonetic conditions are just about
reversed: the back vowels occur in the Indicative and the front vowels
in the Subjunctive. While the conditions for an alternation exist for
stems ending in velars, no such alternations arose. Thus the verbs *llegar*
'to arrive', *pagar* 'to pay', *negar* 'to deny', and *rogar* 'to beg' have Subjunctive forms with the velar (indicated in the spelling by the presence
of *u* after the *g*) (*llegue, pague, niegue, ruegue*). In both cases there is
an alternating environment, but in one case an alternation actually
took hold, and in the other case it did not.

One possible explanation for the difference could be the lexical frequency of the verbs involved. In order for an alternation to be created,
the alternate words must be frequent enough to have somewhat
autonomous representations. For example, the Latin verb *dīcere*
and the Spanish verb *decir*, which exhibit alternations in their conjugations, are of very high frequency. However, a number of other Second
and Third Conjugation verbs, which have alternations established

by the palatalization sound change, are not particularly high in token frequency. And although First Conjugation in general has many more low-frequency verbs than does the Second or Third, many of the First Conjugation verbs we are looking at are not of particularly low frequency. Thus, I doubt that the frequency of the stem is the main factor.

The other relevant difference between those paradigms that established an alternation and those that did not concerns the inflectional categories of the forms with the velar before a front vowel. In the cases where the alternation took hold, the palatalized consonants occur in the more frequently used forms – the Present Indicative, while the nonchanged velars occur in the less used category – the Present Subjunctive.

Where the alternation was not established, the changed velars – the palatals – would have occurred in the less frequent forms of the paradigm (i.e., the Present Subjunctive). This suggests that the failure of the alternation to develop in the First Conjugation may have been due to the lower frequency of the forms with the environment for palatalization. Regular verbs are deeply embedded in the lexicon's network for verbs, but they may not have autonomous forms for low-frequency inflectional categories. Thus, if the Subjunctive forms continued to be formed productively from the stem with the velar, some palatalization may have occurred while the sound change was ongoing, but a palatal alternate may never have been established.

This case illustrates another possible outcome for an alternating environment. The weakness of this example, however, is that the change in question took place in a poorly documented period. Another interpretation of the resulting forms might be that an alternation was indeed established, only to be leveled by regularization on the basis of the Present Indicative forms. The lack of any indication of palatalization in the Subjunctive of the First Conjugation, however, led Menéndez-Pidal (1968:286) to mention that in these verbs, the /k/ and /g/ did not palatalize, assimilate, or disappear as they did in other words. Studies of better documented cases are necessary to determine if and how an alternating environment might block a sound change.

These examples provide evidence for verb stems as emergent units. In order for the lack of a sound change in one token to block a potential sound change in another token, the tokens must be categorized as the 'same' in some sense. I propose that the similarity in question is the result of lexical connections that are established between different forms of the same verb. The predominance of /f/ or /h/, or velars versus palatals, in the tokens of the stem may have the effect of driving out other alternates if they are not strong enough to resist by establishing autonomous representations.

6.4   Phrases and Constructions with Alternations

Much of the effort to understand phonological alternations across word boundaries has focused on discovering the syntactic contexts in which such alternations occur. However, in most cases that have been investigated, no single syntactic correlate has been identified. Even where syntactic environments can be postulated, it is often necessary nonetheless to mention specific lexical items, or to refer to classes of items such as pronouns. The difficulty is now so widely demonstrated that it is considered an accepted part of theory that syntactic and phonological constituents do not coincide (Inkelas and Zec 1990). Thus, phonological rules are said to apply within 'phonological words', which are often arbitrarily defined. In fact, often the only evidence that a certain sequence of words or morphemes constitutes a phonological word is that phonological rules apply within it.

As yet, there is no explanation for why a certain string constitutes a phonological word, while another similar string does not. In addition, the surprising fact that constituency in syntax and phonology do not always coincide has not been explained. Bybee and Scheibman (1999) propose a usage-based solution to this problem: phonological alternations occur between words that are used together often. Words that are often used together become processing units because it is easier to retrieve a larger chunk of language than to piece an utterance together morpheme by morpheme or even word by word each time. It is within such chunks that phonological changes create variant forms of words, and thus alternations. Moreover, it is precisely because these words occur embedded in larger fused units that the changes arise: they are the result of automating production (Boyland 1996).

In fact, the larger claim is that use determines constituency in general. In most cases, frequency of co-occurrence accurately predicts syntactic constituency: adpositions occur next to noun phrases, determiners next to nouns, auxiliaries next to verbs, and so on. Thus a great deal of the phonological fusion that indicates tight constituency occurs where it is predictable from the morphosyntax: postpositions fuse with nouns to form case suffixes, auxiliaries fuse with verbs to form

children learn the pronunciation before they learn the analysis.

tense/aspect/modality affixes, and so on. However, certain cases tend to arise in which items are used together more frequently than their strict syntactic categorization would predict. These are the cases that demonstrate the importance of frequency for determining phonological fusion, for the formation of production units, and as we claim in Bybee and Scheibman (1999), for morphosyntactic constituency.

In the following sections, we examine several well-known cases that involve alternates of words in different contexts. I will argue that in these cases, which include fixed phrases (such as *I don't know*), frequently used sequences involving grammatical morphemes (such as pronouns), and constructions that have undergone grammaticization, the alternates are parts of processing units that do indeed behave like words. Further, I will show that their status as processing units is directly related to their frequency in discourse.

6.4.1   The Reduction of *don't* in American English

A frequently observed reduction in American English is the reduction of the negative auxiliary *don't*. Phonologically, this reduction involves the flapping of the initial /d/, the reduction of the vowel to schwa, and the loss of the final consonants. A syntactic approach to this problem comes up short because, even though the reduction is restricted to environments where *don't* is preceded by its pronominal subject and followed by its verb, only a small class of verbs conditions this reduction. According to Kaisse (1985), these verbs are *like, care, need, want, know*, and a few others. Kaisse (1985:59) notes that frequency of combination with *don't* might be a factor in determining this list of verbs.

On the basis of a study of the reduction of *don't* in naturally occurring discourse, Scheibman (2000a) and Bybee and Scheibman (1999) conclude that the frequency of the phrases in which *don't* is found is the main determinant of the reduction. The study is based on 135 tokens of *don't* in 3 hours and 45 minutes of conversation on 3 different occasions and involved a total of 6 participants. The phonetic variants in focus are [d] versus the flap [ɾ], and the full vowel [o] versus schwa. While the flapped variant was found after all pronouns, some adverbs, and the interrogative *why*, the variants with schwa occurred only after the pronoun *I* and in one case after *why* (in the suggestion, *Why don't you . . .*). Thus, reduction occurs not after all pronouns, but only after the most frequent one (I preceded *don't* in 63% of the cases).

The verbs that condition reduction to schwa also were the most frequent verbs in the data. *Know* with *don't* occurred 39 times, and 29 of these *don't* tokens had the schwa variant. The other verbs occurring with the schwa variant were (in order of frequency): *think, have (to), want, like, mean, feel,* and *care*, all occurring with *I*. All of these also appeared in the data with the full vowel variant. The 10 verbs in the database that occurred most frequently with *I don't* occurred with the schwa variant, with the single exception of *see* in *I don't see*. Thus the phrases *I don't know, I don't think, I don't have, I don't want, I don't like, I don't mean, I don't feel,* and *I don't care* all occurred with a reduced vowel in *don't*.

Kaisse (1985:57) argues that the flapping and final consonant deletion are the result of the regular casual speech processes, while the reduced vowel is part of the lexical representation of the clitic version of *don't*. The reason is that the reduced vowel variant is the one that requires syntactic and (I would add) lexical information to predict its occurrence, as just shown.

Our data strongly suggest that these high-frequency phrases are stored as single automated units and that, because of this storage, the reduced vowel variant of the word *don't* is preserved. Further evidence of the autonomous storage of these phrases is the fact that some of them have meanings or discourse functions that are not transparently derivable from their component morphemes. Scheibman (2000a) demonstrates that *I don't know* is often used as a discourse marker to deferentially yield the floor to others, as in 6.

(6)   Z: well I talked to a guy that's thirty-four in my class,
           and we were talking about the differences,
           just in . . . physiology and how you feel,
           and your best study hours, and the rest you need versus what you do
      O: right (*spoken simultaneously with the preceding*)
      Z: I don't [rə] know
           it's just—
      O: right

In this passage, after a fairly long contribution, Z yields the floor by expressing some uncertainty with *I don't know*, which occurs in reduced form.

Similarly, *I don't think* is usually used in discourse in a less than transparent sense. The utterance *I don't think they'll go for your fantasy*, in which *don't* has a reduced vowel, does not literally mean 'I am not having cognitive activity', but rather 'It is my opinion that they will NOT go for your fantasy'. It is used in discourse as a negative epistemic and can even be used parenthetically (Thompson and Mulac 1991).[7]

An important point about both the phonological and the semantic change in these cases is that neither of them could be registered in the lexicon if there were not already material stored there on which to register the changes. That is, the vowel in *I don't know* could not reduce to schwa in this particular phrase unless the phrase were present in storage. Similarly, a new discourse function could not be assigned to this phrase unless it was already present as an autonomous unit. Thus, both the functional and phonological changes attest to the prior autonomy of these phrases, which arose because of the high frequency of use of these words in combination. That is, I am not claiming that a phrase becomes a stored unit when its reduction reaches a certain point; rather, I am claiming that phrases that are repeatedly used become processing and storage units, but only those that are of very high frequency undergo extreme phonological reduction such as the vowel reduction in this example. Thus, *I don't believe, I don't need*, and so on, which occurred in our data with a full vowel and a flap are probably stored and processed as whole phrases because they are used frequently, but they have not undergone phonological reduction to the same extent as *I don't know* and *I don't think*.

The phonological and the semantic variation have a close but not absolute correspondence. There are some uses of *I don't know* that are transparent semantically, such as *I don't know any woman who hasn't tried it*. The reduced vowel can also occur in these uses. Table 6.11 shows the relation between the transparent versus pragmatic uses of *I don't know* and the full versus reduced vowel variants.

These figures suggest that the phonological reduction is somewhat ahead of the extension to the pragmatic use, since the reduction occurs even in the transparent use of the phrase. The reason for this might be that the two changes are basically independent, with the vowel reduc-

---

[7] Other verbs, such as *believe*, also allow their negation to affect their complement clauses rather than negating the main clause, but do not necessarily condition reduction of the vowel. In our corpus, *I don't believe* occurred twice (compared to 19 occurrences of *I don't think*) and did not have a reduced vowel in either example. As we will see, the phonological reduction and the pragmatic function do not strictly correspond.

Table 6.11. *The Relation between the*
Transparent vs. Pragmatic Uses of I don't know
and the Full vs. Reduced Vowel Variants

	Full Vowel	Reduced Vowel
Transparent use	7	12
Pragmatic use	1	17

tion being largely due to frequency rather than to the functional change.

The range of phonetic variation available for the phrase *I don't know* suggests multiple representations of this unit, ranging from phonetically full to highly reduced. In addition, of course, the lexical units *I, don't*, and *know* are also available for access, so that the same phrase could be constructed from its component parts. In the latter case, only general, productive processes, such as flapping, would be likely to apply. As mentioned earlier, although phonological reduction is an excellent indicator of memory storage of a phrase, it is the frequency of use itself that determines the units of storage and that is the prerequisite to reduction. Thus, the fact that a phrase is not (yet) reduced does not mean that it is not stored in memory as a unit.

6.4.2   String Frequency and Other Measures of Probability

In Section 6.4.1, I argued that the high frequency of strings such as *I don't know* conditions their reduction. Since the phonetic reduction occurs as linguistic material is used, phrases that are used more often will undergo more reduction. Krug (1998) studied a large corpus of spoken British English and found that the most frequently contracted Pronoun + Auxiliary combination was *I'm*, and that this combination was also the most frequently used. He introduced the term 'string frequency' for a measure of the frequency of occurrence of words together. In studies designed to measure the probability of the occurrence of words in text, the relative frequency of two words occurring together in text is called their 'joint probability'. We take up other measures of probability later in this section.

We have seen that when words occur together frequently, they begin to behave phonologically as if they constituted a single word.

Phonetic change takes place within the string, and alternations can develop between the word in the string and the word in other environments. In addition, it seems that the more frequent the string, the more advanced the phonetic changes can be. In the case of *don't* reduction just examined, we found that the highest degree of reduction, the deletion of the flap, occurred only with the most frequent subject, the pronoun *I*.

In addition, in Bybee and Scheibman (1999), we examined the reduction and relations within the phrase *I don't know*. The reduction of the vowel of *don't* depends more on the subject than it does on the following verb. The reduction only occurs with *I* (and in one instance with *why*), but it occurs with a variety of verbs: *know, think, have(to), want, like, mean, care,* and *feel.* Moreover, the deletion of the flap occurs only with *I*, but with a variety of verbs: *know, think, like, mean,* and *feel.*

We also found that an adverb intervening between the subject and *don't* blocks vowel reduction, as seen in the examples in 7, but that an adverb between *don't* and the verb does not, as in 8.

(7)   I really d[o]n't think so.
      I also d[o]n't know anyone ...
(8)   I d[ɔ] even know if I was that horny.

Thus there are multiple pieces of evidence for the tighter cohesion within *I don't* than within *don't know*, although both units show considerable fusion.[8]

Table 6.12 shows that string frequency predicts this difference in cohesion. In our corpus, the string frequency of *I don't* is 88 and the string frequency of *don't know* is 39. Thus, string frequency predicts the greater cohesion of the first two words of the phrase. Note also that fewer types precede *don't* than follow it. Only 5 lexical noun phrases preceded *don't* in this corpus, but 16 verbs occurred only once after *don't*. We do not have appropriate data for determining the transitional probability for the two parts of this phrase. However, in another corpus, we were able to determine that *don't* is the second most frequent word to follow *I*, coming just after *'m* (Scheibman 2000b).

Another approach to the relation between frequency in text and phonological reduction measures the predictability of words given sur-

---

[8] Kaisse (1985:56–57) argues that *don't* cliticizes to the verb rather than the pronoun. Our data suggest otherwise.

Table 6.12. *Number of Items Preceding and Following* don't

Preceding *don't*:	Tokens	Types	Following *don't*:	Tokens	Types
I	88		*know*	39	
Total	138	14	Total	124	30

rounding words. Gregory et al. (1999) and Jurafsky et al. (2001) hypothesize that words are more reduced when they are more predictable or
probable. These studies focus on the relationship between phonological effects and predictability given the preceding and following
word. Some of the factors involved in the relationship between predictability and phonological reduction would be the automation and
lexicalization of frequently occurring strings, along with comprehen-
sion-based factors, which include the fact that more predictable
words carry less information than less predictable ones, and also that
more predictable words can be decoded with less phonological information than less predictable words. It is claimed that these factors
allow the speaker to unleash reductive processes on the more predictable words.

Gregory et al. (1999) find significant relationships between a
measure of 'mutual information' and various reductive processes.
Mutual information counts the number of times that two particular
words occur together and divides that figure by the prior probability
(token frequency) of both words, $p(w, w + 1)/p(w)p(w + 1)$. Thus,
mutual information is like string frequency or joint probability, except
that it also takes into account the overall frequency of each of the two
words, since highly frequent words may also occur in sequence by
chance. Gregory et al. found that flapping of word-final [t] or [d] to [ɾ],
as in *lot of* or *that I*, was affected significantly by mutual information,
but not by any of the other probability measures tested, including word
frequency. Their analysis shows that flapping is a process that applies
more often in highly cohesive word pairs. They also found that final *t/d*
deletion and word duration in monosyllables ending in [t] or [d] were
affected significantly by mutual information.

The production of linguistic material is not neutral with respect to
directionality. Since one word follows another in a temporal sequence,
it is plausible to suppose that the tendency to chunk as much material
as possible proceeds in the same direction as production. Thus, given a

word as a starting point, as much material as possible is pulled in after, or from the right of, that word. It is possible, then, that chunking favors situations where the first element is highly predictive of the second element.

The temporal directionality of speech is of special importance to phonetic processes. The fluency of motor processing derives from the ability to anticipate the next set of gestures and modify current gestures to accommodate the transition. The greater the predictability of the following configuration, the greater the accommodation or anticipation can be. As Bush (2001) points out, the ability to react to common sequences of events by learning to anticipate the second based on the occurrence of the first is ubiquitous in living organisms. This behavior is the basis for a range of phenomena from conditioned responses to inferences of cause and effect.

Saffran et al. (1996) report that infants as young as nine months can identify commonly occurring three-syllable sequences out of strings of syllables that are otherwise randomly occurring. They propose that the syllables that are taken to belong together are identified because in the input, the first is a good predictor of the second, and the second of the third. A measure of this predictability is transitional probability, or the probability that any one item will follow the first. Transitional probability can be calculated from a corpus by dividing the frequency of the two-word sequence by the token frequency of the first word alone, $p(w, w + 1)/p(w)$. In other studies, such as Jurafsky et al. (2001), this measure is called 'joint probability given the previous word'.

Given the inherently linear nature of speech, it seems plausible that predictability given the previous word would have more of an effect on reductive processes than string frequency or mutual information, or predictability given the following word. However, research to date has not revealed any strong indications that transitional probability or predictability given the previous word has more of an effect than other measures of predictability.

Jurafsky et al. (2001) test the effects of joint probability given the previous word and given the following word on the ten most frequent words of English, the function words *a, the, in, of, to, and, that, I, it,* and *you*. The first measure is the same measure as transitional probability, and the second is analogous, except that is the frequency of the word pair divided by the frequency of the second word, $p(w, w + 1)/p(w + 1)$. Jurafsky et al. found that vowel reduction in these function words was highly associated with joint probability given the previous word ($p < .0001$), but that it was also significantly associated with the joint probability given the following word, though the magnitude of the effect was somewhat weaker ($p = .002$). On the other hand, for word duration, the magnitude of effects for predictability given the previous word and given the following word were the same ($p < .0001$).

Bush (2001) studied the occurrence of palatalization of /t/ and /d/ before /y/ in the next word and found both string frequency and transitional probability to be predictive of the occurrence of this variable process. Other studies have pointed to the frequency with which palatalization occurs before the pronoun *you*, but have otherwise been unable to predict when palatalization will occur. Bush's study shows that it occurs most often in the most frequent phrases with the pronoun *you(r)* (e.g., *did you, didn't you, don't you, would you, that you, what you,* and *told you*). In the small database used, palatalization was not restricted to the pronoun *you*, but also occurred in the phrase *last year*. Bush shows that the phrases with *you* have a relatively high transitional probability. However, palatalization was significantly associated with both string frequency and transitional probability, with simple string frequency having a larger effect.

The results of these studies have not yet conclusively shown that any one measure of predictability is any more effective than the others in conditioning reductive phonological processes.

6.4.3   Phonological Reduction in Grammaticizing Constructions

Constructions undergoing grammaticization show enormous frequency increases, which lead both to semantic reduction and phonological reduction (Bybee et al. 1994). Within grammaticizing constructions, the phonological material that occurs contiguously the most reduces and fuses the most. Consider the grammaticizing construction [SUBJECT + *be going to* + VERB]. Conjecturing on the basis of the data on subject and verb position surrounding *don't*, I suggest that the most variable part of this construction is the verb position, that the second most variable is the subject position, that the forms of *be* also vary, but comprise a closed set, and that the *going to* section is invariable. It is not surprising, then, that most of the reduction that has occurred in this construction involves *going to*, which has reduced to [gɚ̃ə] and other variants. The only reduction involving the other elements that I have observed is the reduction of *I'm gonna* to [aimɚ̃ə]. Based on the general high frequency of 1st Person Singular in conversation, I would predict that this construction is used more with *I* than with any other subject.

The greater tendency to reduce invariant sequences would explain why two invariant grammatical morphemes that often occur in sequence would reduce rapidly. Boyland (1996) discusses the fusion of *would have* to [wʊrə], which has been ongoing for several centuries. She finds increasing evidence for the analysis of this sequence as a single unit, including the misspelling *would of* and the inversion in questions of the whole unit, as in *What would've you done, what would've you videotaped?* (Boyland 1996:49).

6.5 Conclusion

In this chapter, we have discussed the differences between words and morphemes with regard to ongoing sound change, arguing that the evidence suggests basically one continuous range of variation per word. The development of allomorphy within words shows that morphemes are not autonomous storage and processing units the way that words are.

We have also seen that variant forms of words, such as the reduced versions of *don't* or *going to* come to be established in frequently occurring phrases and constructions, which are automated processing units, while their full forms are still available for productive concatenation in other constructions. The hypothesis put forward here, then, is that frequency of use explains all cases of external sandhi that appear to take place in particular morphosyntactic or lexical contexts. This hypothesis applies not just to phrases such as *I don't know* or to constructions with invariant parts, such as *gonna*, but also to constructions characterized by alternations, such as the alternation in the English indefinite article, *a/an*. As the Old English number 'one', *ān* grammaticized with a following noun to become the indefinite article, with the final /n/ deleting before a consonant, but remaining before a vowel. The retention of /n/ before a vowel was due to the frequent processing of *an* + vowel-initial noun as a single unit. The result is that the construction [INDEFINITE ARTICLE + NOUN] is characterized by the particular phonological alternation. In Chapter 7, we consider other cases of phonological alternations in constructions and the evidence that they provide for the nature of processing and storage units.

7

Constructions as Processing Units: The Rise and Fall of French Liaison

7.1 Introduction

In this chapter, the example of French liaison is used to illustrate the fact that construction or phrase frequency conditions the development of alternations among variants of the same word, and that frequency also makes such variants resistant to regularization once alternations are established. The chapter concludes with the argument that phonological alternations viewed as having syntactic conditioning are due to the frequency of certain combinations of words and provide evidence for chunks, or units of processing and storage, that are used in speech. (The material in this chapter also appears in Bybee 2001.)

One of the best-studied cases of alternations between versions of the same word under putative syntactic conditions is the case of French liaison. Liaison is the name for the appearance of a word-final consonant before a vowel-initial word in words that in other contexts end in a vowel. Thus, the 3rd Person Singular copula *est* is pronounced [εt] in the examples in 1 and as [ε] in the examples in 2 (the *s* is never pronounced). The examples are from Green and Hintze (1988).

(1) a. le climat est [t] également très différent.
       'The climate is also very different.'
    b. C'est [t] encore un refuge de notables.
       'It's still a refuge for famous people.'
(2) a. C'e(st) le meurtre.
       'It's murder.'
    b. le Conseil Régional qui e(st) donc son assemblée délibérante
       'the Regional Council, which is thus their deliberative
       assembly'

The phonological condition for the appearance of the liaison is before
a vowel-initial word, but only under certain syntactic conditions. In 3
and 4, plural liaison is obligatory for the definite article *les*. However,
in the noun phrase in 3, the plural morpheme on the noun may variably appear before a vowel-initial adjective, while in 4 the presence of
[z] on this same noun is not possible, as the construction involves an
NP subject and its verb.

(3) le[z] enfants ([z]) intelligents   'the intelligent children'
(4) le[z] enfan(ts) arrivent   'the children arrive'

It is often said that liaison contexts involve a tighter syntactic constituency, but it has not been easy to define what this means in formal
terms.

Moreover, in cases such as 1 and 3, where liaison is possible, there
is currently considerable variability. In the databases studied by Ågren
(1973) and by Green and Hintze (1988), speakers at times also omitted
the consonant before a vowel. Such omissions are taken as evidence
that liaison is disappearing in some contexts.

In this section, we examine the evolution of liaison from its origin
as phonetically conditioned consonant deletion to its present state, as
attested in conversation, as a highly lexically and morphologically governed process (Baxter 1975, Delattre 1966, Green and Hintze 1988,
Klausenburger 1984, Morin and Kaye 1982, Post 2000, Tranel 1981). I
argue that the morphosyntactic and lexical contexts in which liaison
became established occurred with high frequency and were thus
sequences that could be stored in memory. Currently, as liaison is being
lost, we see that it is also maintained in the contexts that occur most
frequently.

7.2   Final Consonant Deletion in French

The source of the liaison alternations is the deletion of word-final consonants before another consonant. It is important to note that this was
only a specific instance of the more general deletion of syllable-final
consonants, which was entirely phonetically conditioned. The first wave
of such deletion occurred very early in French, when consonants that
had been final in Latin were lost, as in Latin *pŏntem* 'bridge' and *caput*
'chief'. A subsequent development was the loss of final posttonic
vowels, which created another full set of final consonants (giving *pont*
and *chef* from the Latin words just given). The stops and fricatives in

final position developed two or sometimes three alternates in the environments before a pause, a consonant, or a vowel. Harris (1988) gives the example of *dix* 'ten', which is pronounced [dis] before a pause, [di] before a consonant (*dix femmes* 'ten women') and [diz] before a vowel (*dix élèves* 'ten pupils'). More commonly today, where the alternations persist, the only two variants are the presence and absence of the consonant. However, it is interesting that while this consonant deletion was in progress, the preconsonantal and prepausal conditions were distinguished. The deletion occurred earlier in preconsonantal position than before pause (Klausenburger 1984). This fact suggests that an important phonetic condition for the deletion was the masking provided by a following consonant, and that the spread of deletion to prepausal position was due to the restructuring of the lexical representations. This case is parallel, then, to the Spanish *s* deletion discussed in Chapter 6.2.[1]

The result of this phonetic change was that many words, notably nouns, and some adjectives, lost their final consonants completely. For instance, nouns such as *haricot* 'bean', *buffet* 'sideboard', *bois* 'forest', *goût* 'taste', *tabac* 'tobacco', and *sirop* 'syrup' are pronounced without a final consonant. However, words that occurred frequently in particular grammatical or idiomatic conditions that placed them before a vowel tended to develop an alternation. Word-internally, such conditions existed before the feminine suffix, which was vocalic and thus yielded alternations between masculine and feminine nouns and adjectives, such as found in [pəti] 'small (masc.)' and [pətitə] 'small (fem.)', which today, with the loss of final schwa, yields the alternation [pəti], [pətit].

In sixteenth-century and seventeenth-century French, when final consonant deletion was being implemented, there was a strong tendency, as there is today, for forward resyllabification when a final consonant was followed by a vowel (Encrevé 1983, Green and Hintze 1988). This process, known as *enchaînement*, makes a final consonant syllable-initial when a vowel follows within the same pause group. As we observed in Chapter 6.2, there is a strong tendency toward having a single representation for individual words, the result of which is that many words simply lose their final consonants. However, multiple representations are possible for grammatical words and grammatical

---

[1] See Terrell and Tranel (1978) for further discussion of similarities between Spanish *s* deletion and French liaison.

morphemes, according to the constructions they frequently occur in. In the case of liaison, words or morphemes that frequently occur in constructions that put them in prevocalic position are able to maintain their final consonant in those constructions. Examples are shown in 5 to 12, based on Morin and Kaye (1982) and Tranel (1981:233). The use of the liaison consonant in 5 and 6 is considered obligatory, while in the remaining contexts, it is variable in spoken French.

(5) Determiners
    a. vos [z] enfants   'your children'
    b. les [z] autres   'the others'
    c. un [n] ancien ami   'an old friend'

(6) Clitic pronouns
    a. nous [z] avons   'we have'
    b. ils [z] ont   'they have'
    c. allons [z]-y   'let's go'
    d. chante-t-il?   'does he sing?'

(7) Plural /-z/ in noun-adjective constructions
    a. des enfants [z] intelligents   'intelligent children'
    b. des découvertes [z] inquiétantes   'worrisome discoveries'

(8) Person/number endings
    a. nous vivons [z] à Paris   'we live in Paris'
    b. ils chantent [t] en choeur   'they sing in chorus'

(9) A small set of prenominal adjectives in the Masculine Singular
    a. un petit [t] écureuil   'a little squirrel'
    b. un gros [z] amiral   'a fat admiral'
    c. un long [g] été   'a long summer'

(10) The plurals of the same adjectives
    a. deux petites [z] histoires   'two short stories'
    b. quelques [z] années plus tôt   'a few years earlier'

(11) Prepositions, adverbs, particles
    a. dans [z] un mois   [dãzẽmwa]   'in a month'
    b. pendant [t] un mois   [pãdãtẽmwa]   'for a month'

(12) Fixed phrases
    a. c'est [t] à dire   'that is to say'
    b. pas [z] encore   'not yet'

Despite the variety of morpheme or word types included in this list, it is important to note that there are no purely lexical, or open class items, that exhibit liaison. Rather, the items range from suffixes for Plural to grammatical classes, such as prepositions and small closed classes (e.g., the exceptional prenominal adjectives (see Section 7.4 for further discussion of this small class). Two relevant points can be made about such forms. First, they are all of relatively high frequency, especially in the constructions or phrases in which the liaison consonant appears, and second, they all occur in very specific grammatical constructions. No liaison consonant appears independently of a specific construction. The situation of liaison consonants within specific constructions will be discussed in the next section.

7.3 Grammatical Constructions and Liaison

The roles of morphology, syntax, and lexicon have been widely recognized in accounts of French liaison, but the relative contribution of each has been debated in the literature, and very little has been said about the role of frequency in establishing and maintaining liaison consonants. Perhaps the most monolithic approach is that of Selkirk (1974), which attempts to derive liaison contexts by reference to the placement of word boundaries (#, ##) according to the principles proposed in Chomsky and Halle (1968), which place single word boundaries around members of lexical categories, but not around members of grammatical categories. These principles define a phonological word as the material between instances of two word boundaries (##). Selkirk proposes that liaison occurs only within the phonological word. Because of the way that # is placed, the effect of these principles is that liaison occurs when grammatical and not lexical morphemes are involved. This analysis works well for most cases, but because it treats all instances of liaison as involving grammatical morphemes, it leaves open the question of how to treat prenominal adjectives, since they are technically lexical in generative theory. Kaisse (1985) proposes that liaison takes place in a sequence *ab* if *b* is the head of the phrase and c-commands *a* (that is, if *a* is in the phrase of which *b* is the head). However, the data we examine in this and the next section shows that the variability of liaison is highly affected by the very specific location of the grammatical element in a construction, and that all cases of liaison do not have the same status in terms of their productivity and degree of entrenchment, indicating that a single syntactic principle is not likely to be successful in predicting liaison contexts.

The syntactic principles proposed so far are adequate for the obligatory liaison in 5 and 6, which involve determiners with their nouns and clitic pronouns with their verbs, but it is not possible to extend either of these proposals to cases where liaison is considered variable. Indeed, any syntactic proposal referring to the head of a phrase runs into trouble in connection with both noun-adjective combinations, as in 7, and adjective-noun combinations, as in 9 and 10 (de Jong 1990). Moreover, proposals based on traditional assumptions about constituent structure are unable to explain the fact that liaison occurs almost 99% of the time in a sequence *est [t] un* 'is a' + NOUN, but about 50% of the time in the sequence *je suis[z] un* 'I am a' + NOUN, which presumably has the same constituent structure (data from Ågren 1973).

Another approach is to postulate a level of prosodic organization and stipulate that liaison applies within units so organized – that is, within phonological words or phrases (Selkirk 1986, de Jong 1990). Such proposals were tested in the experiments of Post (2000), but her attempts to find a correspondence between the prosodic unit of phonological word and the occurrence of liaison failed to produce significant results.

Most other authors (Baxter 1975, Green and Hintze 1988, Klausenburger 1984, Morin and Kaye 1982, Tranel 1981) have offered an analysis that refers to both morphosyntactic and lexical factors. Like other alternations that have become lexicalized or morphologized, what was a unitary phonological change has become associated with particular grammatical contexts and is no longer unitary (cf. Chapter 5.2.2). The account offered here is based on these previous treatments and will only mention some of the liaison environments, as the main point is to underscore the role of frequency and phonological material situated in constructions. I assume that frequency of use played a major role in the establishment of liaison alternations, and I will argue on the basis of modern data that frequency of use plays a major role in preserving them. In particular, I will argue, as in Chapter 6.4, that the 'degree of syntactic cohesion' that is often mentioned in studies of liaison is a direct result of the frequency with which the two items surrounding the liaison consonant occur in sequence.

Evidence in support of the view that liaison is morphologized or lexicalized is the fact pointed out in various studies, most explicitly in Encrevé (1983), Morin and Kaye (1982) and Post (2000), but also in Ågren (1973) and Green and Hintze (1988), that liaison consonants can occur both before and after a pause, or with and without forward syllabification or *enchaînement*. In other words, while liaison originally depended upon forward resyllabification, it is not now restricted to occurring within a phonological word. On the other hand, *enchaîne-ment*, which is still a viable process in Modern French, occurs only within pause groups and not across them.

The current approach to liaison takes the construction as the basic unit and, since constructions often contain very specific lexical and grammatical material, attributes the liaison consonant to the construction itself. Constructions are frequently used sequences of morphemes or words that bear a particular semantic or functional relation to one another when used together – a relation that they do not necessarily have outside that construction. Constructions have different degrees of conventionalization, as they come to be established in a language through repeated use. The mechanisms for the establishment of constructions are (i) automation of chunks of linguistic material due to repetition, and (ii) categorization of the items occurring in particular positions in these larger chunks. Because repeated use is a major factor in the formation of constructions, constructions need not have unpredictable meaning – they can simply be often-used chunks of language. However, owing to the autonomy that accompanies repetition and frequency of use, constructions often do take on nontransparent meanings (recall the discussion of *I don't know* in Chapter 6.4).

At one end of a continuum involving constructions are fixed phrases, such as *I don't know* and *c'est à dire* 'that is to say'; nearer the middle are constructions with some grammatical material and a slot that is more open (e.g., the preposition *dans* with its noun phrase object); and, at the most general end, are constructions such as [NOUN + PLURAL + ADJECTIVE], with two slots that are very open. It seems useful to restrict the term 'construction' to sequences that include a relatively open slot and to classify phrases without open slots, such as *c'est à dire*, as fixed phrases. The open slots in constructions are subject to categorization in terms of semantic features (such as motion verb) or grammatical features (such as pronoun). Since constructions arise from frequently used stretches of speech, they usually correspond to traditional constituents, as constituents consist of elements that are frequently used together (determiners and their nouns, prepositions and their objects, etc.). However, it is also possible, as we will see in examining some liaison contexts, for items that are not in the same traditional constituent to be used together frequently, thus showing that it is frequency of co-occurrence, and not constituency, that is the important factor in the maintenance of liaison.

The data used in this discussion is taken from published sources and represents the data set that the authors studied (as in the case of Ågren 1973 or Green and Hintze 1988) or the authors' intuitions (as in the case of Morin and Kaye 1982). Since liaison is a variable phenomenon and increasingly less used in casual speech, the generalizations made here are intended to describe just the data presented in these sources, and not the current situation concerning liaison in the spoken language.

One construction that is much discussed in the liaison literature involves a plural noun followed by vowel-initial adjective. In some cases, a [z] occurs between the noun and adjective, a remnant of the plural marking that has been deleted when a consonant follows. The examples from 7 are repeated here as 13.

(13) a. des enfants [z] intelligents   'intelligent children'
     b. des découvertes [z] inquiétantes   'worrisome discoveries'

Ågren (1973) reports that liaison in such contexts is considered obligatory in certain frequent lexicalized phrases, some of which are proper nouns: *affaires [z] américaines* 'American affairs', *Champs [z] Elysées*, *Nations [z] Unies* 'United Nations', *Jeux [z] Olympiques* 'Olympic Games', and so on. Among the optional contexts, liaison occurs in only 26% of cases with a plural noun followed by an adjective. Most authors regard this construction with liaison as somewhat productive, however, owing to the existence of examples such as these offered by Morin and Kaye (1982), in which the [z] liaison occurs for plural but at some remove from its etymological site.

(14) a. des chefs d'Etat [z] africains   'African heads of state'
     b. les chemins de fer [z] anglais   'the English railways'

Morin and Kaye (1982) argue that the plural liaison occurs not just in lexicalized expressions, but also applies productively in these cases.

The data suggest two constructions for the plural noun–adjective expressions. The more general one contains a plural determiner followed by an unmarked noun and adjective, as indicated in 15.

(15)

	les			
[	*ces*	NOUN	ADJECTIVE	]
	des			Plural
	etc.			

A second, more restricted construction, applies only to vowel-initial adjectives, as in 16.

(16)

	les				
[	ces	NOUN	-z-	[Vowel]-ADJECTIVE	]
	des				Plural
	etc.				

The examples in 14 result from the phrasal nouns *chefs d'Etat* and *chemins de fer* occurring in the NOUN position in this construction.

Besides the restriction of the second construction to vowel-initial adjectives, there is another difference between them: the first construction applies to more items – that is, it has a higher type frequency, which makes it more productive than the second one. Thus, it is not surprising that there is variation in the data resulting from speakers choosing the more general schema even for vowel-initial adjectives in most cases. Still, the more specific schema with the [z] before vowel-initial adjectives is available and is sometimes used. Thus, the loss of liaison resembles regularization of irregular verbs: if the specific schema is not easily accessed, then the more general one, which is stronger and easier to access, is used (see Section 7.4).

In addition to (or perhaps instead of) the second schema for vowel-initial adjectives, there might also be more specific schemas for adjectives that are frequently used with the [z], such as *anglais* or *américain*.

(17)

	les				
[	ces	NOUN	-z-	*anglais*	]
	des				Plural
	etc.				

Another plural construction that results in cases of 'false liaison' consists of the cardinal numbers plus [z] and a noun. As reported in Tranel (1981:214–216), liaison is frequently maintained with the cardinal numbers *deux* [døz] 'two' and *trois* [trwaz] 'three' before vowels when in construction with the following noun and when plurality is indicated. Thus *les deux [z] amis* 'the two friends' has liaison, but *le deux octobre* 'October 2nd' does not. The viability of the [z] as a plural marker in this construction is evidenced in the widely reported use of cardinal numbers without etymological final [z] in this construction. Tranel (1981:216) gives the following examples.

(18) a. quatre enfants   [katzãfã]   'four children'
      b. huit épreuves   [ɥizeprœv]   'eight events'
      c. neuf oeufs   [nœfzø]   'nine eggs'
      d. vingt-cinq années   [vẽtsẽkzane]   'twenty-five years'
      e. trois mille évêques   [trwamilzevɛk]   'three thousand
                                                      bishops'

Not only do these examples show the intrusion of a nonetymological [z], but examples c-e also show that the other final consonant of the number is present. Thus, this construction goes beyond the function of creating optimal syllable structure to a truly morphological use, where the [z] is signaling plurality.

On the basis of examples such as those in 18, Tranel (1981), Morin and Kaye (1982), and Klausenburger (1984) argue for an analysis that inserts the liaison consonant in certain contexts before a vowel, rather than deleting it before a consonant. The solution proposed here is neutral with regard to insertion or deletion. It simply states that a construction exists that contains the [z] after a number and before a vowel-initial noun. This construction could be formulated as in 19.

(19)

    [NUMBER   -z-   [vowel]-NOUN   ]
                                                  Plural

The construction in 19 is a generalization from the conservative usage, in which *deux*, *trois*, *six*, and *dix* were the only numbers that had [z] before vowel-initial nouns. These cardinal numbers, then, form a viable class or gang and attract other numbers into the class. This change resembles an analogical extension such as is observed in the case of the originally regular verb *stick* acquiring a vowel-change Past Tense *stuck*.

As mentioned earlier, Ågren (1973), Morin and Kaye (1982), and Green and Hintze (1988) all report that the liaison consonant can appear even if a pause or hesitation syllable separates the two words of the construction. Green and Hintze (1988:159) report an example with the number *quatre*.

(20) quatre euh . . . [z] obligations   'four uh . . . obligations'

Such examples show that it is possible to pause or hesitate in the middle of a construction, just as it is possible to pause in the middle of a word. Since the words of a construction are usually associated with other instances of the same word, their identity as words is known, and the point between two words is a possible place to pause. The position of the pause in this and other examples reported in the works cited suggests that the liaison consonant is associated more closely with the second word than with the first, its historical source.

Another illustration of the close association of particular liaison consonants with particular constructions is in the reciprocal construction, discussed in Morin and Kaye (1982:318–319). These authors report that liaison is optional after *l'un* 'the one', but only in the reciprocal construction. Elsewhere, liaison is not possible. Thus, in 21 liaison with [n] is an option, but in 22, it is not.

(21) a. Il les a confundus l'un [n] avec l'autre.
          'He mistook them for each other.'
      b. Ils se ressemblent l'un [n] à l'autre.
          'They resemble each other.'
(22) Ils sont venus, l'un avec sa mère, l'autre avec son père.
      'They came, one with his mother, the other with his father.'

These examples in particular show that grammatical morphemes are highly entrenched in the constructions in which they appear, not just in French, but in all cases. A grammatical morpheme is identified as such because of its appearance in certain well-defined grammatical constructions. The history of grammatical morphemes shows that if they occur in different constructions, they move away from one another in phonological shape, meaning, and distributional properties (Heine and Reh 1984, Hopper 1991). In French, there are several grammatical morphemes deriving from *un*, which originally was only the numeral 'one'. *L'un* 'the one', as in 22, where liaison is not possible; the reciprocal, as in 21, where liaison is optional; and the indefinite article *un, une,* for which liaison is considered obligatory even with rare nouns. Each instance is associated with a different construction, and each construction has its own set of conditions for preserving liaison.

7.4 Loss of Liaison as Regularization

Studies of optional liaison, such as Ågren (1973), show a tendency for liaison to be lost in many contexts. As mentioned earlier, the observation is often made that liaison is maintained in cases of 'tighter syntactic cohesion' (Tranel 1981). However, no one has offered a definition of this syntactic cohesion that is detailed enough to make correct predictions across the numerous constructions involved in liaison. It has been noticed and amply documented in Ågren (1973) that uses with higher frequency maintain a higher level of optional liaison than do those that are less frequently used (see also Booij and de Jong 1987). However, no one has yet zeroed in on frequency of use as a causal factor in the establishment, maintenance, or loss of liaison.

My proposal is that liaison, though it takes place between rather than within traditional 'words', is very similar to morphologically and lexically conditioned alternations that occur word-internally. It was established with an original phonetic motivation, and the alternations gradually came to be associated with certain morphosyntactic and lexical contexts. Like other morpholexical alternations, it is subject both to extension to new contexts in cases of productivity and to leveling or loss of the alternations. The frequency factors affecting these ongoing changes are the same as in the cases of word-internal alternations. High type frequency of a construction spurs productivity. Unproductive alternations are gradually leveled or regularized, with low-frequency forms being leveled first and high-frequency tokens resisting the leveling longest.

What makes this case especially interesting is the fact that the units in which the alternations occur are larger than traditional words. For arbitrary alternations to become established and to be maintained in such units, these units must constitute units of storage, just as words do. Thus, the facts of French liaison and other cases of external sandhi are valuable in that they provide evidence for the existence and nature of storage units beyond the traditional word. The evidence presented so far strongly suggests that frequent fixed phrases are storage and processing units, as are constructions containing grammatical morphemes. Among the latter, more specific and more general constructions compete, leading to the gradual loss of the more specific construction – in this case, the one with liaison.

I have already mentioned that grammatical morphemes are entrenched in constructions; to describe this situation, I have proposed that grammatical constructions contain these grammatical morphemes as explicit phonological material. Thus, the same grammatical morphemes in different constructions are independent of one another. The more frequently used a construction is, the greater likelihood that its form will be maintained, rather than being replaced by some more productive construction (Bybee and Thompson 1997). It is not surprising, then, that certain liaison contexts, in particular those involving articles and their noun (as in 5) and those involving clitic pronouns and their verb (as in 6), are obligatory by all accounts and not tending towards loss of liaison. These constructions are those that are apparently regarded as having the tightest syntactic cohesion, but this cohesion could simply be the reflex of frequency of co-occurrence. No relative frequency counts are available to prove this point, but given the fact that almost all noun phrases contain either a definite or indefinite article and that subject and object clitic pronouns are used redundantly in the spoken language (M. Harris 1988:231–232, 235–236), the high frequency of these construction cannot really be in doubt.

Other reasons exist for regarding [ARTICLE + NOUN] constructions and [CLITIC + VERB] constructions as storage and processing units in Modern French. The maintenance of gender distinctions, which are overtly signaled primarily in the Singular article, suggests the storage of the article, both Singular and Plural, with the noun. The special treatment of articles with *h aspiré* words (the lack of liaison with certain vowel-initial nouns) also points to lexical representation of articles with nouns.[2] Studies of spoken French usage demonstrate that the subject and object clitic pronouns are now almost obligatory accompaniments to the verb, behaving perhaps more like prefixes than clitics, again suggesting lexical status (M. Harris 1988:232).

If frequency of co-occurrence is the main factor governing the appearance of the liaison consonant, then we would not expect to find such consonants between two randomly selected lexical items whose probability of co-occurrence is extremely low, and indeed, we do not. One case that might appear to contradict this claim is the small class of prenominal adjectives that link to a following vowel-initial noun, even in the masculine, as illustrated in 9, repeated here as 23.

(23) a. un petit [t] écureuil   'a little squirrel'
     b. un gros [z] amiral   'a fat admiral'
     c. un long [g] été   'a long summer'

The important point about the construction represented by these examples is that it is restricted to a small set of adjectives, listed in 24,

---

[2] If *h aspiré* words behaved as though they were consonant-initial with respect to liaison from all sources and with respect to elision (vowel deletion at the end of the preceding word), then it would make sense to treat them as though they were consonant-initial. However, Tranel reports that the exceptional status of these words is maintained most strongly in those contexts in which the syntactic constituency is tighter (1981:301, note 4).

many of which have a different meaning when used prenominally rather than in the more common postnominal position.

(24) Prenominal adjectives that condition liaison
    bon   'good'
    long   'long'
    nouveau   'new'
    mauvais   'bad'
    grand   'great, big'
    gros   'fat'
    petit   'little'

In a sense, then, these adjectives are partially grammaticized and not fully lexical in this construction. Still, the frequency of such adjectives in this construction and their resulting 'syntactic cohesion' must be lower than some of the other fully grammatical morphemes exhibiting liaison. It is thus predicted that liaison in this context will be maintained less than in other contexts.

A real test of the frequency hypothesis is possible with the data reported in Ågren (1973), where different inflectional forms of the same word with different frequencies and of the same word in different constructions with different frequencies can be compared for the maintenance of liaison. First, consider the forms of the copular verb *être*. Ågren points out that the presence of liaison is directly related to the token frequency of these forms. He gives the data in Table 7.1,

Table 7.1. *Number of Instances of Liaison for the Forms of the Verb* être *'to be'*

	L	NL	Total	Percentage of Liaison
est (3rd Sg. Pres. Ind.)	2,591	77	2,668	97%
sont (3rd Pl. Pres. Ind.)	242	38	280	86%
étant (Pres. Part.)	22	7	29	76%
était (3rd Sg. Impf.)	272	95	367	75%
êtes (2nd Pres. Ind.)	24	10	34	71%
étaient (3rd Pl. Impf.)	36	21	57	63%
sommes (1st Pl. Pres. Ind.)	43	31	74	58%
suis (1st Sg. Pres. Ind.)	65	74	139	47%
serait (3rd Sg. Fut.)	17	24	41	41%
soit (3rd Sg. Pres. Subj.)	22	32	54	41%
j'étais (1st Sg. Impf.)	6	23	21	21%

which shows the number of cases of liaison (L) and non-liaison (NL) and the number of times each item was used in the data he analyzed, listed according to the percentage of cases of liaison.

The correspondence between token frequency and percentage of liaison is quite close, except for two noticeable exceptions, both of which are explained by Ågren. The first is the high percentage of liaison for the relatively infrequent Present Participle *étant*. Here Ågren points out the high percentage of occurrence of liaison in the construction *étant* + Past Participle, which has liaison in 7 out of 8 cases in his data, 4 of which are the fixed phrase *étant entendu* 'being understood'. The other exception is the 1st Person Singular Present Indicative form *suis*, which has fewer instances of liaison than predicted by its token frequency. For this case, Ågren observes that it is common to reduce the sequence *je suis* 'I am' to [ʒsɥi]. In fact, further reduction of this sequence is often noted, even to [ʃɥi]. In Ågren's data, this reduced form tends to occur without liaison. In other words, the new contraction of *je suis* does not end in [z]. It appears that the reduction of this phrase, originally a casual speech phenomenon, is not compatible with liaison, which is, in this case, more common in more formal styles. In addition, however, there is a general tendency for liaison in verbs to involve the consonant [t] and for liaison in noun Plurals to involve [z]. Thus, all verb forms ending in [z] tend to have a lower percentage of liaison than those of comparable frequency involving [t].

The wide range of variation for liaison with the forms in Table 7.1 is especially interesting because these forms are all inflected forms of the same verb, and yet they behave quite differently under liaison conditions.[3] Their usage is regularizing, with the low-frequency forms more likely to undergo regularization than the high-frequency forms. The mechanism by which this occurs is parallel to the way in which irregular inflected forms such as *weep/wept* regularize. As a low-frequency English verb, its irregular Past may not be as easy to access as that of a high-frequency verb would be. Thus, a new Past can be made for it by using the base form and the regular Past Tense construction.

All of the forms of *être* listed in Table 7.1 occur in two variants, one with and one without a final consonant. The variant without a final

---

[3] Ågren found the same pattern among the inflected forms of the auxiliary *avoir* 'to have' and the semi-auxiliaries (as he calls them) *aller* 'to go', *falloir* 'to be necessary', *pouvoir* 'to be able to', *devoir* 'to have to', and *vouloir* 'to want'.

consonant occurs more commonly because it occurs before a consonant. Thus, in any given use of these forms, there is competition
between a construction that is more specific (the one for a word before
a vowel-initial word) and the more general construction (the one for
the word before a consonant-initial word. The latter construction will
apply more often, since consonant-initial words are more common than
vowel-initial ones (by at least 2 to 1). The more specific construction
can be preserved by frequency, which increases its lexical strength, but
there is always the option of using the more general construction, the
one without liaison.

The token frequency of the first element alone does not predict the
occurrence of liaison, nor should we expect it to. Rather, the important
variable is how often the two elements that are linked occur together,
and perhaps also the transitional probability between the first and
second element. For instance, Ågren counted the frequency of liaison
with the auxiliaries *aller* 'to go', *falloir* 'to be necessary', *pouvoir* 'to be
able to', *devoir* 'to have to', and *vouloir* 'to want'. When these are compared to one another, their frequency of occurrence does not correspond neatly with their percentage of liaison. Part of this lack of
correspondence is due to certain high-frequency forms such as *je
voudrais* 'I would like' not participating in liaison because final *s* in verb
forms shows less liaison and also because as a fixed expression, it has
become invariable. However, much of the variation among the auxiliaries is due to different rates of occurrence in specific constructions. All
of these auxiliaries occur with a following infinitive, the most frequent
infinitive of which is *être* 'to be' (226 out of 604 infinitives after an auxiliary). The second most frequently occurring infinitive was *avoir* 'to
have', which occurred 71 times. We would thus expect the highest rates
of liaison with *être*, and indeed this is what is found, as shown in Table
7.2. In fact, occurrences of *être* can be divided into those that constitute
the passive construction and those that are more copular in function.
Ågren found a different percentage of liaison in the two cases.[4]

A frequency effect is evident here, in that *être* is the most common
infinitive to follow these auxiliaries, as well as the most common site
for liaison. These findings are particularly clear with *devoir* and
pouvoir, which occur very frequently with *être*.

[4] In Ågren's chart *être* + Past Participle is distinguished from *être* + other word. I am assuming that most of the cases of the latter are not also passives, though they could be in cases
where the other word is followed by the Past Participle.

Table 7.2. *Ågren's Findings for Auxiliaries and Following Infinitives*

	Avoir		*être* + Past Participle		*être* + Other Word		*Other* Infinitives	
	L	NL	L	NL	L	NL	L	NL
aller	3	3	5	2	2	6	5	16
devoir	9	7	47	3	39	2	19	16
falloir	2	3	1	1	10	4	42	23
pouvoir	18	20	41	4	40	13	60	59
vouloir	3	3	3		2	1	14	53
Total	35	36	97	10	93	26	140	167
Percentage of liaison	50%		91%		78%		46%	

The very high percentage of liaison with *devoir* and *pouvoir* with *être* + Past Participle suggests very specific constructions for these modals and the Passive. The differences between this and the other uses of *être* confirm our statement that grammatical morphemes are very much entrenched in the particular constructions in which they occur. In this case, considerations of function also play a role in identifying constructions. When *devoir* and *pouvoir* are used with the passive, their subjects are not the agents of the main verb and, therefore, their subjects cannot be the agents of whom obligation or ability is being predicated. Note that in these cases, the auxiliary will ordinarily be in the 3rd Person. Thus the sequences *doi[t] être* + Past Participle and *peu [t] être* + Past Participle and their plural counterparts are constructions that have particular semantic readings that differ slightly from those of the same modals in active constructions. Consider 25 from Ågren (1973:83).

(25) Marie-Claire, est-ce que vous pensez que l'homme et la femme doivent [t] être placés sur le même plan intellectuel et social? 'Marie-Claire, do you think that man and woman should be put on the same intellectual and social level?'

This example illustrates the 'root obligation' sense of *devoir* as no specific source for the obligation is expressed. The auxiliary expresses only a very general sense of obligation. Similarly, 26 expresses 'root possibility' – general conditions exist for the possibility of completing the predication (Ågren 1973:86).

(26) Ca prouve, enfin qu'il y a, qu'il y a des choses extraordinaires qui
      peuvent [t] être faites encore.
      'This proves finally that there are, that there are extraordinary
      things that could be done still.'

Both root obligation and root possibility are more grammaticized functions than the obligation and ability meanings from which they arise
(Bybee et al. 1994, Nordquist 1999), and these functions may reinforce
the autonomy of the construction.

Finally, the viability of the liaison [t] in these constructions is
supported by the overgeneralization reported in Morin and Kaye
(1982:324).

(27) Ca doit bien t-être cuit, maintenant
      'It must be cooked by now'

In this example, the modal is fulfilling an epistemic function, which is
a further development from the root obligation reading.

Another interesting difference to observe in Table 7.2 is the difference between the cases where *être* is the following infinitive and those
cases, which are pooled together, in which a variety of lexical infinitives
occur. Although there are more of the latter in all, neither type
frequency nor token frequency of the construction as a whole are the
relevant variables. Since the maintenance of liaison is comparable to
the maintenance of irregularity in inflected forms, it is the token
frequency of the particular sequence that is instrumental in resisting
regularization.

On the other hand, liaison is still used with lexical infinitives about
half the time in the data analyzed. This means that forms such as 3rd
Person Singular *doit* or *peut* occur in constructions that supply the
liaison consonant in case the next word begins with a vowel. That is,
there are two constructions for *doit* (besides the ones mentioned
earlier) – 28a is the more general construction that is used with a
greater variety of infinitives, while 28b is the less general one. The more
general schema is gradually taking over and replacing the less general
one, except in very specific sequences with high token frequency.

(28)

    a. [[dwa]   INFINITIVE   ]
                                         obligation

    b. [[dwa]   -t-   [vowel]-INFINITIVE   ]
                                                  obligation

7.5   Syntactic Cohesion as Frequency of Co-occurrence

The data examined here concerning French liaison support the view that what has been called 'syntactic cohesion' is frequency of co-occurrence, the factor which determines the strength of the association between the first element and the second one. These connections are stored in memory and reinforced by frequent use. The argument for their memory storage is that the principles that we have established for morpholexical alternations operate at what has been taken to be this higher level of organization as well. In particular, the higher the frequency of the phrase or construction, the more likely it is to preserve liaison; the lower its frequency, the more likely it is to lose liaison by the application of a more general construction.

Collocations of words that are used frequently have strong memory representations. Just as morphologically complex words that occur with high frequency are more autonomous from their own paradigms and paradigms of other words, so high-frequency phrases grow more autonomous. That is, the connections between the words and morphemes of such phrases and other instances of the same words or morphemes become weaker. The potential loss of association is heightened both by phonetic and by semantic or functional change. The extreme outcome of this process is seen in grammaticization, where parts of grammaticized constructions are no longer associated with their lexical sources. For instance, English-speaking children have difficulty when they begin to read in identifying the form they know as *gonna* with the three morphemes *go*, *ing*, and *to*. In most liaison contexts, this loss of internal structure is not so extreme, but the syntactic cohesion referred to operates by these same mechanisms: frequent sequences are processed together, and this unity breaks down their relations with related items.

7.6   Taking the Phonology Seriously

As I mentioned earlier, it is common practice to try to predict French liaison, English *don't* reduction, and other cases of words with variants by reference to syntactic constituency and relations. However, all such attempts leave some cases unaccounted for, and many such analyses still require special mention of certain lexical items. Many researchers have concluded from this that the relation between syntactic structure and phonological rule application is indirect (Vogel and Kenesei 1990, among others). Another view, rarely proposed, would be that the relation between syntax and phonology is quite direct, but that we are not operating with the correct syntax. In other words, the phonological evidence could be taken to suggest different syntactic structures. Consider that in determining morphological structure, phonological evidence is often taken into account. Deciding whether or not a grammatical morpheme is an affix often involves some consultation of the phonological fusion between the proposed affix and stem. What would be the consequences of letting the phonological tail wag the syntactic dog?

In many cases, of course, nothing would change. In French, as liaison indicates, determiners go with nouns and clitic pronouns go with verbs. The only innovation I have proposed is that [DETERMINER + NOUN] and [CLITIC PRONOUN + VERB] sequences are stored in memory. Similarly, [ADJECTIVE + NOUN] and [NOUN + PLURAL + ADJECTIVE] sequences are syntactic constituents. However, English sequences of [PRONOUN + AUXILIARY], such as *I don't* and *I'm*, are not usually considered constituents. In fact, the highest-level syntactic break within a clause – that between the subject noun phrase and the verb phrase occurs within this sequence. Yet it is undeniable that auxiliaries contract and fuse with subject pronouns, not with the following verb, even though it is the auxiliary and verb that belong to the same constituent. The reason (Bybee and Scheibman 1999; see also Krug 1998) is that specific instances of [PRONOUN + AUXILIARY] are extremely frequent, much more so than any particular sequences of [AUXILIARY + VERB]. The phonological and usage facts, then, suggest an analysis of English much like that of Quileute, where the forms of subject pronouns are determined by modal functions (Andrade 1933:203ff.).

Along these same lines is another interesting case of French liaison concerning the copular verb in the 3rd Person Singular, *est*. In 47% of the uses of *est*, it occurs in the construction *est un* 'is a' + NOUN. That means the transitional probability of *un* after *est* is quite high (.47). In this sequence, liaison occurs 98.7% of the time, much more frequently than with any other uses of *est*, which strongly suggests a construction in which *est [t] un* is a constituent that precedes a noun. A comparable claim about English would be to say that *is a* is a constituent because of the frequency of use of these two items together. Of course, to say that *est un* or *is a* is a constituent is not to say that *un* + NOUN or *a* + NOUN are not also constituents. There is no reason why two constructions cannot overlap, giving ambiguous constituent analyses in cases such as these.

If we take usage as the determinant of constituency and syntactic hierarchy such that items frequently used together are constituents, then phonology is a valid indicator of constituency, since the same property, frequent co-occurrence, conditions the phonological alternations.

7.7 Conclusion

In a model in which memory storage includes not just individual words, but also phrases and constructions, lexicon and grammar are not strictly separated, but are integrated and subject to the same organizational principles (Bybee 1998, Langacker 1987). Any frequently occurring stretch of speech can be stored in memory and placed into categories with identical and similar units. Categorization occurs at multiple levels. Exemplars of the same word or phrase are mapped onto a single representation. Tokens of the same construction are similarly mapped onto a representation, and the items in the variable positions of the construction contribute to the formation of categories based on their semantic properties. Thus, in the English construction *X is going to Y*, the occurring tokens contribute to the formation of the categories *X* and *Y*. In the French construction [NUMBER + z + [vowel]-NOUN], the occurring tokens create the categories 'number' and 'noun' (Croft to appear).

A focus of this chapter has been alternations conditioned across word boundaries, or external sandhi. Is the analysis of external sandhi given here applicable to all cases? The answer, I believe, is yes. However, it is important to distinguish between phonetically conditioned processes that operate across word boundaries and those lexicalized instances that occur only within fixed phrases or constructions. Phonetically conditioned processes are observable within pause groups, wherever their conditioning environment occurs, both within words and across word boundaries, allowing for some variation. Examples are Spanish *s* aspiration at early stages of development, the spirantization of voiced stops in Spanish, vowel coalescence in Spanish, English flapping of coronal stops, and French *enchaînement* (resyllabification), to name just a few. Lexicalized external sandhi always has its source in phonetically conditioned processes that were originally not restricted to word boundary environments. Once they are thus restricted, they apply to grammatical morphemes, to small lexical classes, and only within specific constructions.

We have also examined the status of words and morphemes in memory storage. Nouns and verbs can emerge through their recurrent appearance in strings of speech and also by their ability to occur in isolation. However, in languages such as English and French, it is doubtful whether nouns and verbs are wholly independent units or whether they occur with certain clitics surrounding them. Thus, it is likely that nouns occur with their determiners as part of the same 'word' and verbs with their clitic pronouns, as in French *je te vois* 'I see you' or English *I see'im*. I have also argued that bound morphemes are never isolated but only occur in the words or constructions in which they appear in speech. Morphemes are identified across contexts by sets of lexical connections that associate both meaning and form.

I have argued in this chapter and the previous one that words, phrases, and constructions all share the same properties, which suggests that they are storage and processing units. Phonological reduction can occur within such units, creating alternations of the subparts of the unit with other instances of the same subparts. Thus 'word-level' phonology can also occur within frequent phrases and constructions. Moreover, given a sufficient level of frequency, constructions and phrases can maintain alternations much as words do. Storage units with high token frequency are conservative with respect to morphosyntactic regularization on the basis of productive patterns, just as multimorphemic words are. In addition, constructions with high type frequency, such as [DETERMINER + NOUN] constructions, can retain alternations. Some may even produce a gang effect, as in the case of the numerals adding a liaison /z/ where none is etymologically motivated (Section 7.3). It appears, then, that when it comes to phonological alternations, constructions and fixed phrases have many of the same properties as inflected words with alternations. This finding strongly suggests that frequent phrases and constructions are stored in memory and accessed in much the same way as inflected words.

8

Universals, Synchrony and Diachrony

8.1 Universals and Explanation

Any modern linguistic theory requires a statement concerning the role of language universals in explaining the nature of language. In the past few decades, many theorists have assumed that certain commonly occurring properties of language are inherent to the language acquisition device possessed by children (Chomsky 1965, 1975, and elsewhere). These innate features of language do not have to be acquired by children, but rather provide the framework around which language-specific structures are built. The notion that human beings bring to the task of language acquisition certain cognitive capacities that make this complex task possible undoubtedly has some validity, but whether these cognitive capacities equate directly to synchronic language universals, or even typological statements, is much more controversial. In this chapter, I argue that the relation between the human capacity for language and universals of language is much more subtle and complex. As I have argued in other works (Bybee 1988b, Bybee et al. 1994), I will argue here that the true universals of language are the dynamic mechanisms that cause language to change in certain systematic ways as it is used and as it is transmitted to new generations. Since linguistic change is regular and highly predictable, the synchronic systems that emerge as a result of the action of these dynamic forces have many properties in common.

The view of language universals presented in this chapter follows from diachronic typology as originally developed by Greenberg (see also Givón 1979, Bybee 1988b). My proposal is that underlying synchronic crosslinguistic patterns are the dynamic mechanisms that cause language to change in certain systematic ways as a result of use. Recent work in morphosyntax as well as phonology shows that linguistic change is regular and highly predictable. In fact, in some domains that have been studied, such as the grammaticization of tense and aspect, it is possible to state universals of change that are much stronger than any valid synchronic universals (Bybee and Dahl 1989). Thus, a new way of studying universals and typology is to hypothesize (on the basis of documented and inferred changes in related and unrelated languages) common unidirectional paths of change (Bybee et al. 1994, Croft 1990, Greenberg 1978a). Underlying these universal paths are recurrent mechanisms of change that operate on linguistic material to change it in predictable ways. Mechanisms of change are processes that occur while language is being used, and these are the processes that create language structure. Examples of mechanisms of change discussed here include the reduction of articulatory gestures (discussed in Chapter 4), the association of phonological material with lexical and morphological units, the formation of classes or gangs, regularization in morphology (all discussed in Chapter 5), and the formation of constructions out of frequently used sequences.[1] The synchronic systems that emerge from multiple applications of these dynamic forces have many properties in common.

In this view language is a self-organizing system, and grammar, including both morphosyntax and phonology, is an emergent property of that system (Lindblom et al. 1984). By postulating a finite set of mechanisms attributable to human neuromotor, perceptual, and cognitive capabilities, which interact with linguistic substance in acquisition and in language use, a range of possible language structures and units will emerge. Since the cognitive and neuromotor capabilities of humans are the same across cultures (even though there are individual differences within cultures), and since the uses to which language is put are similar across cultures, the structures emergent from this interaction will have very similar properties.

Chomsky's program for linguistic theory, which is adopted by most current theories, draws a relationship between language universals and explanation: a theory attains explanatory adequacy when it contains all the universal statements necessary for specifying the grammars of the languages of the world. The theory proposed here also postulates a strong relationship between universals and explanation, and so to the

---

[1] Mechanisms of change identified in grammaticization research also include semantic change by inference (Traugott 1989) and generalization (Bybee et al. 1994).

extent that it identifies the dynamic factors that create and recreate synchronic grammars, it will constitute an explanatory theory of language.

The mechanisms of change that create grammar are directly attributable to certain cognitive abilities, including the ability to categorize tokens of experience, the ability to make inferences, and the ability to use established tools for new means. In addition, certain 'lower-level' processes also contribute to change: habituation, by which an organism ceases to respond at the same level to repeated stimuli, leads to semantic bleaching (Haiman 1994); chunking, by which a frequently repeated sequence of elements becomes a single processing unit, leads to fusion of sequences of elements; and automatization, by which frequently used sequences become easy to access, leads to further reduction (Haiman 1994, Boyland 1996, Bybee to appear). Neuromotor processes such as these result from the genetically given properties of the organism. While these processes make language possible, they are also operative in nonlinguistic behavior and are thus not specific to language. Indeed, some of the abilities crucial to the acquisition and use of language are not even specific to humans.

Mechanisms of change are operative whenever language is being used. Change requires no extra processes, nor is change regarded as extraordinary. Rather the seeds of change are inherent to the system and the way it is used, so that change is ongoing in meaning, function, distribution, and form.

In this chapter, I demonstrate an approach to phonological universals based on these notions. We will observe how certain frequently occurring types of change have the effect of creating similar phonological rules, phoneme inventories, and syllable structures across languages. By identifying a few mechanisms of change that are commonly observed in languages, we come closer to identifying the true universals: the processes that create synchronic systems.

8.2   Searching for Universals

The issue of language universals is difficult because there appear to be so few absolute universals. In the domain of phonology, we cannot move much beyond the statement that all languages utilize consonants and vowels. Perhaps the most specific statements we can make would be to say that all languages have plain stop consonants and low vowels (Maddieson 1984). Yet any linguist with experience with several languages develops strong intuitions about which consonant and vowels, syllables patterns, and alternations are to be expected, and which are unusual.

Various proposals have been put forward to solve the problem of making valid crosslinguistic statements despite the rarity of true absolute universals. Jakobson (1948) and Greenberg in various works (e.g., 1966, 1978b) make extensive use of implicational universals – that is, statements that predict one feature in terms of another: if a language has X, it also has Y. For instance, Greenberg (1978b:257) formulates an implicational universal restated here as follows:

If a language has initial clusters of liquid-obstruent, then it also has initial clusters of obstruent-liquid.

An implicational universal that holds over phonemic inventories is stated in Greenberg (1966:21):

If a language has phonemic nasal vowels, then it also has phonemic oral vowels.

These statements capture the relative markedness of these phonological combinations: #LK is more marked that #KL (where K and L stand for obstruent and liquid, respectively), and nasal vowels are more marked than oral ones. Greenberg views such statements as simple generalizations over data. Jakobson, in contrast, relates such crosslinguistic statements to the order in which children acquire phonological structures, with the less marked being acquired before the more marked.

Chomsky and Halle (1968), following the program laid out for syntax in Chomsky (1965), according to which all speakers have access to the universal aspects of grammar, formulate marking conventions for a universal phonology. These marking conventions, which include statements such as 'minus is the unmarked value for the feature nasal', are considered to be substantive universals and a part of the innate language acquisition device. As language universals, they do not have to be included in the language-specific grammars and do not have to be specifically acquired by children.

One difficulty with the marking conventions is that while some are absolute universals (such as [+high] is [−low], which is true by definition), many of them are not absolute and can be overridden in particular languages. Thus, there are languages with vowels that are [+nasal], and most languages do have stops that are [+nasal]. The marking conventions, then, must be viewed as providing relative values. It is difficult, therefore, to see exactly what sort of innate conditions these are if they can be overridden in many languages. Still, there is something right about the basic idea that the presence or absence of a feature in a given context is more or less likely due to the inherent nature of the human language storage and processing capabilities.

Stampe's Natural Phonology suggested an approach to this problem: he proposed that children are born with an innate set of phonological rules, which must be suppressed in order for children to acquire the phonology of the language of their environment (Stampe 1973). One such rule would state that all vowels are non-nasal, and in order for children to learn nasal vowels, they must learn to suppress this rule. Until they do so, young children produce phonemic nasal vowels as oral vowels. Another such rule states that syllable-final obstruents are voiceless. Children acquiring a language with voiced and voiceless syllable-final obstruents, it is claimed, first pronounce these as voiceless and later suppress the devoicing rule to produce voiced syllable-final obstruents.[2]

Extensions of this approach in Naturalness Theory have been applied to all levels of grammar – phonology, morphology, and syntax (Dressler 1985, Dressler et al. 1987). Naturalness Theory proposes that there are a number of universal preference laws, some of them functional in nature, which are manifest in typological patterns as well as in child language. These preferences are sometimes in conflict, as when articulatory ease conflicts with perceptual distinctness, and such conflicts are resolved in different languages in different ways, giving rise to both commonalities and differences among languages. Dressler seeks to motivate preferences such as morphological transparency and paradigm uniformity in terms of semiotic principles and with reference to ease of processing at various levels. He claims that such principles shape languages and language acquisition, and that, while they are innate in the sense of being particular to human cognition, they are not literally a part of grammar.

A proposal to incorporate these notions into generative grammar arose in the 1990s under the name of Optimality Theory (Prince and Smolensky 1997), in which it is proposed that language is governed by

---

[2] A general problem with both Jakobson's and Stampe's approaches to child language is that careful studies have now revealed that children do not acquire the sounds of their language phoneme by phoneme, but rather word by word (Ferguson and Farwell 1975, Vihman 1996).

a set of universal well-formedness constraints that are innate – 'literally present in every language' (1605). Languages differ in the rankings they impose on the members of this set of constraints. Thus, all languages have constraints prohibiting syllable-final consonants, which can be overcome if the language happens to have syllable-final consonants. In Optimality Theory, the ranked constraints apply in the derivation of words and sentences.

While embracing the goals of Optimality Theory and Naturalness Theory to discover the universal tendencies operating crosslinguistically and their motivations, I am not in complete agreement on how the tendencies or constraints, once discovered, should be incorporated into a theoretical account. In addition, in my view, theories of compétence should be moving closer and closer to plausible theories of performance, but Optimality Theory seems to move in the opposite direction, as the style of derivation is psycholinguistically implausible in the extreme. Thus, I would like to propose a treatment of universals that takes advantage of data from both competence and performance, by proposing that the universal mechanisms that create language are activated in the on-line procedures for using language. That is, I envision a theory that can cope with the subtle relationship between crosslinguistic patterns and the cognitive abilities of human beings that enable them to articulate, perceive, store, and analyze linguistic material.

Some versions of Optimality Theory seem content with putting crosslinguistic generalizations directly into the innate language acquisition device without offering any explanation for them (Prince and Smolensky 1997). However, others are committed to the idea that universal phonological constraints have phonetic motivation or grounding (Hayes 1999, Kirchner 1998). Hayes (1999) discusses the issue of how to incorporate the findings of phonetic research into phonological theory. He raises the question of what the origin of grammar design is and offers two answers: one could attribute grammar design to an invariant Universal Grammar – a product of evolution, or one could look to the level of the individual child who constructs a grammar. Hayes chooses the second path and instead of arguing that phonetically grounded constraints are innate, he suggests that they are discovered inductively by the language learner, who also induces their phonetic grounding. The child, he argues, has direct access to its own production and perception apparatus and can make judgements about the relative difficulty of articulations and perceptual signals. By comparing these judgments to the phonetic map drawn from experience, 'a language learner could in principle use it to construct phonetically grounded constraints' (Hayes 1999:254).

When Hayes asks about the source of grammar design, he suggests two dynamic temporal dimensions that could be taken into account: biological evolution and first language acquisition. I would like to suggest that a third dynamic temporal dimension does most of the work of language design: namely, language change that takes place during language use. In the following, I address the issue of how universals of language can be taken to be the result of patterns of language change.

Consider, for example, the preference for open syllables exhibited crosslinguistically in both phonotactic patterns and in alternations. Optimality Theory proposes a constraint designated as NO CODA to describe this preference. Note that I would designate this generalization as a preference since it is not absolute. The experimental findings on phonotactic knowledge that were discussed in Chapter 4.7 (namely, that this knowledge reflects patterns of frequency in the lexicon) argue against the proposal that phonotactic knowledge can be described accurately by the ordering of constraints. Similarly, alternations such as those found in French liaison (discussed in Chapter 7), while originally motivated by syllable-final weakening and deletion, are now lexically and syntactically governed and not synchronically attributable to a phonetically grounded constraint.

A proposal more compatible with the data is one in which that the crosslinguistic patterns of syllable structure are considered to be the result of a diachronic tendency by which syllable-final consonants gradually weaken and delete. Such changes can be manifested in various ways: a syllable-final nasal can nasalize the preceding vowel and then delete; an [s] can lose its lingual articulation, becoming [h], which then deletes; or a syllable-final obstruent can assimilate to the following obstruent, producing a geminate that then degeminates. The result, however, is the same: an increase in the number of open syllables in the language.

The changes that create open syllables out of closed ones come about gradually. The on-line weakening of coda consonants creates gradual changes in the set of exemplars for each word, producing weaker consonants until gradual deletion occurs. Thus, I suggest that the appropriate universal is that the articulation of coda consonants involve gestures of lesser magnitude or duration than those found in syllable-initial consonants. This tendency has been described by Fujimura (1990), according to whom syllable-initial position is characterized by more forceful articulations, and by Browman and Goldstein (1995:26) as differences in the sequencing and magnitude of syllable-final gestures that 'might be caused by a general reduction of speaking effort over the time course of a unit.' The ultimate explanation for this tendency has not yet been discovered, but when it is, it will also explain the crosslinguistic patterns of phonotactics as well as the fossilized alternations caused by the deletion of syllable-final consonants.

In other words, the fact that open syllables are more common than closed ones and that weakened variants of sounds occur in coda position are neither innate constraints on the language acquisition device nor constraints that the child induces from experience, but rather are the result of a particular pattern of reduction that tends to weaken and eliminate final consonants should they arise. This pattern of reduction is manifested as language is used and gradually affects final consonants, eventually eliminating them. (For more details, see Section 8.5.)

In this view, the explanation for the common patterns that languages share is in the mechanisms that produce those states. Thus, we should investigate the operation of the articulatory, perceptual, storage, and categorizing mechanisms that change language over time. I would propose for phonology, as I have for morphology and for the development of grammar in general, that paths of change can be delineated more precisely than synchronic states can be, and that an essential component to any explanation for universals is reference to the mechanisms of change that create these paths of change (Bybee 1988b). In fact, we can formulate much stronger phonological universals as universals of change than as universals of synchronic descriptions. Such universals can be formulated for purely phonological processes, as we saw in Chapter 4, and also for the interaction of phonology with morphology and syntax, as we saw in Chapters 5 and 6. Thus, the general tendency identified by Browman and Goldstein (1992) and Mowrey and Pagliuca (1995) for gestures to increase in overlap and to decrease in magnitude over time predicts certain paths of change that give rise to variation and alternations. Similarly, the tendency for alternations to become associated with the morphology and lexicon is a diachronic tendency that gives rise to synchronic states in which alternations are lexicalized and morphologized. The tendency to regularize alternations and the minor tendency to form gangs that attract new members also create morphologies of certain types.

Not change!

This model for incorporating a diachronic dimension into linguistic theory is illustrated in the remainder of this chapter for certain phonological domains. In Section 8.3, I examine the possibility of explaining crosslinguistic similarities in phoneme inventories. In Section 8.4, I discuss the mechanisms underlying sound change and their implications for phonological universals. Section 8.5 considers the way that change affects syllable structure, taking up the proposal by Vennemann (1988) that syllable structure changes in certain predictable ways and creates syllables of certain well-defined types. Further evidence for the necessity of diachronic universals is presented in Section 8.6. Finally, in Section 8.7, I examine the way that structural constraints, such as Structure Preservation as proposed for Lexical Phonology, are the natural consequence of the morphologization and lexicalization of sound change.

8.3   Phoneme Inventories

The approach to universals just outlined is quite compatible with the approach taken by Lindblom et al. (1984) and Lindblom (1992), who propose that phoneme inventories are emergent from the interaction of certain phonetic tendencies over time. Lindblom et al. (1984) argue that rather than just assuming that languages have segments, it is necessary to explain why languages have structures that are conveniently describable as segments. Their view is that language is a self-organizing system, and that the phonetic signal evolves over time in such a way as to facilitate both production and perception.

These authors report on a simulation by a model that produces a series of rankings of CV syllables using two production-based criteria and two perception-based criteria. These criteria embody hypotheses about what factors shape phoneme inventories; in other words, in a fully articulated theory, the criteria should correspond in some way to the mechanisms that cause phonetic change that affects phoneme inventories. Lindblom et al. do not attempt this further correspondence and, while I discuss some mechanisms for sound change in the next section, I have not been able to identify in sound change all the factors that are used in the simulation.

The production-based criteria used for the ranking of syllables are sensory discriminability and less extreme articulation. The first of these favors distinct speech sounds that are more distant in the sensory space over those that are located closer to one another. Thus, a set of sounds that are dental, alveolar, and retroflex is less favored than one that contains labials, alveolars, and velars. The second condition favors less extreme deviations from neutral position, choosing, for example, an alveolar over a retroflex and choosing sequences that require less movement, say, between stop closure and vowel. That is, [gu] and [ɟi] require shorter movements than [gi] and [ɟu], respectively.

The two perceptual conditions are perceptual distance and perceptual salience. The first rank-orders all possible pairs of CV events in terms of their possibility for confusion. The second measures the distance between the initial and final auditory spectra and favors the more salient of these transitions – the ones with greater distance between the initial and final points. Note that conditions can work against one another. The articulatory conditions that favor less extreme movement between C and V can have the opposite effect of the perceptual condition that favors more auditory distance between C and V. Note further that these desiderata are simply stated as such – no claim is made as to the particular mechanisms that lead to changes in the dispreferred states.

In their simulation, Lindblom et al. (1984) rated 7 onsets with complete closure (corresponding to stop consonants) and 19 steady state formant sequences (corresponding to vowels) (yielding a total of 133 possible syllables) for the four criteria. In a series of computer trials, each beginning with a different syllable, they found that the fifteen syllables in (1) emerge as the optimal syllables ([ɟ] is a palatal stop):

(1) bi   bɛ   ba   bo   bu
     di   dɛ   da   do   du
     ɟi   ɟɛ   ga   go   gɨ

Among the interesting properties of this set is that, out of the seven points of articulation tested, four emerge as optimal. These include the three points of articulation for stops most common in the languages of the world and the palatal stop, which is a common variant of the velar in just the contexts in which it emerged as optimal. In addition, the five crosslinguistically most common vowels emerge in this simulation. Rather than fifteen syllables all containing different onsets and steady state offsets, the same onsets and offsets are repeated across the fifteen, leading to a pattern from which a small set of consonants and vowels emerge. The symmetry of this set further means that it is describable by a small set of features. Thus, both a coherent set of segments and a small set of features emerges from coupling preference for articulatory ease with perceptual discriminability.

What does this computer simulation correspond to in the evolution of segment systems in real languages? Presumably it corresponds to multiple phonological changes that have the effect of automating production and facilitating perception. To test it on real languages, we must be able to identify changes that are motivated by the factors that Lindblom et al. used in their simulations. Of the two articulatory criteria, the one favoring less extreme articulations could correspond to the common reduction in the magnitude of gestures discussed in Chapter 4. The other, which favors articulations that are not too similar to one another, has not been implicated in sound changes as far as I am aware. Of the two perceptual criteria, the one favoring syllables that are less likely to be confused could lead to the elimination or change of syllables that are difficult to discriminate. The other criterion, which favors salient transitions between consonant and vowel, has not been studied in connection with sound change. In the next section, I consider the interaction of the two criteria that have already been suggested to be important to sound change.

8.4 Two Main Mechanisms for Phonological Change

The theory of emergence outlined here focuses attention on mechanisms that are operative in sound change as the dynamic basis for the creation of segment inventories and phonological patterns. Sound change has not usually been probed with such a goal in mind. Before-and-after studies of change leave us with only post hoc guesses about causes and mechanisms. I have argued in Chapter 4 that patterns of lexical diffusion may be used as diagnostics for mechanisms of phonological change. Closer observation of ongoing changes will no doubt yield further data. For now, I would like to review the mechanisms mentioned earlier that can be further investigated in the context of relevant ongoing sound changes.

Chapter 4 discussed in some detail the proposal by Browman and Goldstein and Mowrey and Pagliuca. Both sets of researchers have proposed that one can understand phonological processes in terms of the sets of muscular gestures that produce speech, and that, furthermore, there are only two types of processes that affect gestural configurations: those that increase the degree of overlap of muscular activity and those that reduce the magnitude of this activity. While these mechanisms appear to be responsible for the majority of attested sound changes, it is important to bear in mind that the articulatory changes they handle all must also have an acoustic-perceptual component, as such changes in articulation cannot be transmitted across speakers except via the acoustic dimension. Thus, no study of articulatory mechanisms is complete without an associated study of the acoustic-perceptual mechanisms of transmission.

Also in Chapter 4, I treated three classes of exceptions to the general articulatory tendencies just described and explicated the mechanisms behind these other, less frequent types of change. First, although they are not common, articulatory strengthenings do occur, as in the case of the strengthening of glides in Spanish dialects. Second, simplification based on perceptual criteria, such as the unrounding of the front rounded mid vowel in Middle English, can be identified as a distinct mechanism, because of the pattern of lexical diffusion evidenced in this change. Third, generalization of a highly frequent pattern, such as the tendency of French final vowels to be tense, is a mechanism that produces phonological change even though it resembles analogical change more than sound change. Given the criteria identified in Lindblom et al.'s simulation, it is the second of these mechanisms that is potentially the most important in shaping phonological systems.

Suppose we could identify a few basic articulatory and perceptual mechanisms that govern all or most phonological processes and change. We would still have to ask why the phonological systems of the languages of the world differ from one another. As in other complex systems, these simple mechanisms of change create a wide range of states for a variety of reasons. First, at any given moment in time in any given language, these mechanisms have different material to work on. A [t] in one language is dental, in another alveolar; in one language it might be aspirated with a long delay in VOT, and in another it might be unaspirated. Second, there are crosslinguistically common paths of change for particular sounds, such as /p/ > /pf/ > /f/ > /h/, but a particular language at any given time might be at a different stage on such a path than other languages. One language might have a stable /p/ (English), another language might have affricated its /p/ to /pf/ (northern dialects of German), another language might have reached the /f/ stage (southern dialects of German), while another may have weakened /p/ to just voicelessness (Japanese). Synchronically, it is difficult to see any connection among these languages, but they may be following the same path of change. Third, these mechanisms work under different conditions, especially prosodic ones, such as stress and rhythm, which influence phonology. In fact, since timing is involved in most processes, the presence or absence of duration due to stress will have an effect on how a particular phonological change is manifested. It is hoped that the investigation of factors such as these will help us understand why, for example, intervocalic stops voice in some languages, spirantize in others, and flap in yet others.

Another factor to consider is that the phonetic details of a language are not universal but rather conventionalized for each language. Even though they originate in the universal mechanisms of reduction and compression that are characteristic of all motor behavior, that and apply in all languages, by the time they become salient parts of a phonology, they are already emancipated from their original phonetic function. They are language-specific and differ across languages in details of phonetic outcome or distribution.

8.4.1   Interaction of Mechanisms

The literature on universals often mentions the tension created by competing tendencies (Dressler 1985, Stampe 1973, Vennemann 1988, 1993) or, in the markedness literature, the tension between context-free markedness and context-sensitive markedness (Schachter 1968). That is, what is considered natural in context, say, voicing in intervocalic stops, is the opposite of the general tendency for stops to be voiceless. This can be thought of as the interaction between two mechanisms of change that apply successively. One mechanism is the overlapping of gestures that is motivated by the automation of articulation; the counteracting mechanism is the simplification of complex coarticulations, motivated either by perception or by articulation itself.

Complex or marked sounds arise by the retiming and/or reduction of gestures. The compression of gestures in particular may result in the piling up of articulations that create economy for the mature speaker who also knows the unpacked version of the articulation, but may, at the same time, create perception and production problems for the new user of the language. As a result, such articulations tend to be simplified over time. Examples of complex articulations created by overlap and reduction of gestures are nasalized vowels, palatal consonants, and secondary articulations (rounding, palatalization, velarization) – all examples of marked segments and all prone to further change.

Markedness conditions stated in terms of implicational universals derive from this interaction of context-sensitive coarticulation and context-free reinterpretation. The more marked segments are created from the less marked ones in certain contexts. It follows, then, that a language must have the less marked sounds before acquiring the more marked ones. The more marked sounds will also occur in a more restricted environment and thus have a lower text frequency (Greenberg 1966). Thus, the existence of nasal vowels in a language implies the existence of oral vowels, since nasal vowels are created out of oral ones in certain environments. The existence of front rounded vowels implies the existence of front unrounded and back rounded vowels, since these (especially the latter) are the source for front rounded vowels.

Some particular examples implicate child language acquisition in the simplification of complex articulations. Consider the example of the pronunciation of *doesn't, isn't* and *didn't* in many American dialects. The alveolar closure of the [n] is anticipated and totally overlaps the fricative articulation in the first two items, giving a complex articulation involving the sequencing of alveolar and glottal closure: *doesn't* [dʌdʔnt], *isn't* [ɪdʔnt], and *didn't* [dɪdʔnt]. I have observed young speakers of such a dialect produce a simplified sequence of [dʌ̃t], [ɪ̃t], [dɪ̃t] for these negative auxiliaries.

Children acquiring their first language often make substitutions of one sound for another similar sound, usually replacing a more marked segment with a less marked one. Nasalized vowels are usually produced first as non-nasalized, front rounded vowels are produced as front unrounded, fricatives are produced as stops, and so on. In fact, child language acquisition is often cited as a possible source of phonological change. However, there are several problems with this proposal.

First, the set of phonological substitutions found in child language is quite different than that found in sound change or in adult phonologies (Drachman 1978). Take consonant harmony, in which the consonants of a word are produced at the same place of articulation. This phenomenon is common in child language, as in [gʌg] for *bug*, [gɔg] for *dog*, and [bʌb] for *tub* (Menn 1989:82), but does not occur in adult phonology or in sound change. Radical cluster reduction is also common in child language ([bɛd] for *bread*), but rare in sound change. The substitution of stops for fricatives ([du] for *shoe*) is common in child language (Menn 1989:78), but not attested in sound change or in adult language. Conversely, assimilations and reductions common in adult phonologies and in sound change have not been observed in child language unless they are already present in the language that the child is acquiring.

There are, however, some substitutions that children make that do occur as sound changes. Two examples come to mind: the denasalization of nasal vowels and the unrounding of front rounded vowels, both of which are considered late acquisitions. Substitutions that persist into late stages of acquisition would be the ones that are most likely to have a permanent effect on the language.

As argued in Chapter 4, one possible criterion for identifying a type of sound change produced by a mechanism distinct from articulatory compression and reduction is lexical diffusion. Sound change produced by reduction and compression of gestures affects high-frequency words earlier and to a greater extent than it affects low-frequency words because reductive sound change occurs in real time as words are used. Words that are used more are more exposed to the possibilities of articulatory reduction and fusion. However, there are some sound changes that appear to have the opposite pattern of lexical diffusion, affecting low-frequency words first (Phillips 1984). In this way, they resemble regularization changes in morphology that reflect imperfect learning due to a low frequency in the input. Such changes, then, might be characterized as having their source in language acquisition, and they might also have a perceptual motivation.

The example that Phillips (1984) gives suggests that a series of diachronic changes may have the effect of creating more complex segments by the increased overlap of gestures and may then resolve this complexity by further loss of gestures. The monophthongization of Old English *eo* to [œ] was a retiming of gestures such that the lip-rounding gesture was anticipated and came to overlap the tongue-fronting gesture. The resulting vowel had a complex articulation that was not supported by other vowels in the language, as Middle English had no other front rounded vowels. As mentioned in Chapter 4.4.4, Gilbert and Wyman (1975) found that the front rounded vowel [œ] was the most difficult to discriminate for children and it was often confused with [ɛ]. If such vowels present an acquisition problem, their further change may come about through imperfect learning, in which case infrequent words will be affected before frequent words.

Thus, some patterns of change may represent the successive application of opposing mechanisms. First, a mechanism applies that creates overlapped articulations that are highly complex or perceptually weak, followed by a mechanism that simplifies these articulations.

8.4.2   Summary on Segment Inventories   Absolute

As mentioned earlier, there are very few absolute universals of segment inventories. It is possible, however, to formulate implicational universals that hold without exception, and it is possible to identify numerous statistical tendencies (Maddieson 1984). The absence of absolute universals and the gradualness of change both phonetically and lexically makes it appear unlikely that specific innate constraints are behind the patterns that are observable. Moreover, since segment inventories change over time, it appears more likely that what is behind the synchronic patterns are certain universal mechanisms of change that work on linguistic material to create the observable patterns.

The simulation of Lindblom et al. (1984) implied certain mechanisms that balanced articulatory and perceptual factors. I have not found direct evidence for the operation of all of these criteria as mechanisms of change, but we seem to have clear evidence for distinguishing two types of phonological change: one type that automates production by overlapping and reducing muscular events, and another type that simplifies consonants and vowels by eliminating some of the gestures that have been compressed. The question of the precise mechanisms that operate in any such change is important because only by understanding the mechanisms will we be able to explain how languages arrive at their current states. I have proposed here that one key factor in identifying mechanisms of change is lexical diffusion, since different mechanisms create different patterns of diffusion of change through the lexicon.   fast speech

8.5   Syllable Structure

8.5.1   Preference Laws

child v impl. t.

Common crosslinguistic patterns of syllable structure are also the product of characteristic patterns of change. Vennemann (1988) proposes a close relationship between patterns of phonological change and the typology of syllable structure. Linguistic change is motivated by preference scales on a variety of parameters. Since change follows these well-defined preferences, the range of syllable types found in the languages of the world is constrained. For example, a three-part preference law governs the codas of syllables, according to which a syllable coda is preferred:

    (i) the smaller the number of consonants in the coda,
    (ii) the greater the sonority (or the less the consonantal strength) of the offset, and
    (iii) the more sharply the sonority increases (or the consonantal strength decreases) from the offset towards the preceding nucleus.

Many different sound changes contribute to preferred codas. Some examples are the loss of syllable-final consonants, as when Spanish syllable-final [s] weakens to [h] and then deletes; the deletion of English final [t] and [d] in words like *and, hand, second*, and the sonorization of postnuclear consonants, as when English *milk* is produced as [mɪʊk] or when Latin *factum* becomes Portuguese *feito*.

The occurrence of such changes creates crosslinguistic regularities in syllable structure. The greater preference for loss of syllable-final consonants over syllable-initial ones leads to the generalization that languages allow a greater range of consonants in syllable-initial position than in syllable-final position, that some languages lack syllable codas, but that no languages lack syllable onsets. In addition, more subtle generalizations emerge from this pattern of change. For instance, with some exceptions, if a language allows syllable-final obstruents, it also allows syllable-final glides, liquids, and nasals. This follows from the fact that syllable-final obstruents can be converted into more sonorous consonants, or even vowels, but sonorants are not converted into obstruents in syllable-final position.

Although Vennemann (1988) explicates this relation between change and universals of syllable structure, he offers no explanation for the observed patterns, but rather defers explanations for the preferences to phoneticians. The relationship he envisions between the preference laws and particular sound changes is made clear in Vennemann (1993): language change is improvement on some parameter (see also Dressler 1990). The implication is that languages change in order to be in accord with the preference laws. Thus Spanish syllable-final [s] weakens to [h] and disappears because a syllable coda with no consonants is preferred over one with a consonant.

While the formulation of specific preference laws for syllable structure is an important achievement, it seems to me that a step in the reasoning has been omitted if we move directly from the observed patterns of syllables to the teleological assertion that changes occur in order to create these observed patterns. Clearly the changes do create these observed patterns, but something else must cause the changes to occur. Behind the synchronic patterns are highly predictable types of changes, and behind the changes are a few mechanisms of change, whose source is in the perceptual and neuromotor systems that make language possible.

We have already identified some of the ingredients we need for an explanation of changes affecting syllable codas. First, we have noted that phonological change is reductive in nature, both in terms of the magnitude of the gestures involved and in the time taken to execute them. Second, syllables are produced with a concentration of energy at the beginning and a diminution of energy at the end, making codas the more likely site for reductive processes. One pattern that this distribution of energy creates is that observed by Browman and Goldstein (1992, 1995): syllable-initial gestures are more synchronous than syllable-final gestures, which tend to be sequenced from more open to less open, even when these gestures comprise what is usually regarded as a single segment (see Chapter 4.6). This sequencing of postnuclear gestures makes syllable-final consonants more sonorous than syllable-initial ones. Another pattern that is created by the reduced energy in syllable codas is the reduction in magnitude of gestures, which leads to losses such as that observed in [s] > [h] (as in Spanish) or [l] > [ʊ] (as in English *milk* or *film*). In both of these cases, the tongue tip gestures are gradually reduced and eventually lost.

8.5.2 Paths of Change

In addition to specifying preferences for syllable structure, it is also possible to specify the particular changes that create this syllable structure. Vennemann (1988) lists numerous examples, all of which are crosslinguistically common. In Vennemann's theory, the preference laws are basic, and the particular changes are just means for achieving the preferred states. An emergentist's view, on the other hand, would be that the changes themselves, or the mechanisms behind them, are more basic, and that the cross-linguistically common patterns of syllable structure are emergent properties that arise from the multiple applications of these mechanisms. This view suits the data better since there are many languages that do not have 'preferred' syllables. In a sample of 74 languages picked to be maximally unrelated genetically,

7 (about 10%) allow the same consonants in codas that they allow in onsets and 40 (about half the sample) allow the strongest consonants (namely, stops) contrasting at least two points of articulation.[3] Indeed, Vennemann relies primarily on evidence from language change, rather than synchronic states, to establish preference scales (Vennemann 1993:325).

My proposal is that there are universal paths of change for phonology, just as there are for morphosyntax (Bybee et al. 1994). Once discovered and stated, these universal paths of change constitute much more powerful universals than any that can be formulated to cover the synchronic states of languages. Moreover, these paths of change provide explanations for particular synchronic states. Let us see how the paths of change that affect syllable structure can be used to explain the range of possible synchronic states.

Since the series of changes affecting syllable structure produces a cycle, we can select any arbitrary starting point to illustrate their effects. Consider a language that has primarily words of the type CVCV. If this language is a stress language, one of the vowels in this word will begin to reduce, as vowel reduction is extremely common in stress languages (Bybee et al. 1998). The culmination of vowel reduction is, of course, vowel deletion, which can create syllable-final consonants or consonant clusters: CVCV > CVC or CCV. That vowel deletion is the major source of syllable-final consonants and consonant clusters in general is supported by a correlation in the GRAMCATS database between languages with stress and languages with a greater number of syllable-final consonant positions ($p < .05$) and between stress languages and the number of consonant positions in the syllable in total ($p < .05$). No correlation was found between stress and the size of initial consonant clusters, probably because in the sample, languages with initial and penultimate stress, which would condition CVCV > CVC, made up 77% of the stress languages, whereas those with final stress, which would condition CVCV > CCV, only 15% (Bybee et al. 1998).

Once syllable-final consonants are established, they begin to undergo weakening processes. At first, such processes are allophonic in nature: when vowel deletion has freshly occurred, stops that have

---

[3] The sample used for this survey is the GRAMCATS sample, which contains 76 languages randomly selected within genetic groups to be maximally unrelated genetically (Bybee et al. 1994). Only 74 languages were actually used, due to the absence of reliable phonological information in two of the reference grammars used for the study.

been put into syllable-final position may be released and then later come to be unreleased. Contrasts in glottal states for syllable-final stops seem difficult to maintain both articulatorily and perceptually, so it is common to have neutralization of glottal state for stops in syllable-final position. For instance, in the GRAMCATS sample, out of the 37 languages that have more than one stop series and allow stops in syllable-final position, 16 allow all glottal states contrasting in the language to occur there, but 21 neutralize such contrasts. Of these, 12 have voicing contrasts but only allow voiceless stops syllable-finally.[4] Three contrast voiced, voiceless, and aspirated stops, but only allow voiceless unaspirated in syllable-final position.[5] Shuswap, Maidu, and Abkhaz neutralize some glottalized stops syllable-finally, and Dakota has no glottalized, aspirated, or unaspirated voiceless stops in this position, but only plain voiced stops. Cantonese and Alyawarra neutralize the aspiration distinction finally, allowing only unaspirated stops.

Common paths of change for the supraglottal features of syllable-final consonants involve reduction of two types: a type that results in a total deletion and one that moves towards greater sonority. The former involves both substantive and temporal reduction, and the latter involves primarily substantive reduction with the maintenance of temporal duration (in the terms of Mowrey and Pagliuca 1995; see Chapter 4).

Paths that move toward total deletion in syllable-final position include the following:

(i)   Total assimilation of a syllable-final obstruent to the following one, giving rise to geminate consonants. In degemination, the process is complete.

$C_iC_j \quad > \quad C_jC_j \quad > \quad C_j$

Latin		Old Spanish		Modern Spanish	
ipse	>	isse	> esse	> ese	'that'
gypsu	>		yesso	> yeso	'gypsum'
septembre	> settembre			> setiembre	'September'
scriptura	> *escrittura			> escritura	'writing'

(Menéndez-Pidal 1968:142)

---

[4] The languages are Basque, Kanakuru, Alawa, Palaung, Halia, Tanga, Buli, Ono, Bongu, Chepang, Uigur and Atchin.

[5] The languages are Lao, Haka, and Nung.

(ii)   Gradual decay of supraglottal gestures while maintaining, at least
       for a while, some glottal articulations

Standard Spanish		Dialectal Spanish		
[esto]	>	[ehto]		'this'
[mizma]	>	[mifima]		'same'
[entonses]	>	[entonseh]	> [entonse]	'then'

Careful English		Casual English	
[bætmæn]		[bæʔmæn]	'Batman'
[bækpæk]		[bæʔpæk]	'backpack'
[pɪknɪk]		[pɪʔnɪk]	'picnic'

(iii) Loss of final nasal consonant with or without nasalization of the
       vowel
       In Northern Italian dialects, a nasal after a stressed vowel is lost
       (Hajek 1997:86).

Latin			Milan	Lugo	Bergamo
CANE	>	[ka:n]	[kã:]	[kɛ̃:]	[ka(:)]

The nasal may delete in unstressed syllables without affecting the
vowel:

Latin			Riminese	Cairese
ASINU	>	['asin]	['ɛ:znə]	['ɐ:zu]

Sonorization of syllable-final consonants results in liquids, glides, or
lengthened vowels.

(i)   Obstruents can become liquids or glides by the weakening of
       certain gestures.

Latin	Old Spanish	Portuguese	Modern Spanish	
DEBITA	debda		deuda	'debt'
FACTU		feito	hecho	'fact, done'
LACTUCA		leituga	lechuga	'lettuce'

In Hausa, syllable-final labials and velars become [w], and dentals
become [r] (Vennemann 1988:26).

Syllable-final		Syllable-initial	
makawɲiya	'a blind one (fem.)'	makāfo	'a blind one (masc.)'
talawči	'poverty'	talaka	'a poor one'

15√5 × 15√5

75 1125 × 5625

hawni	'left side'	bahago	'a left-handed one'
farke	'merchant'	fatāke	'merchants'
marmaza	'very fast'	maza	'fast'
harše	'tongue'	halusa	'tongues'

(ii) Liquids can become glides by the loss or retiming of lingual gestures, as in Brazilian Portuguese.

[azuladu]	'bluish'	[azuw]	'blue'
[pexfiladu]	'lined up'	[pexfiw]	'profile'
[mɛladu]	'molasses'	[mɛw]	'honey'

(iii) Final consonants can lose lingual gestures without temporal reduction (or, as usually stated, consonants delete with compensatory lengthening of vowels). A comparison of the Dolakha and Kathmandu dialects of Newari illustrates this change (Genetti 1994:43).

Dolakha	**Kathmandu**	
jāŋgal	jhāāgaa	'bird'
nugar	nugaa	'heart'
kok	kwaa	'crow'

These examples show that there are multiple ways in which the number of open syllables can be increased in a language. These paths of change and the mechanisms underlying them create the crosslinguistic syllable structure patterns that are observable in the comparison of synchronic language states. There are three tiers of phenomena, as shown in Figure 8.1, each one giving rise to the next.

Knowledge of universals may be gleaned from information at any one of these tiers, but our basic goal should be the discovery of the mechanisms that create language. Thus the study of phenomena closest to the mechanisms of change will be the most revealing – that is, phonological change itself. Language-particular synchronic states and even broadly crosslinguistic data provide only indirect evidence for the true universals of human language.

SYNCHRONIC CROSSLINGUISTIC GENERALIZATIONS

⇑

UNIVERSAL PATHS OF CHANGE

⇑

UNIVERSAL MECHANISMS OF CHANGE

Figure 8.1. The relations among three tiers of crosslinguistic phenomena.

8.6 More Evidence against Universals as Purely Synchronic

I have been arguing here for an essential diachronic component for the understanding of language universals and typology. Other current theories, such as Optimality Theory, posit synchronic universals that are crosslinguistic observations incorporated directly into the grammar, without further analysis that might reveal what sort of mechanism underlies the crosslinguistic patterns. I have argued in Section 8.2 that the observation of the crosslinguistic pattern is not itself the universal, but rather that the mechanisms of change and the factors involved in activating that mechanism to create the pattern are the more basic universals.

Further evidence for the necessity of positing a diachronic dimension for universals is the fact that there are diachronic paths whose synchronic manifestations do not lead to observations that one would want to label as 'universals'. An interesting example concerns the status of [h] as a syllable-final consonant. In English /h/ is restricted to syllable-initial position, while in Spanish we find changes that create syllable-final [h] where none existed previously, giving a syllable-final [h] but no syllable-initial one. Is [h] both favored and disfavored in syllable codas?

The crosslinguistic facts are equally ambiguous when viewed synchronically. In the 45 languages of the GRAMCATS sample that have an /h/ and that allow syllable-final consonants, we have the following situation:

(i) 7 languages allow all consonants in coda position, including /h/.

(ii) 12 languages allow /h/ but have restrictions on other consonants: 4 of these allow /h/ but have heavy restrictions on other consonants (Chacobo allows only fricatives, Koho allows no obstruents at all, Palantla Chinantec allows only velars, Slave allows only /ʔ/ and /h/).

(iii) 1 language allows /h/ in syllable-final but not in syllable-initial position (Palaung).

(iv) 25 languages do not have syllable-final /h/: 10 of these have heavy restrictions on coda position, but 15 allow many other consonants in this position.

More languages exclude /h/ from codas than allow it, but a significant minority (the languages in ii and iii) not only allows /h/ there, but seems to favor it in the sense that it is one of a small set of allowed coda consonants. No implicational universals can be formulated to cover the situation. It cannot be said that /h/ in codas implies the existence of obstruents in codas (as, say, nasals do), nor is the reverse true. There are simply no synchronic universals concerning /h/ in the codas of syllables.

However, there are diachronic universals that are missed if only synchronic patterns of syllable structure are described. The reason that /h/ occupies an ambiguous position as a coda consonant is that it is both the product of change and the target of further changes. A single path of change covers both its appearance in codas and its disappearance from them. I suggest that the fricatives /s/, /f/, and /x/ tend to lose their supraglottal articulation in all positions, but earlier where more reduction occurs (that is, syllable-finally). The resulting /h/ then has a tendency itself to be lost, again, in all positions, but more so in syllable-final position. Thus, a single one path of reduction /f/, /s/, /x/ > /h/ > ø covers all of these possibilities and explains why some languages do not allow /h/ in codas and others allow /h/ but exclude other consonants. It also makes predictions about further changes – namely, that syllable-final voiceless fricatives reduce to /h/ and that syllable-final /h/ is eventually lost.

This example underscores the difference between synchronic constraints and a theory of diachronic typology. The path of change /s/, /f/, /x/ > /h/ > ø does not exist in any language per se, but the mechanisms that underlie it – the tendency toward reduction of gestures – does exist in all languages at all times. For a constraint-based theory, this path of change could be broken up into two constraints that could be ranked differently in different languages to allow or disallow /h/ in a coda. But what would be missed in such an account would be the clear relationship between the two constraints. Moreover, no predictions about future states of the language would be made, whereas a path of change gives us a clear set of predictions about future changes.

Paths of change are not innate. The mechanisms behind them might have some innate components, but these may not be specific to language. Even the mechanisms proposed to be universal in the sense that they are essential to human language need experience with language before they can begin to operate. The changes we have discussed in this chapter occur in real time as language is used.

8.7   Diachronic Sources for Formal Universals: The Phonemic Principle and Structure Preservation

Even formal or structural universals are the result of common paths of change and the interaction of common paths of change. A diachronic approach explains both the general formal or structural tendencies and the fact that most such tendencies are only tendencies – they cannot be formulated as absolute because they have exceptions.

Take as an example the phonemic principle. The strictest application of this principle would predict that all phonemes contrast in all positions, that allophones are in complementary distribution and can be predicted in phonetic terms, and that every phone has a unique assignment to a phoneme. The facts show that all languages have some phonemes that behave this way, but some that do not. Some have a very restricted distribution (e.g., /h/ in English), some have variants that seem to require nonphonetic information (/x/ and [ç] in German), and some are not uniquely assignable to a phoneme (the flap in English).

Why does the phonemic principle work at all? Phonemes have allophones because of changes that occur in particular phonetic contexts; because these changes are determined by phonetic context, variants of phonemes are in complementary distribution and predictable in phonetic terms. Because of the way phonetic change (sound change) operates, some variants are reduced to zero in some contexts ([h] in syllable-final position), resulting in phonemes with a restricted distribution. Other phonemes only arise in certain positions (e.g., [ŋ] in English), again giving distributional gaps. Some sound changes neutralize contrast in certain positions. Thus, this structural principle and its manifestations are emergent from the properties of sound change.

In addition, as we saw in earlier chapters, sound changes begin to become involved with lexical and morphological material very early in their development, creating situations where word boundaries or specific morphemes predict the phonetic shape of erstwhile phonemes. Thus, for any given synchronic slice in any language, we find that the phonemic principle works quite well for the majority of contrasts and for predictable phonetic variants, but that in addition, there are certain lexical and morphological environments where the principle breaks down. The resulting issues, such as whether English [ŋ] or German [ç] are phonemes, have attracted much attention as linguists try to analyze them in ways that make it possible to maintain the principles as absolutes.

But if the principles are viewed as emergent from the nature of the diachronic processes that create synchronic states, then there is no reason to expect them to be absolute. Rather, we expect further change and can even predict its direction in many cases because we have identified universal paths of change.

Consider the principle discussed in the context of Lexical Phonology as Structure Preservation, which stipulates that 'any rule that introduces marked specifications of lexically non-distinctive features must be postlexical' (Kiparsky 1985:93). In other words, lexical rules manipulate the contrastive features of the language, and any rule that changes or adds noncontrastive features must apply at the end of the derivation. This principle describes the tendency (for it is only a tendency) for morphologically and lexically conditioned alternations to be alternations between phonemes, while alternations among allophones have phonetic conditioning. This tendency was also identified by American structuralists, for whom morphophonemics involved alternations between phonemes, and who attempted to rule out the use of morphological information in the assignment of allophones to phonemes. However, such constraints on synchronic grammars have always been controversial because exceptions crop up that are not easily explained away.

If we view this tendency as the result of certain diachronic trends, we both explain why it holds in general and predict the existence of exceptions of certain well-defined types. Since alternations of all types are created by sound change, they are initially conditioned phonetically and, as we saw in Chapters 5 and 6, only gradually take on lexical, morphological, or syntactic associations. This is one major universal path of change: a movement from phonetic conditioning to nonphonetic conditioning. Another major generalization over specific phonetic paths of change is an increase in the phonetic distance between the unchanged variant and the variant affected by the change (Hooper 1976a, Janda 1999). Thus a velar might first palatalize to [kʲ], but then later move on to [č] and, as in the history of Spanish, continue to [ts], which changes to [θ] or [s], eventually creating an alternation between /k/ and /s/ (*electríco, electricidad*).[6] In this process, either new phones are created that are sufficiently different phonetically from their sources to be regarded as separate phonemes, or the altered phones merge with already existing phonemes. At the same time, they come to contrast with what were originally their sources. The fact that these paths of change progress in parallel with the morphologization, increasing phonetic distance, and the establishment of new contrasts,

---

[6] It is admittedly difficult to state objective criteria for phonetic distance since what is allophonic in one language might be contrastive in another. However, by the specification of particular paths of phonetic change, we can eventually gauge how far a change has moved beyond its original form.

all occurring simultaneously, leads to a situation in which lexicalized or morphologized alternations usually affect what are also established phonemic contrasts in the language.

While these parallel changes are ongoing, however, we often have situations whose analyses are controversial, because they display some intermediate set of properties. We have already discussed the case of German [ç], which is largely predictable, but occurs outside its phonetic environment in one particular morpheme, the diminutive *-chen* (see Chapter 3.6), and which, at least in some dialects is further removed from its source [x], by becoming palato-alveolar [š]. Another case we discussed is vowel length in English, which is becoming marginally contrastive (Chapter 3.4.2). These cases can all be explained by reference to their position along these parallel and universal paths of change. That is, since lexicalization occurs gradually, Structure Preservation cannot be an absolute constraint. However, because several changes are usually occurring in parallel – lexicalization, increased phonetic differentiation, and development of contrast – the situation described by Structure Preservation usually holds.

The diachronic viewpoint, then, provides an explanation both for the structural tendencies and for the exceptions to them. As mentioned earlier, the real job is to understand the mechanisms of change that create these common paths of development. Phonetic alternations arise from the automating tendencies that reduce and compress articulatory gestures. Further changes may result from the reinterpretation of complex coarticulated gestures as simpler configurations, moving a segment farther away from its 'starting point'. The tendency to lexicalize and morphologize phonetic alternations follows from memory representations that include both phonetic detail and information about grammatical context as well as from the tendency to form lexical and morphological classes or categories with strings of phonologically and semantically related material. The operation of these processes in context, as language is used, creates the layers of phonetics, phonology, and morphophonology that we see in language after language. These well-attested structures are just the result of the interaction of common trajectories of change, which themselves are fueled by the human neuromotor ability to produce complex motor sequences by storing and automating recurring stretches of behavior and by the cognitive ability to categorize and organize stretches of linguistic experience in memory.

References

Abler, W. 1989. On the particulate principle of self-diversifying systems. Journal of Social and Biological Structures 12.1–13.

Ågren, John. 1973. Etude sur quelques liaisons facultatives dans le français de conversation radiophonique: fréquence et facteurs, Uppsala: Acta Universitatis Upsaliensis. Studia Romanica Upsaliensia 10.

Alegre, Maria, and Peter Gordon. 1999a. Frequency effects and the representational status of regular inflections. Journal of Memory and Language 40.41–61.

Alegre, Maria, and Peter Gordon. 1999b. Rule-based versus associative processes in derivational morphology. Brain and Language 68.347–54.

Andersen, Henning. 1973. Abductive and deductive change. Language 49.765–93.

Anderson, John R. 1993. Rules of the mind. Hillsdale, NJ: Erlbaum.

Andrade, Manuel J. 1933. Quileute. New York: Columbia University Press.

Aske, Jon. 1990. Disembodied rules vs. patterns in the lexicon: testing the psychological reality of Spanish stress rules. Berkeley Linguistics Society 16.30–45.

Baayen, R., and Rochelle Lieber. 1991. Productivity and English derivation: a corpus-based study. Linguistics 29.801–43.

Baxter, A. R. W. 1975. Some aspects of naturalness in phonological theory. Oxford University B. Litt. thesis.

Bergen, Dick van. 1995. Acoustic and lexical vowel reduction. University of Amsterdam dissertation.

Bills, Garland D. 1997. New Mexican Spanish: demise of the earliest European variety in the United States. American Speech 72.154–71.

Bloomfield, Leonard. 1933. Language. Chicago: University of Chicago Press.

Booij, Geert. 2000. Lexical storage and phonological change. The nature of words, ed. by Kristin Hanson and Sharon Inkelas, Stanford, CA: CSLI.

Booij, Geert, and Dann de Jong. 1987. The domain of liaison: theories and data. Linguistics 25.1005–25.

Boyland, Joyce Tang. 1996. Morphosyntactic change in progress: a psycholinguistic approach. Berkeley: University of California dissertation.

Browman, Catherine P., and Louis M. Goldstein. 1990. Tiers in articulatory phonology, with some implications for casual speech. Papers in Laboratory Phonology I: between the grammar and physics of speech, ed. by John

Kingston and Mary Beckman, 341–76. Cambridge: Cambridge University Press.

Browman, Catherine P., and Louis M. Goldstein. 1991. Gestural structures: distinctiveness, phonological processes, and historical change. Modularity and the motor theory of speech perception, ed. by I. Mattingly and M. Studdert-Kennedy, 313–38. Hillsdale, NJ: Erlbaum.

Browman, Catherine P., and Louis M. Goldstein. 1992. Articulatory phonology: an overview. Phonetica 49.155–80.

Browman, Catherine P., and Louis M. Goldstein. 1995. Gestural syllable position effects in American English. Producing speech: contemporary issues, for Katherine Safford Harris, ed. by F. Bell-Berti and L. J. Raphael, 19–34. Woodbury, NY: American Institute of Physics.

Brown, Esther. 1999a. The posterioriation of labials in Spanish: a frequency account. Albuquerque, University of New Mexico, ms.

Brown, Esther. 1999b. The role of alternating phonetic environments and word frequency in the development of Latin *f-* in Spanish. Paper presented at the 2nd Annual Meeting of the High Desert Linguistic Society, Albuquerque, NM.

Burzio, Luigi. 1996. Surface constraints versus underlying representation. Current trends in phonology: models and methods, ed. by Jacques Durand and Bernard Laks, 123–41. Salford: European Studies Research Institute.

Bush, Nathan. 2001. Frequency effects and word-boundary palatalization in English. Frequency and the emergence of linguistic structure, ed. by Joan Bybee and Paul Hopper, 255–80. Amsterdam: Benjamins.

Bybee, Joan L. 1985. Morphology: a study of the relation between meaning and form. Philadelphia: Benjamins.

Bybee, Joan L. 1988a. Morphology as lexical organization. Theoretical morphology, ed. by M. Hammond and M. Noonan, 119–41. San Diego, CA: Academic Press.

Bybee, Joan L. 1988b. The diachronic dimension in explanation. Explaining language universals, ed. by J. Hawkins, 350–79. New York: Blackwell.

Bybee, Joan L. 1994. A view of phonology from a cognitive and functional perspective. Cognitive Linguistics 5.285–305.

Bybee, Joan L. 1995. Regular morphology and the lexicon. Language and Cognitive Processes 10.425–55.

Bybee, Joan L. 1998. The emergent lexicon. Chicago Linguistic Society 34: the panels, ed. by M. Gruber, D. Higgins, K. Olson, and T. Wysocki, 421–35. Chicago: Chicago Linguistic Society.

Bybee, Joan L. 1999. Usage-based phonology. Functionalism and formalism in linguistics, volume 1: general papers, ed. by Michael Darnell et al., 211–42. Amsterdam: Benjamins.

Bybee, Joan L. 2000a. Lexicalization of sound change and alternating environments. Papers in Laboratory Phonology V: acquisition and the lexicon, ed. by Michael Broe and Janet Pierrehumbert, 250–68. Cambridge: Cambridge University Press.

Bybee, Joan L. 2000b. The phonology of the lexicon: evidence from lexical diffusion. Usage-based models of language, ed. by M. Barlow and S. Kemmer, 65–85. Stanford, CA: CSLI.

Bybee, Joan. 2001. Frequency effects on French liaison. Frequency and the emergence of linguistic structure, ed. by Joan Bybee and Paul Hopper, 337–59. Amsterdam: John Benjamins.

Bybee, Joan L. To appear. Mechanisms of change in grammaticization: the role of frequency. Handbook of historical linguistics, ed. by Richard Janda and Brian Joseph. Oxford: Blackwell.

Bybee, Joan L., and Mary Alexandra Brewer. 1980. Explanation in morphophonemics: changes in Provençal and Spanish preterite forms. Lingua 52.201–42.

Bybee, Joan L., Paromita Chakraborti, Dagmar Jung, and Joanne Scheibman. 1998. Prosody and segmental effect: some paths of evolution for word stress. Studies in Language 22.267–314.

Bybee, Joan L., and Östen Dahl. 1989. The creation of tense and aspect systems in the languages of the world. Studies in Language 13.51–103.

Bybee, Joan L., and Carol L. Moder. 1983. Morphological classes as natural categories. Language 59.251–70.

Bybee, Joan L., and Elly Pardo. 1981. On lexical and morphological conditioning of alternations: a nonce-probe experiment with Spanish verbs. Linguistics 19.937–68.

Bybee, Joan L., and Dan I. Slobin. 1982. Rules and schemas in the development and use of the English past tense. Language 58.265–89.

Bybee, Joan L., Revere Perkins, and William Pagliuca. 1994. The evolution of grammar: tense, aspect and modality in the languages of the world. Chicago: University of Chicago Press.

Bybee, Joan L., and Joanne Scheibman. 1999. The effect of usage on degree of constituency: the reduction of *don't* in American English. Linguistics 37.575–96.

Bybee, Joan L., and Sandra Thompson. 2000. Three frequency effects in syntax. Berkeley Linguistics Society 23.65–85.

Carramazza, A., and G. Yeni-Komshian. 1974. Bilingual switching: the phonological level. Canadian Journal of Psychology 28.310–18.

Chen, Matthew. 1970. Vowel length variation as a function of the voicing of the consonant environment. Phonetica 22.129–59.

Chomsky, Noam. 1965. Aspects of the theory of syntax. Cambridge, MA: MIT Press.

Chomsky, Noam. 1975. Reflections on language, New York: Pantheon Books.

Chomsky, Noam. 1995. The Minimalist Program. Cambridge, MA: MIT Press.

Chomsky, Noam, and Morris Halle. 1968. The sound pattern of English. New York: Harper and Row.

Clahsen, Harald. 1999. Lexical entries and rules of language: a multidisciplinary study of German inflection. Behavioral and Brain Sciences 22.991–1060.

Clahsen, Harald, and M. Rothweiler. 1992. Inflectional rules in children's grammars: evidence from the development of participles in German. Morphology Yearbook 1–34.

Cole, Jennifer, and José Ignacio Hualde. 1998. The object of lexical acquisition: a UR-free model. Chicago Linguistic Society 34: the panels, ed. by M. Gruber, D. Higgins, K. Olson, and T. Wysocki, 447–58. Chicago: Chicago Linguistic Society.

Coleman, John. 1996. The psychological reality of language-specific constraints. Paper presented at the 4th Phonology Meeting, University of Manchester, Manchester, England.

Coleman, John, and Janet Pierrehumbert. 1997. Stochastic phonological grammars and acceptability. Computational phonology: Proceedings of the 3rd Meeting of the ACL Special Interest Group in Computational Phonology, 49–56. Somerset, NJ: Association for Computational Linguistics.

Comrie, Bernard. 1976. Aspect. Cambridge: Cambridge University Press.

Comrie, Bernard. 1985. Tense. Cambridge: Cambridge University Press.

Croft, William. 1990. Typology and universals. Cambridge: Cambridge University Press.

Croft, William. To appear. Radical Construction Grammar: Syntactic theory in typological perspective. Oxford: Oxford University Press.

D'Introno, Francisco, and Juan Manuel Sosa. 1986. Elisión de la /d/ en el español de Caracas: aspectos sociolingüísticos e implicaciones teóricas. Estudios sobre la fonología del español del Caribe, ed. by Rafael A. Núñez Cedeño, Iraset Páez Urdaneta, and Jorge Guitart, 135–63. Ediciones La Casa de Bello.

Dahl, Östen. 1985. Tense and aspect systems. Oxford: Blackwell.

Daugherty, K. G., and M. S. Seidenberg. 1994. Beyond rules and exceptions: a connectionist modeling approach to inflectional morphology. The reality of linguistic rules, ed. by S. D. Lima, R. L. Corrigan, and G. K. Iverson, 353–88. Amsterdam: Benjamins.

Delattre, Pierre. 1966. Studies in French and comparative phonetics. The Hague: Mouton.

Denes, P. 1955. Effect of duration on the perception of voicing. Journal of the Acoustical Society of America 27.761–64.

Derwing, Bruce L., and William Baker. 1977. The psychological basis for morphological rules. Language learning and thought, ed. by John Macnamara, 85–110. New York: Academic Press.

Drachman, Gaberell. 1978. Child language and language change: a conjecture and some refutations. Recent development in historical phonology, ed. by Jacek Fisiak, 123–44. The Hague: Mouton.

Dressler, Wolfgang U. 1977. Morphologization of phonological processes. Linguistic studies offered to Joseph Greenberg, ed. by A. Juilland, 313–37. Saratoga, NY: Anma Libri II.

Dressler, Wolfgang U. 1985. Morphonology: the dynamics of derivation. Ann Arbor, MI: Karoma.

Dressler, Wolfgang U. 1990. The cognitive perspective of 'naturalist' linguistic models. Cognitive Linguistics 1.75–98.

Dressler, Wolfgang U., Willi Mayerthaler, Oswald Pangl, and Wolfgang U. Wurzel. 1987. Leitmotifs in natural morphology. Amsterdam: Benjamins.

DuBois, John. 1985. Competing motivations. Iconicity in syntax, ed. by John Haiman, 343–65. Amsterdam: Benjamins.

Eddington, David. 1996. Diphthongization in Spanish derivational morphology: an empirical investigation. Hispanic Linguistics 87.1–35.

Encrevé, Pierre. 1988. La liaison avec et sans enchaînement: phonologie tridimensionnelle et usage du français. Paris: Seuil.

Erman, Britt, and Beatrice Warren. 1999. The idiom principle and the open choice principle. Text 20.29–62.

Ferguson, Charles A., and Carol B. Farwell. 1975. Words and sounds in early language acquisition. Language 51.419–39.

Fougeron, Cécile, and Patricia A. Keating. 1997. Articulatory strengthening at edges of prosodic domains. Journal of the Acoustical Society of America 101.3728–40.

Fowler, Carol A., and Jonathan Housum. 1987. Talkers' signaling of 'new' and 'old' words in speech and listeners' perception and use of the distinction. Journal of Memory and Language 26.489–504.

Fox, Barbara. 1995. On the embodied nature of grammar: embodied being-in-the-world. Paper presented at the Conference on Functional Approaches to Grammar, University of New Mexico, Albuquerque, NM.

Francis, W. Nelson, and Henry Kučera. 1982. Frequency analysis of English usage, Boston, MA: Houghton Mifflin.

Frisch, Stefan, Nathan R. Large, Bushra Zawaydeh, and David B. Pisoni. 2001. Frequency and the emergence of linguistic structure, ed. by Joan Bybee and Paul Hopper, 159–79. Amsterdam: Benjamins.

Fujimura, Osamu. 1990. Methods and goals of speech production research. Language and Speech 33.195–258.

Genetti, Carol. 1994. A descriptive and historical account of the Dolakha Newari dialect, Tokyo: Institute for the Study of Languages and Cultures of Asia and Africa.

Gilbert, John H., and Virginia J. Wyman. 1975. Discrimination learning of nasalized and non-nasalized vowels by five-, six- and seven-year-old children. Phonetica 31.65–80.

Givón, Talmy. 1979. On understanding grammar. New York: Academic Press.

Goldberg, Adele. 1995. Constructions: a Construction Grammar approach to argument structure. Chicago: University of Chicago Press.

Goldsmith, John. 1976. Autosegmental phonology. Cambridge MA: MIT dissertation.

Goldsmith, John. 1979. The aims of autosegmental phonology. Current approaches to phonological theory, ed. by Daniel A. Dinnsen, 202–22. Bloomington, IN: Indiana University Press.

Gonnerman, Laura M. 1999. Morphology and the lexicon: exploring the semantics-phonology interface. Los Angeles: University of Southern California dissertation.

Green, John N., and Marie-Anne Hintze. 1988. A reconsideration of liaison and enchaînement. Occasional Papers 136–68. University of Essex: Department of Languages and Linguistics.

Greenberg, Joseph. 1966. Language universals: with special reference to feature hierarchies. The Hague: Mouton.

Greenberg, Joseph. 1978a. How does a language acquire gender markers? Universals of human language, volume 3: Word structure, ed. by Joseph Greenberg, Charles A. Ferguson, and Edith A. Moravcsik, 47–82. Stanford, CA: Stanford University Press.

Greenberg, Joseph. 1978b. Some generalizations concerning initial and final consonant clusters. Universals of human language, volume 2: Phonology, ed. by Joseph Greenberg, Charles A. Ferguson, and Edith A. Moravcsik, 243–79. Stanford, CA: Stanford University Press.

Greenberg, Joseph., and James J. Jenkins. 1964. Studies in the psychological correlate of the sound system of American English. Word 20.157–77.

Gregory, Michelle, William D. Raymond, Alan Bell, Eric Fosler-Lussier, and Daniel Jurafsky. 1999. The effects of collocational strength and contextual predictability in lexical production. Chicago Linguistic Society 35.151–66. Chicago: Chicago Linguistic Society.

Guillaume, P. 1927/1973. The development of formal elements in the child's speech. Studies of child language development, ed. by Charles A. Ferguson and Daniel I. Slobin, 240–51. New York: Holt, Rinehart, and Winston.

Gürel, Ayşe. 1999. Decomposition: To what extent? The case of Turkish. Brain and Language 68.218–24.

Guy, Gregory. 1980. Variation in the group and the individual: the case of final stop deletion. Locating language in time and space, ed. by William Labov, 1–36. New York: Academic Press.

Guy, Gregory. 1991a. Explanation in variable phonology: an exponential model of morphological constraints. Language Variation and Change 3.1–22.

Guy, Gregory. 1991b. Contextual conditioning in variable lexical phonology. Language Variation and Change 3.223–39.

Haiman, John. 1994. Ritualization and the development of language. Perspectives on grammaticalization, ed. by William Pagliuca, 3–28. Amsterdam: Benjamins.

Haiman, John. 1995. Moods and metamessages: alienation as a mood. Modality in grammar and discourse, ed. by Joan Bybee and Suzanne Fleischman, 329–45. Amsterdam: Benjamins.

Haiman, John. 1998. Talk is cheap. Oxford: Oxford University Press.

Hajek, John. 1997. Universals of sound change in nasalization. Publications of the Philological Society 31. Oxford: Blackwell.

Hall, Tracy Alan. 1989. Lexical phonology and the distribution of German [ç] and [x]. Phonology 6.1–17.

Hammond, Michael. 1999. Lexical frequency and rhythm. Functionalism and formalism in linguistics, volume I: General papers, ed. by Michael Darnell et al. 329–58. Amsterdam: Benjamins.

Hankamer, Jorge. 1992. Morphological parsing and the lexicon. Lexical representation and process, ed. by W. Marslen-Wilson, 392–408. Cambridge, MA: MIT Press.

Hare, Mary L., Michael Ford, and William D. Marslen-Wilson. 2001. Frequency effects and the representation of regular verbs. Frequency and the emergence of linguistic structure, ed. by Joan Bybee and Paul Hopper, 181–200. Amsterdam: Benjamins.

Harris, John. 1989. Towards a lexical analysis of sound change in progress. Journal of Linguistics 25.35–56.

Harris, Martin. 1988. French. The Romance languages, ed. by Martin Harris and Nigel Vincent, 209–45. Oxford: Oxford University Press.

Hay, Jennifer, Janet Pierrehumbert, and Mary Beckman. To appear. Speech perception, well-formedness and the statistics of the lexicon. Papers in Laboratory Phonology VI, ed. by J. Local, R. Ogden, and R. Temple. Cambridge: Cambridge University Press.

Hayes, Bruce. 1990. Precompiled phrasal phonology. The phonology-syntax connection, ed. by Sharon Inkelas and Draga Zec, 85–108. Chicago: University of Chicago Press.

Hayes, Bruce. 1999. Phonetically-driven phonology: the role of Optimality Theory and grounding. Functionalism and formalism in linguistics, volume I: General papers, ed. by Michael Darnell et al., 243–86. Amsterdam: Benjamins.

Heine, Bernd, and Mechthild Reh. 1984. Grammaticalization and reanalysis in African languages, Hamburg: Helmut Buske.

Hoard, James. 1971. Aspiration, tenseness and syllabication in English. Language 47.133–40.

Hooper, Joan Bybee. 1976a. Introduction to Natural Generative Phonology, New York: Academic Press.

Hooper, Joan Bybee. 1976b. Word frequency in lexical diffusion and the source of morphophonological change. Current progress in historical linguistics, ed. by W. Christie, 96–105. Amsterdam: North Holland.

Hooper, Joan Bybee. 1977. Substantive evidence for linearity: vowel length and nasality in English. Chicago Linguistic Society 13, ed. by W. Beach, S. Fox, and S. Philosoph, 152–64. Chicago: Chicago Linguistic Society.

Hooper, Joan Bybee. 1981. The empirical determination of phonological representations. The cognitive representation of speech, ed. by Terry Myers, John Laver, and John M. Anderson, 347–57. Amsterdam: North Holland.

Hopper, Paul J. 1987. Emergent grammar. Berkeley Linguistics Society 13.139–57.

Hopper, Paul J. 1991. On some principles of grammaticization. Approaches to grammaticalization, vol. 1, ed. by Elizabeth Traugott and Bernd Heine, 17–35. Amsterdam: Benjamins.

Hopper, Paul. 1994. Phonogenesis. Perspectives on grammaticalization, ed. by William Pagliuca, 29–45. Amsterdam: Benjamins.

Hopper, Paul, and Sandra Thompson. 1984. The discourse basis for lexical categories in universal grammar. Language 60.703–52.

Hualde, José Ignacio. 2000. Linguistic rules and psychological reality. Chicago Linguistic Society 36, vol. 1: the main session, ed. by John Boyle, Jung-Hyuck Lee, and Arika Okrent.

Hyman, Larry. 1975. Phonology: theory and analysis, New York: Holt, Rinehart, and Winston.

Hyman, Larry. 1977. On the nature of linguistic stress. Studies in stress and accent, ed. by Larry Hyman, 37–82. Los Angeles: University of Southern California.

Inkelas, Sharon, and Draga Zec. 1990. The phonology-syntax connection. Chicago: University of Chicago Press.

Ito, Junko, and R. Armin Mester. 1995. Japanese phonology. The handbook of phonological theory, ed. by John A. Goldsmith, 817–38. Oxford: Blackwell.

Jakobson, Roman. 1939. Signe zéro. Reprinted 1971 in Roman Jakobson, Selected writings II, 211–19. The Hague: Mouton.

Jakobson, Roman. 1957. Shifters, verbal categories and the Russian verb. Reprinted in Roman Jakobson, Selected writings II, 130–47. The Hague: Mouton.

Jakobson, Roman. 1966. Quest for the essence of language. Reprinted in Roman Jakobson, Selected writings II, 345–59. The Hague: Mouton.

Jakobson, Roman. 1968. Child language, aphasia and language universals. The Hague: Mouton.

Jakobson, Roman, and Morris Halle. 1956. Fundamentals of language. The Hague: Mouton.

Janda, Richard D. 1999. Accounts of phonemic split have been greatly exaggerated – but not enough. Proceedings of the 14th International Congress of Phonetic Sciences. 329–32.

Jespersen, Otto. 1942. A modern English grammar on historical principles. London: Allen and Unwin.

Johnson, Keith. 1997. Speech perception without speaker normalization. Talker variability in speech processing, ed. by Keith Johnson and John W. Mullennix, 145–65. San Diego, CA: Academic Press.

Johnson, Keith, and John W. Mullennix. 1997. Talker variability in speech processing. San Diego, CA: Academic Press.

Johnson, Theodore. 1983. Phonological free variation, word frequency and lexical diffusion. Seattle: University of Washington dissertation.

Jong, Daan de. 1990. The syntax-phonology interface and French liaison. Linguistics 28.57–88.

Juilland, Alphonse, and E. Chang-Rodriguez. 1964. Frequency dictionary of Spanish words. London: Mouton.

Jurafsky, Daniel, Alan Bell, Michelle Gregory, and William D. Raymond. 2001. Probabilistic relations between words: evidence from reduction in lexical production. Frequency and the emergence of linguistic structure, ed. by Joan Bybee and Paul Hopper, 229–53. Amsterdam: Benjamins.

Kaisse, Ellen. 1985. Connected speech: the interaction of syntax and phonology. San Diego, CA: Academic Press.

Keller, Rudi. 1994. On language change: the invisible hand in language, translated by Brigitte Nerlich. London and New York: Routledge.

Kernan, K. T., and B. G. Blount. 1966. The acquisition of Spanish grammar by Mexican children. Anthropological Linguistics 8.1–14.

Kiparsky, Paul. 1971. Historical linguistics. A survey of linguistic science, ed. by W. Dingwall, 576–635. College Park, MD: University of Maryland Press.

Kiparsky, Paul. 1973. 'Elsewhere' in phonology. A festschrift for Morris Halle, ed. by Paul Kiparsky and Stephen Anderson, 93–106. New York: Holt, Rinehart, and Winston.

Kiparsky, Paul. 1982. Lexical phonology and morphology. Linguistics in the morning calm, ed. by I. S. Yang, 3–91. Seoul: Hanshin.

Kiparsky, Paul. 1985. Some consequences of lexical phonology. Phonology Yearbook 2.85–138.

Kiparsky, Paul. 1995. The phonological basis of sound change. The handbook of phonological theory, ed. by John Goldsmith, 640–70. Oxford: Blackwell.

Kirchner, Robert. 1997. Contrastiveness and faithfulness. Phonology 14.83–111.

Kirchner, Robert. 1998. An effort-based approach to consonant lenition. Los Angeles, CA: UCLA dissertation.

Klausenburger, Jürgen. 1979. Morphologization: studies in Latin and Romance morphonology. Tübingen: Niemeyer.

Klausenburger, Jürgen. 1984. French liaison and linguistic theory. Stuttgart: Franz Steiner.

Köpcke, Klaus-Michael. 1988. Schemas in German plural formation. Lingua 74.303–35.

Krug, Manfred. 1998. String frequency: a cognitive motivating factor in coalescence, language processing and linguistic change. Journal of English Linguistics 26.286–320.

Labov, William. 1981. Resolving the Neogrammarian controversy. Language 57.267–308.

Labov, William. 1994. Principles of linguistic change: internal factors. Oxford: Blackwell.

Lahiri, A., and W. Marslen-Wilson. 1991. The mental representation of lexical form: a phonological approach to the recognition lexicon. Cognition 38.245–94.

Lakoff, George. 1987. Women, fire and dangerous things: what categories reveal about the mind. Chicago: University of Chicago Press.

Langacker, Ronald. 1987. Foundations of cognitive grammar, volume 1: theoretical prerequisites. Stanford, CA: Stanford University Press.

Langacker, Ronald. 2000. A dynamic usage-based model. Usage-based models of language, ed. by M. Barlow and S. Kemmer, 1–63. Stanford, CA: CSLI.

Leopold, W. 1948. Speech development of a bilingual child: a linguist's record, 4 volumes. Evanston, IL: Northwestern University Press.

Lindblom, Björn. 1992. Phonological units as adaptive emergents of lexical development. Phonological development: models, research, implications, ed. by Charles Ferguson, Lise Menn, and Carol Stoel-Gammon, 131–63. Timonium, MD: York Press.

Lindblom, Björn, Peter MacNeilage, and Michael Studdert-Kennedy. 1984. Self-organizing processes and the explanation of phonological universals. Explanations for language universals, ed. by Brian Butterworth, Bernard Comrie, and Östen Dahl, 181–203. New York: Mouton.

Lipski, John M. 1994. Latin American Spanish, London and New York: Longman.

Lobben, M. 1991, Pluralization of Hausa nouns, viewed from psycholinguistic experiments and child language data. University of Oslo Master of Philosophy thesis.

Luce, Paul A., and Jan Charles-Luce. 1985. Contextual effects on vowel duration, closure duration, and the consonant-vowel ratio in speech production. Journal of the Acoustical Society of America 78.1949–57.

MacFarland, Talke, and Janet Pierrehumbert. 1991. On ich-Laut, ach-Laut and Structure Preservation. Phonology 8.171–80.

MacWhinney, Brian. 1978. The acquisition of morphophonology. Monographs of the Society for Research in Child Development vol. 43, ser. no. 174. Chicago: University of Chicago Press.

Maddieson, Ian. 1984. Patterns of sounds. Cambridge: Cambridge University Press.

Magni, Elisabetta. To appear. Paradigm organization and lexical connections in the development of the Italian *passato remoto*. Yearbook of Morphology.

Malécot, André. 1960. Vowel nasality as a distinctive feature in American English. Language 36.222–29.

Mańczak, Witold. 1980. Laws of analogy. Historical morphology, ed. by Jacek Fisiak, 283–88. Berlin: Mouton de Gruyter.

Marchman, Virginia A., and Elizabeth Bates. 1994. Continuity in lexical and morphological development: a test of the critical mass hypothesis. Journal of Child Language 21.339–66.

Marcus, G. F., S. Pinker, M. Ullman, M. Hollander, T. J. Rosen, F. Xu, and H. Clahsen. 1992. Overregularization in language acquisition. Monographs of the Society for Research in Child Development 57. Chicago: University of Chicago Press.

Marcus, G. F., U. Brinkmann, H. Clahsen, R. Wiese, A. Woest, and S. Pinker. 1995. German inflection: the exception that proves the rule. Cognitive Psychology 29.189–256.

Menéndez-Pidal, Ramón. 1968/1904. Manual de gramática histórica española. Madrid: Espasa-Calpe.

Menn, Lise. 1989. Phonological development: learning sounds and sound patterns. The development of language, 2nd Edition, ed. by Jean Berko Gleason, 59–100. New York: Macmillan.

Menn, Lise, and Brian MacWhinney. 1984. The repeated morph constraint: toward an explanation. Language 60.519–41.

Miller, Joanne. 1994. On the internal structure of phonetic categories: a progress report. Cognition 50.271–85.

Moder, Carol Lynn. 1992. Productivity and categorization in morphological classes, Buffalo, NY: SUNY dissertation.

Moonwomon, Birch. 1992. The mechanism of lexical diffusion. Paper presented at the Annual Meeting of the Linguistic Society of America, Philadelphia.

Morin, Yves-Charles, and Jonathan D. Kaye. 1982. The syntactic bases for French liaison. Journal of Linguistics 18.291–330.

Morin, Yves-Charles, Marie-Claude Langlois, and Marie-Eve Varin. 1990. Tensing of word-final [ɔ] to [o] in French: the phonologization of a morphophonological rule. Romance Philology 43.507–28.

Moulton, William. 1947. Juncture in modern standard German. Language 23.212–16.

Mowrey, Richard, and William Pagliuca. 1995. The reductive character of articulatory evolution. Rivista di Linguistica 7.37–124.

Nordquist, Dawn. 1999. A synchronic study of *have to* and *got to* with diachronic implications. Paper presented at the 2nd Annual High Desert Linguistic Society Student Conference, University of New Mexico, Albuquerque.

Nosofsky, R.M. 1988. Similarity, frequency and category representation. Journal of Experimental Psychology: Learning, Memory and Cognition 14.54–65.

Ohala, John J. 1981. The listener as a source of sound change. Papers from the Parasession on Language and Language Behavior, Chicago Linguistic Society, ed. by C. Masek, R. Hendrick, and M. Miller, 178–203. Chicago: Chicago Linguistic Society.

Ohala, John J. 1992. The segment: primitive or derived? Papers in Laboratory Phonology II: gesture, segment, prosody, ed. by Gerald J. Docherty and D. Robert Ladd, 166–89. Cambridge: Cambridge University Press.

Ohala, John J., and Manjari Ohala. 1995. Speech perception and lexical representation: the role of vowel nasalization in Hindi and English. Phonology and phonetic evidence, papers in Laboratory Phonology IV, ed. by Bruce Connell and Amalia Arvaniti, 41–60. Cambridge: Cambridge University Press.

Pagliuca, William. 1982. Prolegomena to a theory of articulatory evolution. Buffalo, NY: SUNY dissertation.

Pagliuca, William, and Richard Mowrey. 1987. Articulatory evolution. Papers from the 7th International Conference on Historical Linguistics, ed. by A. G. Ramat, O. Carruba, and G. Bernini, 459–72. Amsterdam: Benjamins.

Palmeri, Thomas J., Stephen D. Goldinger, and David B. Pisoni. 1993. Episodic encoding of voice attributes and recognition memory for spoken words. Journal of Experimental Psychology: Learning, Memory, and Cognition 19.309–28.

Pawley, Andrew, and Frances Hodgetts Syder. 1983. Two puzzles for linguistic theory: nativelike selection and nativelike fluency. Language and communication, ed. by Jack C. Richards and Richard W. Schmidt, 191–226. London: Longman.

Phillips, Betty. 1981. Lexical diffusion and Southern *tune, duke, news*. American Speech 56.72–8.

Phillips, Betty S. 1984. Word frequency and the actuation of sound change. Language 60.320–42.

Phillips, Betty S. 2001. Lexical diffusion, lexical frequency, and lexical analysis. Frequency and the emergence of linguistic structure, ed. by Joan Bybee and Paul Hopper, 123–36. Amsterdam: Benjamins.

Pierrehumbert, Janet. 1994a. Knowledge of variation. Papers from the Parasession on Variation, 30th Meeting of the Chicago Linguistic Society, 232–56. Chicago: Chicago Linguistic Society.

Pierrehumbert, Janet. 1994b. Syllable structure and word structure: a study of triconsonantal clusters in English. Phonological structure and phonetic form: papers in Laboratory Phonology III, ed. by Patricia Keating, 68–190. Cambridge: Cambridge University Press.

Pierrehumbert, Janet. 1999. Formalizing functionalism. Functionalism and formalism in linguistics, volume I: General papers, ed. by Michael Darnell et al., 287–304. Amsterdam: Benjamins.

Pierrehumbert, Janet. 2001. Exemplar dynamics: word frequency, lenition and contrast. Frequency and the emergence of linguistic structure, ed. by J. Bybee and P. Hopper. 137–57. Amsterdam: Benjamins.

Pinker, Steven. 1991. Rules of language. Science 253.530–35.

Pisoni, David. 1990. Effects of talker variability on speech perception: implications for current research and theory. Proceedings of the International Conference on Spoken Language Processing, ed. by H. Fujisaki, Kobe.

Pisoni, David B. Howard C. Nusbaum, Paul A. Luce, and Louisa M. Slowiaczek. 1985. Speech perception, word recognition and the structure of the lexicon. Speech Communication 4.75–95.

Plooij, F. X. 1978. Traits of language in wild chimpanzees? Action, gesture, and symbol, ed. by A. Lock, 111–32. London: Academic Press.

Port, Robert F., and Jonathan Dalby. 1982. Consonant/vowel ratio as a cue for voicing in English. Perception and Psychophysics 32.141–52.

Postal, Paul M. 1968. Aspects of phonological theory. New York: Harper and Row.

Post, Brechtje. 2000. Tonal and phrasal structures in French Intonation. The Hague: Thesus.

Prasada, Sandeep, and Steven Pinker. 1993. Generalisation of regular and irregular morphological patterns. Language and Cognitive Processes 8.1–15.

Prince, Alan, and Paul Smolensky. 1993. Optimality Theory: constraint interaction in generative grammar. Rutgers, NJ: Rutgers University ms.

Prince, Alan, and Paul Smolensky. 1997. Optimality: from neural networks to Universal Grammar. Science 275.1604–10.

Rosch, Eleanor. 1973. Natural categories. Cognitive Psychology 4.328–50.

Rosch, Eleanor. 1978. Principles of categorization. Cognition and categorization, ed. by Eleanor Rosch and Barbara B. Lloyd, 27–47. Hillsdale, NJ: Erlbaum.

Rumelhart, D., and J. McClelland. 1986. On learning the past tenses of English verbs: implicit rules or parallel distributed processing? Parallel distributed processing: explorations in the microstructure of cognition, ed. by J. McClelland, D. Rumelhart, and the PDP Research Group, 216–71. Cambridge, MA: MIT Press.

Sadock, Jerrold. 1980. Noun incorporation in Greenlandic. Language 56.300–19.

Saffran, Jenny R., Richard N. Aslin, and Elissa L. Newport. 1996. Statistical learning by 8-month-old infants. Science 274.1926–28.

Saussure, Ferdinand de. 1916. Cours de linguistique général. Paris: Payot.

Schacter, Daniel L., and Barbara A. Church. 1992. Auditory priming: implicit and explicit memory for words and voices. Journal of Experimental Psychology: Learning, Memory, and Cognition 18.915–30.

Schachter, Paul. 1968. Natural assimilation rules in Akan. International Journal of American Linguistics 35.342–55.

Scheibman, Joanne. 2000a. I dunno but . . . a usage-based account of the phonological reduction of *don't* in conversation. Journal of Pragmatics 32.105–24.

Scheibman, Joanne. 2000b. Structural patterns of subjectivity in American English conversation. Albuquerque: University of New Mexico dissertation.

Selkirk, Elizabeth. 1974. French liaison and the X̄-notation. Linguistic Inquiry 5.573–90.

Selkirk, Elizabeth. 1986. On derived domains in sentence phonology. Phonology Yearbook 3.371–405.

Sereno, Joan A., and Allard Jongman. 1997. Processing of English inflectional morphology. Memory and Cognition 25.425–37.

Skousen, Royal. 1989. Analogical modeling of language. Dordrecht: Kluwer.

Skousen, Royal. 1992. Analogy and structure. Dordrecht: Kluwer.

Smith, Neilson B. 1973. The acquisition of phonology: a case study. Cambridge: Cambridge University Press.

Sproat, R., and O. Fujimura. 1993. Allophonic variation in English /l/ and its implications for phonetic implementation. Journal of Phonetics 21.291–311.

Stampe, David. 1973. A dissertation on natural phonology. University of Chicago dissertation.

Stemberger, Joseph P. 1981. Morphological haplology. Language 57.791–817.

Stemberger, Joseph P., and Brian MacWhinney. 1986. Frequency and the lexical storage of regularly inflected forms. Memory and Cognition 14.17–26.

Stemberger, Joseph P., and Brian MacWhinney. 1988. Are inflected forms stored in the lexicon? Theoretical morphology: approaches in modern lingusitics, ed. by Michael Hammond and Michael Noonan, 101–16. San Diego, CA: Academic Press.

Steriade, Donca. 2000. Paradigm uniformity and the phonetics-phonology boundary. Papers in Laboratory Phonology V: Acquisition and the lexicon, ed. by Michael Broe and Janet Pierrehumbert, 313–34. Cambridge: Cambridge University Press.

Studdert-Kennedy, Michael. 1987. The phoneme as a perceptuomotor structure. Language, perception and production, ed. by A. Allport, D. MacKay, W. Prinz, and E. Scheerer, 67–84. New York: Academic Press.

Studdert-Kennedy, Michael. 1998. The particulate origins of language generativity: from syllable to gesture. Approaches to the evolution of language, ed. by James Hurford, Michael Studdert-Kennedy, and Chris Knight, 202–21. Cambridge: Cambridge University Press.

Studdert-Kennedy, M., A. M. Liberman, K. S. Harris, and F. S. Cooper. 1970. Motor theory of speech perception: a reply to Lane's critical review. Psychological Review 77.234–49.

Terrell, Tracy. 1977. Constraints on the aspiration and deletion of final /s/ in Cuban and Puerto Rican Spanish. The Bilingual Review 4.35–51.

Terrell, Tracy. 1978. La aspiración y elisión de /s/ en el español porteño. Anuario de Letras 16.41–66.

Terrell, Tracy. 1979. Final /s/ in Cuban Spanish. Hispania 62.599–612.

Terrell, Tracy, and Bernard Tranel. 1978. Parallelisms between liaison in French and /s/-aspiration and deletion in Caribbean Spanish dialects. Recherches Linguistiques à Montréal (Montreal Working Papers in Linguistics) 10.31–50.

Thompson, Sandra A., and Anthony Mulac. 1991. A quantitative perspective on the grammaticization of epistemic parentheticals in English. Approaches to grammaticalization, vol. II, ed. by Elizabeth Traugott and Bernd Heine, 313–30. Amsterdam: Benjamins.

Tiersma, Peter. 1982. Local and general markedness. Language 58.832–49.

Timberlake, Alan. 1978. Uniform and alternating environments in phonological change. Folia Slavica 2.312–28.

Tomasello, Michael, A. C. Kruger, and H. H. Ratner. 1993. Cultural learning. Brain and Behavioral Sciences 16.495–552.

Tranel, Bernard. 1981. Concreteness in generative phonology: Evidence from French. Berkeley, CA: University of California Press.

Traugott, Elizabeth Closs. 1989. On the rise of epistemic meaning: an example of subjectification in semantic change. Language 65.31–55.

Treiman, R., B. Kessler, S. Knewasser, R. Tincoff, and M. Bowman. 2000. Adults' sensitivity to phonotactic probabilities Papers in Laboratory Phonology V: Acquisition and the lexicon. ed. by Michael Broe and Janet Pierrehumbert. Cambridge: Cambridge University Press.

Vachek, Josef. 1964. On some basic principles of 'classical' phonology, Reprinted 1972 in Phonological theory: evolution and current practice, ed. by Adam Makkai, 424–41. New York: Holt, Rinehart, and Winston.

Vennemann, Theo. 1971. Natural generative phonology. Paper presented at the Annual Meeting of the Linguistic Society of America, St. Louis, MO.

Vennemann, Theo. 1972a. Phonetic detail in assimilation: problems in Germanic phonology. Language 48.863–92.

Vennemann, Theo. 1972b. Rule inversion. Lingua 29.209–42.

Vennemann, Theo. 1974. Words and syllables in natural generative phonology. Parasession on Natural Phonology, ed. by A. Bruck, R. Fox, and M. Lagaly, 346–74. Chicago: Chicago Linguistic Society.

Vennemann, Theo. 1988. Preference laws for syllable structure and the explanation of sound change. Berlin: Mouton de Gruyter.

Vennemann, Theo. 1993. Language change as language improvement. Historical linguistics: problems and perspectives, ed. by Charles Jones, 319–44. London and New York: Longman.

Vihman, Marilyn May. 1996. Phonological development: the origins of language in the child. Oxford: Blackwell.

Vitevitch, Michael S., Paul A. Luce, Jan Charles-Luce, and David Kemmerer. 1997. Phonotactics and syllable stress: implications for the processing of spoken nonsense words. Language and Speech 40.47–62.

Vogel, Irene, and István Kenesei. 1990. Syntax and semantics in phonology. The phonology-syntax connection, ed. by Sharon Inkelas and Draga Zec, 339–63. Chicago: University of Chicago Press.

Wang, H. S., and Bruce L. Derwing. 1994. Some vowel schemas in three English morphological classes: experimental evidence. In honor of Professor William S.-Y. Wang: interdisciplinary studies on language and language change, ed. by M. Y. Chen and O. C. L. Tzeng, 561–75. Taipei: Pyramid Press.

Zager, David. 1980. A real time process model of morphological change. Buffalo, NY: SUNY dissertation.

Zimmerman, S. A., and S. M. Sapon. 1958. Note on vowel duration seen cross-linguistically. Journal of the Acoustical Society of America 30.152–3.

Zsiga, Elizabeth C. 1995. An acoustic and electropalatographic study of lexical and postlexical palatalization in American English. Phonology and phonetic evidence: papers in Laboratory Phonology IV, ed. by Bruce Connell and Amalia Arvaniti, 282–302. Cambridge: Cambridge University Press.

Zsiga, Elizabeth C. 2000. Phonetic alignment constraints: consonant overlap and palatalization in English and Russian. *Journal of Phonetics* 28.69–102.

Zubin, David, and Klaus-Michael Köpcke. 1981. Gender: a less than arbitrary grammatical category. Chicago Linguistic Society 17.439–49. Chicago: Chicago Linguistic Society.

Zue, Victor W., and Martha Laferriere. 1979. Acoustic study of medial /t,d/ in American English. Journal of the Acoustical Society of America 66.1039–50.

Zwicky, Arnold. 1972. Note on a phonological hierarchy in English. Linguistic change and generative theory, ed. by Robert P. Stockwell and Ronald S. Macaulay, 275–301. Bloomington, IN: Indiana University Press.

Author Index

231

Subject Index

Languages Index

12
4

48

Tradition of diff. in phonology: regularity vs.
   variation (Neogrammarians vs. dialectol-
   ogists.)
Weinreich / Pike vs. Harris, Bloch
   Chomsky / Halle vs. Vachek
Hooper vs. OT / TG : one U-form vs.
   variation
connectionism vs. generativism

Hooper idea

Critique
   formalization (schema?)
   Local frequency
   Individual variation
   Why redundancy is deleted - NOT economy
       B. provides evidence
       But - of change contrast